TOWARD A THEORY OF HUMAN RIGHTS

In *Toward a Theory of Human Rights*, Michael Perry pursues three important, related inquiries:

- Is there a *non-religious* (secular) basis for the morality of human rights?
- What is the relationship between the *morality* of human rights and the *law* of human rights? Perry here addresses the controversial issues of capital punishment, abortion, and same-sex unions.
- What is the proper role of courts in protecting constitutionally entrenched human rights? Perry pays special attention to the role of the United States Supreme Court.

Toward a Theory of Human Rights makes a significant contribution both to the study of human rights and to constitutional theory.

Michael J. Perry holds a Robert W. Woodruff Chair at Emory University, where he teaches in the law school. He has written more than sixty articles and essays and is the author of nine books, including *Love and Power: The Role of Religion and Morality in American Politics* (1991); *The Idea of Human Rights* (1998); *We the People: The Fourteenth Amendment and the Supreme Court* (1999); and *Under God? Religious Faith and Liberal Democracy* (2003).

Toward a Theory of Human Rights

Religion, Law, Courts

MICHAEL J. PERRY

Emory University

CAMBRIDGE
UNIVERSITY PRESS

 # 64390388

CAMBRIDGE UNIVERSITY PRESS
Cambridge, New York, Melbourne, Madrid, Cape Town, Singapore, São Paulo

Cambridge University Press
32 Avenue of the Americas, New York, NY 10013-2473, USA

www.cambridge.org
Information on this title: www.cambridge.org/9780521865517

First published 2007
Reprinted 2007

Printed in the United States of America

A catalog record for this publication is available from the British Library.

Library of Congress Cataloging in Publication Data
Perry, Michael J.
Toward a theory of human rights : religion, law, courts / Michael J. Perry.
p. cm.
Includes bibliographical references.
ISBN-13: 978-0-521-86551-7 (hardback)
ISBN-10: 0-521-86551-4 (hardback)
1. Human rights. 2. Justice. I. Title
JC571.P4215 2006 2007
323.01–dc22 2006004940

ISBN 978-0-521-86551-7 hardback

For my students,
past, present, future

I give you a new commandment: love one another; you must love one another just as I have loved you.

John 13:34

Just as a mother protects her child with her own life, in a similar way we should extend an unlimited heart to all beings.

Buddhist teaching

Contents

Acknowledgments

I am grateful to many people in many venues – too many people and venues to list here individually – for their helpful comments as I was writing this book.

I am especially grateful to Chris Eberle, Steve Smith, and George Wright; to the participants in the April 2005 Roundtable sponsored by the Center for the Study of Law and Religion at Emory University, and to my dear colleague and friend John Witte, Director of the Center; and to the students at Wake Forest (2001–03), Emory (2003–05), and Alabama (2005) with whom I was privileged to discuss drafts of this book.

Finally, I want to express my gratitude to my editor, Andy Beck, who welcomed both this book and my previous one to Cambridge University Press, and to Ronald Cohen, whose editorial work on the manuscript was exemplary.

Introduction

[W]e [do not] have a clear theory of human rights. On the contrary, . . . the necessary work is just beginning.

John Searle[1]

This book has three parts. Part One (Chapters 1–3) is about the morality of human rights; Part Two (Chapters 4–7), about the relation of the morality of human rights to the law of human rights; and Part Three (Chapters 8–9), about the proper role of courts in protecting the law of human rights.

Part One. In Chapter 1, I discuss the morality of human rights, which holds that each and every born human being has inherent dignity and is inviolable.[2] In Chapter 2, I elaborate a religious ground for the morality of human rights. In Chapter 3, I inquire as to whether there is a non-religious ground for the morality of human rights. That there is a religious ground for the morality of human rights – indeed, more than one – is clear. (The eminent philosopher Charles Taylor has argued that the "affirmation of universal human rights" that characterizes "modern liberal political culture" represents an "authentic development[] of the gospel. . . .")[3] It is far from clear, however, that there is a non-religious ground – a *secular* ground – for the morality of human rights. Indeed, the claim that every born human being has inherent dignity and is inviolable is deeply problematic for many secular thinkers, because the claim is difficult – perhaps to the point of being impossible – to align with one of their reigning intellectual convictions – what Bernard Williams called "Nietzsche's thought": "[T]here is, not only no God, but no metaphysical order of any kind. . . ."[4]

Part Two. How do we get from the morality of human rights to the law of human rights: What laws should we who affirm the morality of human rights, *because* we affirm it, press our government – our elected representatives – to enact? What policies should we press them to adopt? What laws and policies should we press them to avoid? I pursue this inquiry in a general way in Chapter 4. Then, in Chapters 5–7, I focus on three major controversies that engage and divide contemporary American politics: What laws/policies should we who affirm the morality of human rights press our elected representatives to enact/adopt with respect to capital punishment (Chapter 5), abortion (Chapter 6), and same-sex unions (Chapter 7)?

Part Three. Many constitutional provisions entrench human rights; that is, they entrench rights-claims – principally rights-claims directed at government – about what may not be done to, or about what must be done for, human beings. Such provisions often give rise to heated controversy. Three examples from the United States: Does capital punishment violate the cruel and unusual punishments clause of the Eighth Amendment to the United States Constitution? Does a criminal ban on pre-viability abortions violate the due process clause of the Fourteenth Amendment? Does a legislature's refusal to extend the benefit of law to same-sex unions violate the equal protection clause of the Fourteenth Amendment? No constitutional questions are more controversial in the United States today than these three.

In Chapter 8, I inquire about the proper role of courts in adjudicating such controversies; I inquire, that is, about the proper role of courts in protecting constitutionally entrenched human rights. In Chapter 9, I focus on a particular court, the Supreme Court of the United States: What role should the Supreme Court play in protecting constitutionally entrenched human rights?

MORALITY, LEGALITY, AND RIGHTS-TALK[5]

I confess to a bias against *moral*-rights-talk – a bias that reflects my socialization many years ago into the world of lawyers, where legal rights are generally taken to be the paradigm of rights, and moral rights (so-called) are often "thought of as phony rights, as lacking key features [in particular, enforceability] that real rights have."[6] But can we talk about the morality of human rights without engaging in moral-rights-talk?

There is an undeniably important role for rights-talk when we are talking about the *law* of human rights – that is, there is an important, even essential, role for *legal*-rights-talk. After all, the law of human rights, like law generally, consists of many legal "rights"; it consists, that is, of many legal *rights-claims*: claims, for example, about what A must refrain from doing to B if A does not want to make himself vulnerable to certain negative legal consequences, such as imprisonment. (A claim about what A must not do to B is a rights-claim, because a claim that A has a legal *duty* (obligation) not to do X to B is a claim that B has a legal *right* that B not do X to him.) But it is far from obvious that there is an important, much less essential, role for moral-rights-talk when we are talking about the *morality* of human rights. Consider these claims: (1) Every (born) human being has inherent dignity and is inviolable (not-to-be-violated). (2) To rape a human being is to violate her. (3) We who affirm that every human being has inherent dignity and is inviolable, *because* we affirm it, have conclusive reason to do what we can, all things considered, to try to prevent human beings from violating human beings. None of these claims is, as articulated, a rights-claim; none is a claim about what one must do, or refrain from doing, to someone else if one wants to avoid certain negative consequences to oneself.

Now, this is not to say that none of these claims can be translated into the language of rights. If one has a strong preference for moral-rights-talk, one may want to undertake a translation. For example, one may want to translate the claim that "to rape a human being is to violate her" into the claim that "to rape a human being is to violate her human right – her right as a human being – not to be raped." There's nothing wrong with such a translation, as long as we are alert to what the ensuing rights-talk – *moral*-rights-talk, talk about *moral* rights – means and doesn't mean, as distinct from what *legal*-rights-talk means.

In any event, we can talk about the *morality* of human rights without engaging in moral-rights-talk – and, because of my lawyer's bias against moral-rights-talk, I prefer to talk about the morality of human rights without engaging in moral-rights-talk. When I say "the morality of human rights," I'm referring to *the morality that supports the law of human rights.* In Chapter 4, as I noted earlier, I address in a general way the question of how we get from the morality of human rights – from the claim that every human being has inherent dignity and is inviolable – to the law of human rights: What laws should we who affirm the morality of human rights, *because* we affirm it, press our government – our elected representatives – to enact? What policies should we press them to adopt? What laws and policies should we press them to avoid?

TOWARD A THEORY OF HUMAN RIGHTS

PART ONE

❧

THE MORALITY OF HUMAN RIGHTS

According to Niklas Luhmann, the language of reverence has been discredited by the downfall of metaphysics. Logically taken further, that means that "the postulate that all human life is holy no longer exists." The predominantly religious structures which provided the foundations of the concept of dignity, creatureliness and being in the image of God are no longer compellingly binding or even illuminating in the secular world.

Regina Ammicht-Quinn[1]

Richard Rorty, the leading postmodernist liberal theorist, . . . concedes that liberalism, once so jealous of its autonomy from Biblical faith, is in fact parasitic upon it. In his essay "Postmodern Bourgeois Liberalism," he describes secular liberals like himself as "freeloading atheists." They continue to rely on the Judeo-Christian legacy of concern with human dignity despite their rejection of the revealed truth that alone could support this concern. . . . For Rorty, God is dead but secularized Christian morality continues. This is precisely one of the scenarios envisaged by Nietzsche in *The Gay Science*: "God is dead, but given the way men are there may still be caves for thousands of years in which his shadow will be shown." True, only 125 of those years have now passed, but on the evidence of Rorty's thought, it's hard to believe that this sort of shadow play still has centuries to run.

Clifford Orwin[2]

ℒ

The Morality of Human Rights

Notwithstanding their European origins, . . . [i]n Asia, Africa, and South America, [human rights now] constitute the only language in which the opponents and victims of murderous regimes and civil wars can raise their voices against violence, repression, and persecution, against injuries to their human dignity.

Jürgen Habermas[1]

The name of my state of origin – Kentucky – has been said to derive from a Native American word meaning "a dark and bloody ground".[2] An apt name for our century of origin is a dark and bloody time – indeed, *the* dark and bloody time: The twentieth century "'was the bloodiest in human existence,' . . . not only because of the total number of deaths attributed to wars – 109 million – but because of the fraction of the population killed by conflicts, more than 10 times more than during the 16th century."[3] The list of twentieth-century horrors, which plods on at mind-numbing length, includes much more than wars, however. As the century began, King Leopold II of Belgium was presiding over a holocaust in the Congo; it is estimated that between 1880 and 1920, as a result of a system of slave labor, the population of the Congo "dropped by approximately ten million people."[4] From 1915 to 1923, the Ottoman Turks, who were Muslim, committed genocide against the Armenian minority, who were Christian.[5] Not counting deaths inflicted in battle, Stalin was responsible for the deaths of more than 42 million people (1929–53); Mao, more than 37 million (1923–76); Hitler, more than 20 million (1933–45), including more than 10 million Slavs and about 5.5 million Jews.[6] One need only mention these countries to recall some more recent atrocities: Cambodia (1975–79), Bosnia (1992–95), Rwanda (1994).[7] Sadly, this recital only scratches the surface.[8] For an exhaustive and exhausting account of the grim details, one should consult the two-volume *Encyclopedia of Genocide*, which reports:

> In total, during the first eighty-eight years of [the twentieth] century, almost 170 million men, women, and children were shot, beaten, tortured, knifed, burned, starved, frozen, crushed, or worked to death; buried alive, drowned, hanged, bombed, or killed in any other of the myriad other ways governments have inflicted deaths on unarmed, helpless citizens and foreigners. Depending on whether one used high or more conservative estimates, the dead could conceivably be more than 360 million people. It is as though our species has been devastated by a modern Black Plague.[9]

In the midst of the countless grotesque inhumanities of the twentieth century, however, there is a heartening story, amply recounted elsewhere:[10] the emergence, in international law, of the morality of human rights. The morality of human rights is not new; in one or another version, the morality is very old.[11] But the emergence of the morality in international law, in the period since the end of World War II, is a profoundly important development: "Until World War II, most legal scholars and governments affirmed the general proposition, albeit not in so many words, that international law did not impede the natural right of each equal sovereign to be monstrous to his or her subjects."[12] The twentieth century, therefore, was not only the dark and bloody time; the second half of the twentieth century was also the time in which a growing number of human beings the world over responded to the savage horrors of the twentieth century by affirming the morality of human rights.[13] The emergence of the morality of human rights makes the moral landscape of the twentieth century a touch less bleak.

Although it is only one morality among many, the morality of human rights has become the dominant morality of our time. Indeed, unlike any morality before it, the morality of human rights has become a truly global morality; as the passage by Jürgen Habermas at the beginning of this chapter reflects, the language of human rights has become the moral lingua franca. Nonetheless, the morality of human rights is not well understood.

What does the morality of human rights hold? The International Bill of Rights, as it is informally known, consists of three documents: the Universal Declaration of Human Rights, the International Covenant on Civil and Political Rights, and the International Covenant on Economic, Social, and Cultural Rights.[14] The Universal Declaration refers in its preamble to "the inherent dignity . . . of all members of the human family" and states in Article 1 that "[a]ll members of the human family are born free and equal in dignity and rights . . . and should act towards one another in a spirit of brotherhood." The two covenants each refer in their preambles to "the inherent dignity . . . of all members of the human family" and to "the inherent dignity of the human person" – from which, the covenants insist, "the equal and inalienable rights of all members of the human family . . . derive."[15] As the International Bill of Rights makes clear, then, there is a twofold claim at the heart of the morality of human rights. The first part of the claim is that each and every (born) human being – each and every member of the species homo sapiens sapiens[16] – has inherent dignity.[17] The second part of the claim, which is implicit, is that the inherent dignity of human beings has a normative force for us, in this sense: We should live our lives in accordance with the fact that every human being has inherent dignity; that is, we should respect – we have conclusive reason to respect – the inherent dignity of every human being.

To say that every human being has *inherent* dignity is to say that the dignity that every human being has does not inhere in – it does not depend on – anything as particular as a human being's "race, colour, sex, language, religion, political or other opinion, national or social origin, property, birth or other status."[18] But to say this is not to say what the inherent dignity of every human being does depend on. What is the source, the ground, of this dignity – and of the normative force this dignity has for us? Why – in virtue of what – is it the case both that every human being has inherent dignity and that should we live our lives accordingly, that is, in a way that respects this dignity? (The International Bill of Rights is famously silent on this question. This is not surprising, given the plurality of religious and non-religious views among those who profess commitment to the Universal Declaration and the two covenants.[19]) I turn to this difficult, contested question in the next two chapters.

The twofold conviction that every human being has inherent dignity and that we should live our lives accordingly is so fundamental to the morality of human rights that when I say, in this book, "the morality of human rights," I am referring to this conviction.

There is another way to state the conviction: Every human being has inherent dignity and is "inviolable": not-to-be-violated.[20] According to the morality of human rights, if one's reason for doing something to, or for not doing something for, a human being (call him Daniel) denies, implicitly if not explicitly, that Daniel has inherent dignity, one fails to respect Daniel's inherent dignity; in that sense, one "violates" Daniel. (The Nazis explicitly denied that Jews had inherent dignity.[21] Even if Bosnian Serbs did not explicitly deny that Bosnian Muslims had inherent dignity, they implicitly denied it: How else to understand what Bosnian Serbs did to Bosnian Muslims – the humiliation, rape, torture, and murder? In that sense, what Bosnian Serbs did to Bosnian

Muslims constituted a practical denial – an existential denial – of the inherent dignity of Bosnian Muslims.) In the context of the morality of human rights, and therefore of this book, to say that (1) every human being has inherent dignity and we should live our lives accordingly (that is, in a way that respects this dignity) is to say that (2) every human being has inherent dignity and is inviolable: not-to-be-violated, in the sense of "violate" just indicated. To affirm the morality of human rights is to affirm the twofold claim that every human being has inherent dignity and is inviolable.

ᘐ

The Morality of Human Rights: A Religious Ground

Only someone who is religious can speak seriously of the sacred, but such talk informs the thoughts of most of us whether or not we are religious, for it shapes our thoughts about the way in which human beings limit our will as does nothing else in nature. If we are not religious, we will often search for one of the inadequate expressions which are available to us to say what we hope will be a secular equivalent of it. We may say that all human beings are inestimably precious, that they are ends in themselves, that they are owed unconditional respect, that they possess inalienable rights, and, of course, that they possess inalienable dignity. In my judgment these are ways of trying to say what we feel a need to say when we are estranged from the conceptual resources we need to say it. Be that as it may: each of them is problematic and contentious. Not one of them has the simple power of the religious ways of speaking.

Where does that power come from. Not, I am quite sure, from esoteric theological or philosophical elaborations of what it means for something to be sacred. It derives from the unashamedly anthropomorphic character of the claim that we are sacred because God loves us, his children.

Raimond Gaita[1]

As I explained in Chapter 1, the fundamental, twofold conviction at the heart of the morality of human rights holds that each and every (born) human being – each and every member of the species homo sapiens sapiens – has inherent dignity and is inviolable: not-to-be-violated. (Again, one violates a human being, according to the morality of human rights, if one's reason for doing something to, or for not doing something for, a human being denies, implicitly if not explicitly, that the human being has inherent dignity.) Now, the claim that every (born) human being has inherent dignity is controversial.[2] (The claim that every human being, unborn as well as born, has inherent dignity – which claim I address in Chapter 6, where I discuss abortion – is, of course, even more controversial.) Not everyone agrees that every human being has inherent dignity and is inviolable. Some believe that – or act as if, or both – no human being has inherent dignity. Others believe that – or act as if, or both – only some human beings have it: the members of one's own tribe, for example, or of one's own nation.[3] The claim that every human being has inherent dignity and is inviolable needs to be defended. *Why* is it the case – *in virtue of what* is it the case – that every human being has inherent dignity and is inviolable?[4]

I want to sketch a religious defense of – a religious ground for – the conviction that every human being has inherent dignity and that we should live our lives accordingly. (Recall from the Introduction that the claim "every human being has inherent dignity and is inviolable" and the claim "every human being has inherent dignity and we should live our lives accordingly" are equivalent claims.) The ground I am about to sketch is certainly not the only religious ground for the morality of human rights. (A similar ground could be developed on the basis of Jewish materials,[5] for example, or of Islamic materials.[6]) It is, however, the religious ground with which I am most familiar.

Let us imagine a religious believer named Sarah. Sarah affirms that every human being has inherent dignity and that we should live our lives accordingly. (For a reason that will soon be apparent, Sarah prefers to say that every human being "is sacred." Nonetheless, for Sarah, each predicate – "has inherent dignity," "is sacred" – is fully equivalent to the other; Sarah translates each predicate into the other without remainder.) In affirming this, Sarah affirms the morality of human rights. Predictably, Sarah's affirmation elicits this inquiry: "Why – in virtue of what – does every human being have inherent dignity?" Sarah gives a religious explanation: Speaking the words of *The First Letter of John*, Sarah says that "God is love." ("Whoever fails to love does not know God, because God is love." 1 John 4:8.[7] "God is love, and whoever remains in love remains in God and God in him." 1 John 4:16.)[8] Moreover, God's act of creating and sustaining the universe is an act of love,[9] and we human beings are the beloved children of God and sisters and brothers to one another.[10] (As Hilary Putnam has noted, the moral image central to what Putnam calls the Jerusalem-based religions "stresse[s] equality and also fraternity, as in the metaphor of the whole human race as One Family, of all women and men as sisters and brothers.")[11] Every human being has inherent dignity, says Sarah, because, and in the sense that, every human being is a beloved child of God and a sister/brother to every other human being.[12] Sarah is fully aware that she is speaking analogically, but that is the best anyone can do, she insists, in speaking about who/what God is[13] – as in "Gracious God, gentle in your power and strong in your tenderness, you have brought us forth from the womb of your being and breathed into us the breath of life."[14]

Sarah's explanation provokes yet a further inquiry, an inquiry about the source of the normativity – the source of the "should" – in the claim that we *should* live our lives in a way that respects the inherent dignity of every human being: "Let's assume, for the sake of discussion, that every human being has inherent dignity because, and in the sense that, every human being is a beloved child of God and a sister/brother to every other human being. So what? Why should it matter to me – to the way I live my life – that every human being has inherent dignity, that every human being is a beloved child of God and a sister/brother to me?" In responding to this important question about the source of normativity, Sarah – who "understands the authority of moral claims to be warranted not by divine dictates but by their contribution to human flourishing"[15] – states her belief that the God who loves us has created us to love one another.[16] (We are created not only to achieve union, in love, with one another; we are also created, Sarah believes, to achieve union, in love, with God. Sarah understands this state to be "not an ontological unity such that either the lover or the beloved ceases to have his own individual existence[, but rather] a unity at the level of affection or will by which one person *affectively* takes the other to be part of himself and the goods of the other to be his own goods.")[17] Given our created nature – given what we have been created *for* – the most fitting way of life for us human beings, the most deeply satisfying way of life of which we are capable, as children of God and sisters and brothers to one another, is one in which we embrace Jesus's commandment, reported in John 13:34, to "love one another . . . just as I have loved you."[18] By becoming persons of a certain sort – persons who discern one another as bearers of inherent dignity and love one another as such – we fulfill our created nature.[19] "We are well aware that we have passed over from death to life because we love our brothers. Whoever does not love, remains in death." (1 John 3:14.)[20] Indeed, Sarah believes that in some situations, we love most truly and fully – and therefore we live most truly and fully – by taking the path that will probably or even certainly lead to our dying. "Greater love than this hath no man . . ."[21]

(Sarah also believes that the ultimate fulfillment of our created nature – which, she believes, is mystical union, in love, with God and with one another[22] – can be neither fully achieved nor even fully understood in our earthly life.[23] "Now we see only reflections in a mirror, mere riddles, but then we shall be seeing face to face. Now, I can know only imperfectly; but then I shall know just as fully as I am myself known." (I Corinthians 13:12.) But in our earthly life, Sarah believes, we can make an important beginning.)[24]

The "love" in Jesus's counsel to "love one another" is not *eros* or *philia*, but *agape*.[25] To love another in the sense of *agape* is *to see her (or him) in a certain way* (that is, as a child of God and sister/brother to oneself) and, therefore, *to act toward her in a certain way*.[26] *Agape* "discloses to us the full humanity of others. To become properly aware of that full humanity is to become incapable of treating it with contempt, cruelty, or indifference. The full awareness of others' humanity that love involves is an essentially motivating perception."[27] The "one another" in Jesus's counsel is radically inclusive: "You have heard how it was said, You will love your neighbor and hate your enemy. But I say this to you, love your enemies and pray for those who persecute you; so that you may be children of your Father in heaven, for he causes his sun to rise on the bad as well as the good, and sends down rain to fall on the upright and the wicked alike.... You must therefore set no bounds to your love, just as your heavenly Father sets none to his." (Matthew 5:43–48.)[28]

As it happens, Sarah embodies Jesus's extravagant counsel to "love one another just as I have loved you." She loves all human beings. Sarah loves even "the Other": She loves not only those for whom she has personal affection, or those with whom she works or has other dealings, or those among whom she lives; she loves even those who are most remote, who are unfamiliar, strange, alien, those who, because they are so distant or weak or both, will never play any concrete role, for good or ill, in Sarah's life. ("The claims of the intimate circle are real and important enough. Yet the movement from intimacy, and to faces we do not know, still carries the ring of a certain local confinement. For there are the people as well whose faces we never encounter, but whom we have ample means of knowing *about*.... [T]heir claims too, in trouble, unheeded, are a cause for shame.")[29] Sarah loves even those from whom she is most estranged and toward whom she feels most antagonistic: those whose ideologies and projects and acts she judges to be not merely morally objectionable, but morally abominable. ("[T]he language of love...compels us to affirm that even...the most radical evil-doers...are fully our fellow human beings.")[30] Sarah loves even her enemies; indeed, Sarah loves even those who have violated her, who have failed to respect her inherent dignity. Sarah is fond of quoting Graham Greene to her incredulous friends: "When you visualized a man or a woman carefully, you could always begin to feel pity.... When you saw the corners of the eyes, the shape of the mouth, how the hair grew, it was impossible to hate. Hate was just a failure of imagination."[31]

Such love – such a state of being, such an orientation in the world – is, obviously, an ideal. Moreover, it is, for most human beings, an extremely demanding ideal; for many persons, it is also an implausible ideal.[32] Why should anyone embrace the ideal? Why should anyone want to become (or to remain) such a person – a person who, like Sarah, loves even the Other? This is, existentially if not intellectually, the fundamental moral question for anyone: Why should I want to become the sort of person who makes the choices, who does the things, that I am being told I should make/do. And, in fact, Sarah's interlocutor presses her with this question: "Why should I want to become the sort of person who, like you, loves the Other? What reason do I have to do *that*?"[33] Because this is essentially the question about the source of the normativity in the claim that we should live our lives in a way that respects the inherent dignity of every human being, Sarah is puzzled; she thought that she had already answered the question. Sarah patiently rehearses her answer, an answer that appeals ultimately to one's commitment to one's own authentic well-being: "The most deeply satisfying way of life of which we are capable is one in which we 'love one another just as I have loved you.' By becoming persons who love one another, we fulfill – we perfect – our created nature and thereby achieve our truest, deepest, most enduring happiness."[34] Now it is Sarah's turn to ask a question of her interlocutor: "What further reason could you possibly want for becoming (or remaining) the sort of person who loves the Other?"

> When he was deliberating about how to live, St. Augustine asked, "What does anything matter, if it does not have to do with happiness?" His question requires explanation, because he is not advising selfishness nor the reduction of other people to utilities, and even qualification, because other things can have some weight. All the same, the answer he expects is obviously right: only a happy life matters conclusively. If I had a clear view of it, I could have no motive to decline it, I could regret nothing by accepting it, I would have nothing about which to deliberate further.[35]

A clarification may be helpful here. Does Sarah do what she does for the Other – for example, does she contribute to Bread for the World as a way of feeding the hungry – for a *self-regarding* reason? Does she do so, say, because it makes her happy to do so? She does not. (This is not to say that feeding the hungry doesn't make Sarah happy. It does. But this is not why she feeds the hungry.) Given the sort of person she is, the reason – the *other-regarding* reason – Sarah feeds the hungry is: "The hungry are my sisters and brothers; I love them." Now, a different question: Why is Sarah committed to being the sort of person she is, and why does she believe that everyone should want to be such a person? *Pace* Augustine, Sarah's answer to this question *is* self-regarding: "As persons who love one another, we fulfill our created nature and thereby achieve our truest, deepest, most enduring happiness."[36] According to Sarah, it is not individual acts of love that necessarily make one happy; it is, rather, becoming a person who loves the Other "just as I have loved you."

"[S]elf-fulfillment happens when we are engaged from beyond ourselves. Self-fulfillment ultimately depends on self-transcendence. This is essentially the claim that is made by religion, that the meaning of our lives is to be found beyond ourselves."[37]

It bears emphasizing that Sarah does not believe that she should be the sort of person she is because God has issued a command to her to be that sort of person – a command that, because God is entitled to rule, to legislate, she is obligated to obey. For Sarah, God is not best understood in such terms. A theistic religious vision does not necessarily include, though some conventional theistic religious visions do include, a conception of God as supreme legislator, issuing directives for human conduct.[38] For Sarah, for whom God is love, not supreme legislator, some choices are good for us to make (or not to make) – and therefore we ought (or ought not) to make them – not because God commands (or forbids) them, but because God is who God is, because the universe – the universe created and sustained by God who is love in an act that is an expression of God/love – is what it is, and, in particular, because we human beings are who we are. For Sarah, "[t]he Law of God is not what God legislates but what God is, just as the Law of Gravity is not what gravity legislates but what gravity is."[39] Sarah believes that because God is who God is, because the universe is what it is, and because we are who we are, and not because of anything commanded by God as supreme legislator, the most fitting way of life for us human beings – the most deeply satisfying way of life of which we are capable – is one in which we children of God, we sisters and brothers, "love one another just as I have loved you."

SARAH'S RELIGIOUS GROUND FOR THE MORALITY OF HUMAN RIGHTS reminds us that in the real world, if not in every academic moralist's study, fundamental moral questions are intimately related to religious (or metaphysical) questions; there is no way to address fundamental moral questions without also addressing, if only implicitly, religious questions.[40] (This is *not* to say that one must give a religious answer to a religious question, such as, Does God exist? Obviously many people do not give religious answers to religious questions.)[41]) In the real world, one's response to fundamental moral questions has long been intimately bound up with one's response – one's answers – to certain other fundamental questions: Who are we? Where did we come from; what is our origin, our beginning? Where are we going; what is our destiny, our end?[42] What is the meaning of suffering? Of evil? Of death? And there is the cardinal question, the question that comprises many of the others: Is human life ultimately meaningful or, instead, ultimately bereft of meaning,

meaningless, absurd?[43] If any questions are fundamental, *these* questions –
"religious or limit questions"[44] – are fundamental. Such questions – "naive"
questions, "questions with no answers," "barriers that cannot be breached"[45] –
are "the most serious and difficult . . . that any human being or society must
face . . ."[46] John Paul II was surely right in his encyclical, *Fides et Ratio*, that
such questions "have their common source in the quest for meaning which
has always compelled the human heart" and that "the answer given to these
questions decides the direction which people seek to give to their lives."[47]

3

∾

The Morality of Human Rights:
A Non-Religious Ground?

Attempts to found a morality outside religion are similar to what children do when, wishing to replant something they like, they tear it out without the roots and plant it, rootless, in the soil. . . . [R]eligion is a particular relationship that man establishes between his own separate personality and the infinite universe, or its origin. And morality is the permanent guide to life that follows from this relationship.

Leo Tolstoy[1]

The masses blink and say: "We are all equal. – Man is but man, before God – we are all equal." Before God! But now this God has died.

Friedrich Nietzsche[2]

There are many for whom Sarah's religious ground for the morality of human rights – her religious ground for insisting that every human being, even the Other, has inherent dignity and that we should live our lives accordingly – holds no appeal. For many of these, Sarah's ground holds no appeal precisely because it is *religious*.[3]

What ground can someone give who is not a religious believer and, so, rejects Sarah's and any other religious ground? (We could also ask what ground one can give who, though a religious believer, professes religious beliefs different from Sarah's – a Buddhist, for example.[4] But that's not the question that engages me here.) Can any non-religious ground bear the weight of the twofold claim, which both Sarah and the International Bill of Rights make, that every human being has inherent dignity and is inviolable. (Again, the claim "every human being has inherent dignity and is inviolable" and the claim "every human being has inherent dignity and we should live our lives accordingly" are equivalent claims.) In particular, is there anything one who is not a religious believer can say that is functionally equivalent to "the unashamedly anthropomorphic . . . claim that we are sacred because God loves us, his children."[5] As Australian philosopher Raimond Gaita, who is an atheist,[6] observes in the passage I've used as the epigraph for the preceding section of this chapter: "If we are not religious, we will often search for one of the inadequate expressions which are available to us to say what we hope will be a secular equivalent of [the religious articulation that all human beings, as beloved children of God, are sacred]." Examples of the hoped-for secular equivalent: "We may say that all human beings are inestimably precious, that they are ends in themselves, that they are owed unconditional respect, that they possess inalienable rights, and, of course, that they possess inalienable dignity." In Gaita's reluctant judgment, "these are ways of trying to say what we feel a need to say when we are estranged from the conceptual [i.e., religious] resources we need to say it."

Now, to doubt that any non-religious ground can bear the weight of the claim that every human being has inherent dignity and is inviolable is not to doubt that a non-believer can both affirm that every human being has inherent dignity and live her life accordingly. Nonetheless, as the Polish philosopher Leszek Kolakowski has written:

> When Pierre Bayle argued that morality does not depend on religion, he was speaking mainly of psychological independence; he pointed out that atheists are capable of achieving the highest moral standards . . . and of putting to shame most of the faithful Christians. That is obviously true as far as it goes, *but this matter-of-fact argument leaves the question of validity intact; neither does it solve the question of the effective sources of the moral strength and moral convictions of those 'virtuous pagans.'*[7]

This chapter is about what Kolakowski calls "the question of validity."[8] As to the other question Kolakowski identifies – "the question of the effective sources of the moral strength and moral convictions of those 'virtuous pagans'" – Jürgen Habermas offers only a bleak response:

> Who or what gives us the courage for such a total engagement that in situations of degradation and deprivation is already being expressed when the destitute and deprived summon the energy each morning to carry on anew? The question about the meaning of life is not meaningless. Nevertheless, the circumstance that penultimate arguments inspire no great confidence is not enough for the grounding of a hope that can be kept alive only in a religious language. The thoughts and expectations directed toward the common good have, after metaphysics has collapsed, only an unstable status.[9]

A NON-RELIGIOUS GROUND?

Glenn Tinder is skeptical that there can be a non-religious ground for the claim that every human being has inherent dignity:

> Nietzsche's stature is owing to the courage and profundity that enabled him to make all this unmistakably clear. He delineated with overpowering eloquence the consequences of giving up Christianity, *and every like view of the universe and humanity*. His approval of those consequences and his hatred of Christianity give force to his argument. Many would like to think that there are no consequences – that we can continue treasuring the life and welfare, the civil rights and political authority, of every person without believing in a God who renders such attitudes and conduct compelling. Nietzsche shows that we cannot. We cannot give up the Christian God – *and the transcendence given other names in other faiths* – and go on as before. We must give up Christian morality too. If the God-man is nothing more than an illusion, the same thing is true of the idea that every individual possesses incalculable worth. The standard of *agape* collapses. It becomes explicable only on Nietzsche's terms: as a device by which the weak and failing exact from the strong and distinguished a deference they do not deserve. Thus the spiritual center of Western politics fades and vanishes.[10]

Is Tinder right? The point here is *not* that morality cannot survive the death of God. There is not just one morality in the world; there are many. Nor is the point that one cannot be good unless one believes in God. As Kolakowski's comments earlier remind us, many people who do not believe in God are good, even saintly,[11] just as many people who believe in God – including many Christians, as Archbishop Desmond Tutu has recently reminded us – are not good.[12] The point is just that what ground one who is not a religious believer can give for the claim that every human being has inherent dignity is obscure. Especially obscure is what ground a resolute atheist can give.

Imagine a cosmology according to which the universe is, finally and radically, meaningless[13] – or, even if meaningful in some sense, not meaningful in a way hospitable to our deepest yearnings for what Abraham Heschel called "ultimate relationship, ultimate belonging."[14] Consider, for example, Clarence Darrow's bleak vision (as recounted by Paul Edwards):

> Darrow, one of the most compassionate men who ever lived, . . . concluded that life was an "awful joke." . . . Darrow offered as one of his reasons the apparent aimlessness of all that happens. "This weary old world goes on, begetting, with birth and with living and with death," he remarked in his moving plea for the boy-murderers Loeb and Leopold, "and all of it is blind from the beginning to the end." Elsewhere he wrote: "Life is like a ship on the sea, tossed by every wave and by every wind; a ship headed for no port and no harbor, with no rudder, no compass, no pilot; simply floating for a time, then lost in the waves." In addition to

the aimlessness of life and the universe, there is the fact of death. "I love my friends," wrote Darrow, "but they all must come to a tragic end." Death is more terrible the more one is attached to things in the world. Life, he concludes, is "not worthwhile," and he adds . . . that "it is an unpleasant interruption of nothing, and the best thing you can say of it is that it does not last long."[15]

One prominent contemporary proponent of a Darrowian cosmology – the physicist and Nobel laureate Steven Weinberg – "finds his own world-view 'chilling and impersonal.' He cannot understand people who treat the absence of God and of God's heaven as unimportant."[16]

Where is there a place in a cosmological view such as Darrow's or Weinberg's for the morality of human rights to gain a foothold? For one who believes that the universe is utterly bereft of transcendent meaning, why – in virtue of what – is it the case that every human being has inherent dignity? Richard Posner apparently shares my lack of comprehension: "Thomas Nagel is a self-proclaimed atheist, yet he thinks that no one could *really* believe that 'we each have value only to ourselves and to those who care about us.' Well, to whom then? Who confers value on us without caring for us in the way that we care for friends, family, and sometimes members of larger human communities? Who else but the God in whom Nagel does not believe?"[17] I am inclined to concur in R.H. Tawney's view (except that where Tawney says "all" morality, I'd say something like "our" morality): "The essence of all morality is this: to believe that every human being is of infinite importance, and therefore that no consideration of expediency can justify the oppression of one by another. But to believe this it is necessary to believe in God."[18]

One need not be a religious believer to concur in Tawney's view. Jeffrie Murphy, for example, insists that it is, for him, "very difficult – perhaps impossible – to embrace religious convictions," but he nonetheless claims that "the liberal theory of rights requires a doctrine of human dignity, preciousness and sacredness that cannot be utterly detached from a belief in God or at least from a world view that would be properly called religious in some metaphysically profound sense." Murphy continues: "[T]he idea that fundamental moral values may require [religious] convictions is not one to be welcomed with joy [by nonreligious enthusiasts of the liberal theory of rights]. This idea generates tensions and appears to force choices that some of us would prefer not to make. *But it still might be true for all of that.*"[19] Raimond Gaita says much the same thing:

The secular philosophical tradition speaks of inalienable rights, inalienable dignity and of persons as ends in themselves. These are, I believe, ways of whistling in the dark, ways of trying to make secure to reason what reason cannot finally underwrite. Religious traditions speak of the sacredness of each human being, but I doubt that sanctity is a concept that has a secure home outside those traditions.[20]

Nietzsche asked: "Now suppose that belief in God has vanished: the question presents itself anew: 'who speaks?'"[21] Echoing Nietzsche's question a horrific century later, Art Leff wrote:

> Napalming babies is bad.
> Starving the poor is wicked.
> Buying and selling each other is depraved.
> Those who stood up to and died resisting Hitler, Stalin, Amin,
> and Pol Pot – and General Custer too – have earned salvation.
> Those who acquiesced deserve to be damned.
> There is in the world such a thing as evil.
> [All together now:] Sez who?
> God help us.[22]

JOHN FINNIS

John Finnis, a Roman Catholic who works within the Thomistic natural-law tradition,[23] "believes that a major contribution of his account of ethics is its demonstration of clear and reliable moral truths about moral actions . . . that appeal to all rational persons independent of . . . religious beliefs."[24] If Finnis's account of ethics actually succeeds in demonstrating "clear and reliable moral truths about moral actions that appeal to all rational persons independent of religious beliefs," perhaps Finnis's account can be conscripted to provide non-religious support for the morality of human rights. Does Finnis's account succeed?

In *Natural Law and Natural Rights*, Finnis argues that no one should intentionally harm (one or another aspect of) the well-being of another, because to do so would be to act contrary to the requirement "of fundamental impartiality among the human subjects who are or may be partakers of [the basic human goods]."[25] Assuming that to intentionally harm the well-being of another is to act contrary to the requirement of fundamental impartiality, why is fundamental impartiality a requirement? Put another way: Why should I avoid acting contrary to the requirement? Until Finnis has answered this question, he has not specified the source of the normativity – the source of the "should" – in the claim that no one should intentionally harm the well-being of any human being.[26] The totality of Finnis's brief answer to this fundamental question is that it is *unreasonable* for a human being, who presumably values his own well-being, to intentionally harm the well-being of another human being: "[My own well-being] is [not] of more value than the well-being of others, simply because it is mine: intelligence and reasonableness can find no basis in the fact that A is A and not B (that I am I and not you) for evaluating (our) well-being differentially."[27]

Let us put aside the possibility that being "reasonable" may not be one's overriding goal in life. Even on its own terms, Finnis's answer doesn't work. One may reply to Finnis: "My own well-being is not of more value *to whom* than the well-being of others?[28] My own well-being – or the well-being of someone I love, like my child – may well be of more value *to me* than your well-being; or, your well-being may be of no value to me; in some situations, your well-being – your continued existence – may be a disvalue to me. (Your well-being is probably of more value *to you* than my well-being; or, my well-being may be of no value to you; or, my continued existence may be a disvalue to you.) If your well-being is of no value to me, it is not necessarily 'unreasonable' for me to intentionally harm your well-being in an effort to achieve something of great importance to me or to someone I love."[29] In 1985, Jeffrey Goldsworthy made substantially this criticism of Finnis's argument in an essay in the *American Journal of Jurisprudence.*[30] Goldsworthy concluded: "[John] Finnis has tried to do in two pages what ... others have devoted entire books to: ... show that egoism is inherently self-contradictory or irrational. All of these attempts have failed. It is surprising that Finnis deals with such a problematic and contentious issue in such a brief and casual fashion."[31] Finnis's failure does not inspire confidence that the resources of the natural-law tradition in which he participates are up to the challenge of providing a non-religious ground for the morality of human rights.[32]

I doubt that a natural-law morality of human rights can stand without theological support. Finnis is a religious believer, and we can easily imagine him providing theological support.[33] In particular, we can easily imagine Finnis endorsing Sarah's religious ground – or one very much like it. (Finnis might want to say something like this, for example: "My own well-being is not of more value *to God* than the well-being of others. I am not *more* sacred than other human beings.") But then Finnis's ground would be religious. "As they should have foreseen, philosophers who, like [Germain] Grisez and Finnis, attempt to argue that God need not be invoked in [debates about moral obligation] are no more able to avoid him than was Kant, who, attempting to show that morality needs no metaphysical foundations (in his understanding of metaphysical), had to allow that without the ultimate sanction of God, his moral universe would collapse ..."[34]

RONALD DWORKIN

John Finnis is one of the most prominent moral philosophers now teaching in an English-speaking law school.[35] Two other scholars fit the same profile: Ronald Dworkin and Martha Nussbaum. Has either Dworkin or Nussbaum done what Finnis has not done – provide an argument that can serve as a non-religious ground for the morality of human rights?[36] Let's look first at Dworkin.

In writing about abortion and euthanasia, Dworkin asserts that "[w]e almost all accept, as the inarticulate assumption behind much of our experience and conviction, that human life in all its forms is *sacred*..."[37] "For some of us," writes Dworkin, the sacredness of human life "is a matter of religious faith; for others, of secular but deep philosophical belief."[38] According to Dworkin, "there is a secular as well as a religious interpretation of the idea that human life is sacred[;]"[39] the conviction that every human being (or, as Dworkin says, "life") is sacred "may be, and commonly is, interpreted in a secular as well as in a conventionally religious way."[40]

Dworkin elaborates: "[T]he nerve of the sacred lies in the value we attach to a process or enterprise or project rather than to its results considered independently from how they were produced."[41] The sacredness of human beings is rooted, for non-religious persons, in two basic facts about human beings. First, every human being is "the highest product of natural creation. . . . [T]he idea that human beings are special among natural creations is offered to explain why it is horrible that even a single human individual life should be extinguished."[42] Second, "each developed human being is the product not just of natural creation, but also of the kind of deliberative human creative force that we honor in honoring art."[43] "The idea that each individual human life is inviolable is therefore rooted . . . in two combined and intersecting bases of the sacred: natural *and* human creation."[44]

> The life of a single human organism commands respect and protection, then, no matter in what form or shape, because of the complex creative investment it represents and because of our wonder at the . . . processes that produce new lives from old ones, at the processes of nation and community and language through which a human being will come to absorb and continue hundreds of generations of cultures and forms of life and value, and, finally, when mental life has begun and flourishes, at the process of internal personal creation and judgment by which a person will make and remake himself, a mysterious, inescapable process in which we each participate, and which is therefore the most powerful and inevitable source of empathy and communion we have with every other creature who faces the same frightening challenge. The horror we feel in the willful destruction of a human life reflects our

shared inarticulate sense of the intrinsic importance of each of these dimensions of investment.[45]

Again, the conviction that lies at the heart of the morality of human rights has two parts, the first of which is that every human being has inherent dignity. For Sarah, every human being has inherent dignity because, and in the sense that, every human being is a child of God and a sister/brother to every other human being. For Dworkin, every human being is sacred because, and in the sense that, even if, *pace* Darrow and Weinberg, the universe is nothing but a cosmic process bereft of ultimate meaning, every human being is nonetheless, according to Dworkin, "a creative masterpiece"[46] – a masterpiece of "natural *and* human creation."[47] Thus, Sarah gives a religious explanation, and Dworkin, a secular explanation, in support of the first part of the conviction.

Sarah also gives a religious explanation in support of the second part of the conviction, which holds that we should live our lives accordingly: in a way that respects the inherent dignity that every human being has. According to Sarah, it is because God is who God is, because the universe is what it is, and because we are who we are that the most fitting way of life for us human beings – the most deeply satisfying way of life of which we are capable – is one in which we children of God, we sisters and brothers, are persons who "love one another just as I have loved you." Sarah's specification of the source of normativity is religious.

What is Dworkin's secular specification of the source of normativity? Recall Dworkin's statement that "the nerve of the sacred lies in the value we attach to a process or enterprise or project rather than to its results considered independently from how they were produced."[48] Recall too his statement that "[t]he life of a single human organism commands respect and protection . . . because of our wonder at the . . . processes that produce new lives from old ones . . ."[49] The non-religious source of normativity, for Dworkin, is the great value "we" attach to every human being understood as a creative masterpiece; it is "our" wonder at the processes that produce new lives from old ones. Given that we greatly value every human being intrinsically – that is, as an end in herself – we should respect (that is, we have conclusive reason to respect) every human being. But to whom is Dworkin referring with his "we" and "our"? Did the Nazis value the Jews intrinsically? The conspicuous problem with Dworkin's specification of the source of normativity – and therefore with his secular argument – is that Dworkin assumes a consensus among human agents that does not exist and has never existed: Many people do not value every human being – or even most human beings – intrinsically. Dworkin's non-religious specification of the source of normativity – his reliance on what "we" value – is a kind of whistling in the dark.

MARTHA NUSSBAUM

Martha Nussbaum, a moral philosopher engaged by issues of human rights, specifies substantially the same source of normativity that Dworkin specifies. Nussbaum writes that "the good of other human beings is an end worth pursuing in its own right, apart from its effect on [one's] own pleasure or happiness."[50] (It is clear in her essay that by "other human beings" Nussbaum means not just *some* other human beings but *all* other human beings.) But *why* is "the good of other human beings . . . an end worth pursuing in its own right"? Nussbaum reports in the final paragraph of her essay that "it seems to be a mark of the human being to care for others and feel disturbance when bad things happen to them."[51] One might say, following Nussbaum, that whether or not we should pursue the good of others as an end in itself, we should, at a minimum, not act contrary to the good of others. For Nussbaum, the source of normativity – the source of the "should" in this claim – is that we "care for others and feel disturbance when bad things happen to them." This care/feeling, she says, is rooted in "the basic social emotion" of "compassion."[52]

The subversive question "Who is this 'we'?" again intrudes. Did the Nazis care about Jews and feel disturbed when bad things happened to – indeed, were inflicted on – Jews? We could ask the same question about so many other pairings: Turks/Armenians in the early part of the twentieth century, for example; Serbs/Muslims and Hutus/Tutsis in the last decade of the century. It is certainly a mark of the normal human being to care for *some* other human beings – for example, and especially, the members of one's own family or clan or tribe. But it is certainly not a mark of all (normal) human beings – it is not a mark of "the human being" as such – to care for *all* other human beings and to feel disturbance when bad things happen to them.[53] Listen to Claude Lévi-Strauss:

> [T]he concept of an all inclusive humanity, which makes no distinction between races or cultures, appeared very late in the history of mankind and did not spread very widely across the face of the globe. . . . For the majority of the human species, and for tens of thousands of years, the idea that humanity includes every human being on the face of the earth does not exist at all. The designation stops at the border of each tribe, or linguistic group, sometimes even at the edge of a village. So common is the practice that many of the peoples we call primitive call themselves by a name which means "men" (or sometimes . . . "the good ones," the "excellent ones," the "fully complete ones"), thus implying that the other tribes, groups, and villages do not partake in human virtue or even human nature, but are, for the most part, "bad people," "nasty people," "land monkeys," or "lice eggs." They often go so far as to deprive the stranger of any connection to the real world at all by making him a

"ghost" or an "apparition." Thus curious situations arise in which each interlocutor rejects the other as cruelly as he himself is rejected.[54]

As if to affirm Lévi-Strauss's point, Richard Rorty has contrasted "the rather rare figure of the psychopath, the person who has no concern for any human being other than himself[,]" to "the much more common case: the person whose treatment of a rather narrow range of featherless bipeds is morally impeccable, but who remains indifferent to the suffering of those outside this range, the ones he or she thinks of as pseudohumans."[55] According to Rorty, moral philosophy, to its detriment, has "systematically neglected" the latter in favor of the former.[56]

The consensus (or human sentiments) on which Nussbaum relies (we "care for others and feel disturbance when bad things happen to them"), like the substantially similar consensus on which Dworkin relies ("the value we attach to" all human life), is, alas, a phantom. ("To present the-good-of-fellows as the object of a desire which all people have, a desire from which no one could escape, is to divest the thesis of much of its attraction. We are all too familiar with counterexamples.")[57] And no phantom can begin to fill the void left by the death of God. Nietzsche declared: "Naiveté: as if morality could survive when the *God* who sanctions it is missing! The 'beyond' absolutely necessary if faith in morality is to be maintained."[58] Philippa Foot is right on target when she says about much contemporary secular moral philosophy: "Few contemporary moral philosophers . . . have really joined battle with Nietzsche about morality. By and large we have just gone on taking moral judgements for granted as if nothing had happened. We, the philosopher watchdogs, have mostly failed to bark . . ."[59]

EVOLUTIONARY BIOLOGY

Finnis, Dworkin, and Nussbaum have each failed to provide an argument – in particular, each has failed to provide a specification of the source of normativity – that can serve as a non-religious ground for the morality of human rights, for the claim that every human being has inherent dignity and is inviolable. Might an argument rooted in evolutionary biology serve as a non-religious ground?

An atheist or agnostic might respond to Sarah along these lines: "I agree with some of what you say: Like you, I believe that by being persons who love one another, to that extent we fulfill our nature and thereby achieve our truest, deepest, most enduring happiness. But I disagree with you that we human beings have a 'created' nature: a nature created by God. I believe that we have only an *evolved* nature: the nature that evolution has bequeathed us. Nonetheless, given the nature that blind evolution has fortuitously bequeathed us, the most fitting way of life for us human beings, the most deeply satisfying way of life of which we are capable, is one in which we love one another – 'one another' in your radically inclusivist sense, which includes even the Other. This fact, coupled with our commitment to our own authentic well-being, is the source – the non-religious source – of normativity. True, I can't prove that human beings have the evolved nature I believe they have, though it is a matter of conviction for me that they do have it. (Look at all those fulfilled other-lovers: They have a serenity and centeredness that cannot fail to impress.) However, I am no worse off in this regard than you are, Sarah: You can't prove that human beings have the created nature you believe they have; nonetheless, it is a matter of conviction for you that they do have it."[60] Unlike Dworkin's and Nussbaum's positions, this non-religious position does not rely on the demonstrably false claim that "we" attach value to all human life (Dworkin) or "care for [all] others and feel disturbance when bad things happen to them" (Nussbaum).

In my judgment, the fundamental problem with this position, by comparison with Sarah's, is this: In the absence of a larger metaphysical context with which it coheres – indeed, in which it makes sense as an integral part of the whole – the alleged invariable connection between "being persons who love one another (in the radical sense of 'one another')" and "fulfilling (perfecting, completing) our nature" seems contrived; it seems too good to be true. Sarah's religious position is embedded in – and it has whatever plausibility or implausibility it has because of its embeddedness in – a broader family of religious claims, especially the claims that (a) every human being is a beloved child of God and a sister/brother to every other human being, and (b) human beings are created by God to love one another. By contrast, it is a presupposition of the non-religious position that the universe is just what Clarence Darrow and Steven Weinberg (among others) have proclaimed it to be: a cosmic process bereft of ultimate meaning. As Darrow put it: "This weary old world goes on, begetting, with birth and with living and with death, and all of it is blind from the beginning to the end."[61] Far from being created "in the image of God",[62] human beings are merely the unplanned, unintended yield of random mutation and natural selection. But, lo and behold, it just happens that the evolved nature of human beings is such that being a person who "loves one another just as I have loved you" is the most deeply satisfying way of life of which human beings are capable. This free floating non-religious position seems so ad hoc, as if those who espouse the position were determined to cleave to a consoling belief about human nature long after the religious vision in which the belief has traditionally been embedded has ceased to have, for them, credibility.[63]

Now, few would deny that the social nature of human beings is such that a person who is part of a network of loving family and friends is better off in consequence thereof than one who is not. But this is a far cry from claiming that the evolved nature of human beings is such that being a person who "loves one another just as I have loved you" (in the radical sense of "one another") is the most deeply satisfying way of life of which human beings are capable.[64]

In any event, and for whatever reason, the non-religious position I've sketched here is not a position that either Dworkin or Nussbaum espouses. As far as I am aware, it is not a position that any contemporary secular moral philosopher has advanced. Is this some evidence of the implausibility of the position?

WE MUST BE CAREFUL NOT TO CONFUSE THE QUESTION OF THE GROUND of the morality of human rights – which is the fundamental question addressed in this chapter as well as in the preceding one – with the different question of the ground or grounds of one or another human-rights-claim. Even if there is no non-religious (secular) ground for the morality of human rights, there are no doubt secular reasons – indeed, self-regarding secular reasons – for wanting the law, including international law, to protect some human-rights-claims. In an address to the World Conference on Human Rights in June 1993, U.S. Secretary of State Warren Christopher argued that "[a] world of democracies would be a safer world. . . . States that respect human rights and operate on democratic principles tend to be the world's most peaceful and stable. On the other hand, the worst violators of human rights tend to be the world's aggressors and proliferators. These states export threats to global security, whether in the shape of terrorism, massive refugee flows, or environmental pollution. Denying human rights not only lays waste to human lives; it creates instability that travels across borders."[65] However, self-regarding rationales for protecting some human-rights-claims may bear much less weight than we would like to think: "[Self-regarding] arguments are hard to prove and not fully persuasive. Despite considerable effort, it has been difficult to construct a wholly convincing 'selfish' rationale for major U.S. national commitments to promote the human rights of foreigners."[66] In any event, the question I've pursued in this chapter is not whether there are secular grounds for some human-rights-claims, but whether there is a secular ground for *the morality of human rights* – a secular ground, that is, for the claim that each and every human being has inherent dignity and is inviolable.

My goal here has not been to prove that there is no secular ground for the morality of human rights. (How does one prove a negative?) My goal, rather, has been simply to suggest that it is far from clear that there is such a ground. *If* there is no non-religious ground, and *if* any religious ground, including Sarah's, is a metaphysical fantasy, then there is no ground for the morality of human rights, no warrant for the claim that every human being has inherent dignity and is inviolable. What then? Would it matter? Not according to Richard Rorty. Is he right?

RORTY'S CALL TO ABANDON "HUMAN RIGHTS FOUNDATIONALISM"

Richard Rorty would certainly reject the evolutionary-biological position I just sketched, because he would reject any position that relies on the idea of *human* nature, including one, like Nussbaum's, that relies on the idea of *human* sentiments. Rorty denies what, according to Rorty,

> historicist thinkers [ever since Hegel] have denied[:] that there is such a thing as "human nature" or the "deepest level of the self." Their strategy has been to insist that socialization, and thus historical circumstance, goes all the way down, that there is nothing 'beneath' socialization or prior to history which is definatory of the human. Such writers tell us that the question "What is it to be a human being?" should be replaced by questions like "What is it to inhabit a rich twentieth-century democratic society?"[67]

Rorty writes approvingly of "this historicist turn," which, he says, "has helped free us, gradually but steadily, from theology and metaphysics – from the temptation to look for an escape from time and chance. It has helped us substitute Freedom for Truth as the goal of thinking and of social progress."[68] In his embrace of the cause of human rights, Rorty does rely on sentiments, but not on *human* sentiments, the existence of which he denies. Rather, Rorty relies on what we may call "Eurocentric" sentiments: the sentiments of twenty-first-century North Americans and Western Europeans. Rorty refers, at one point, to "our Eurocentric human rights culture."[69] As Bernard Williams observed: "Rorty is so insistent that we cannot, in philosophy, simply be talking about human beings, as opposed to human beings at a given time. . . . Rorty . . . contrasts the approach of taking some philosophical problem and asking . . . 'What does it show us about being *human*?' and asking, on the other hand, 'What does the persistence of such problems show us about *being twentieth-century Europeans*?'"[70]

Earlier I asked what ground one who is not a religious believer might try to provide for the morality of human rights. Rorty is not a religious believer; his answer: *Don't bother.* Rorty recommends that we abandon what he calls "human rights foundationalism,"[71] which, in his estimation, has proven to be a futile project.[72] Worse, it is an "outmoded" project.[73] There is, Rorty suggests, a better project for those of us who embrace the cause of human rights: "We see our task as a matter of making our own culture – the human rights culture – more self-conscious and more powerful, rather than demonstrating its superiority to other cultures by an appeal to something transcultural," such as human nature, created or evolved.[74] We should try to convert others to our human rights culture, says Rorty – to our local "we," to our Eurocentric sentiments and preferences – partly through a process of "manipulating sentiments, [of] sentimental education,"[75] a process in which we tell "sad and sentimental stories."[76] Rorty suggests that

> the rhetoric we Westerners use in trying to get everyone to be more like us would be improved if we were more frankly ethnocentric, and less professedly universalist. It would be better to say: Here is what we in the West look like as a result of ceasing to hold slaves, beginning to educate women, separating church and state, and so on. Here is what happened after we started treating certain distinctions between people as arbitrary rather than fraught with moral significance. If you would try treating them that way, you might like the results.[77]

For many (most?) of us who embrace the cause of human rights, the fundamental wrong done, when the inherent dignity of any human being is not respected – when any human being is violated – is not that our local ("Eurocentric") sentiments are offended. The fundamental wrong done is that, somehow, the very order of the world – the *normative* order of the world – is transgressed. ("Outside our philosophical study . . . we don't think we're merely 'expressing our acceptance' of norms calling for mutual respect and social justice when we make (sometimes great) personal sacrifices in order to comply with these norms. We act as if we think that the authority of these norms is not 'in our heads' or traceable only to social conventions and our (cognitive or affective) reactions to them, but 'real.'")[78] For many of us who embrace the cause of human rights, the fundamental wrong done at Auschwitz and the other Nazi death camps, for example, was not that our local sentiments were offended, but that the normative order of the world was violated. Given Sarah's understanding of the normative order of the world, Auschwitz constitutes, for Sarah, a terrible violation of who God is, of what the universe is, and, in particular, of who we human beings are.

Now, we might be quite wrong to believe – it might be a false belief – that the world has a normative order that one transgresses whenever one violates any human being. But if we are wrong, if our belief is false – at least, if we have no reason to be other than agnostic about the issue – and if we nonetheless coerce others, and perhaps even, at the limit, kill others, in the name of protecting the inherent dignity of human beings, then, *pace* Rorty, aren't we coercing and killing in the name of nothing but our Eurocentric sentiments and preferences, our Eurocentric human rights culture? Does Rorty want us to say something like this: "It's a brutal world out there. It's either them or us – either their sentiments and culture or ours. It's not that might makes right. It's that there is no right, only might. May our might, not theirs, prevail!" Rorty did once say something like that: "[W]hen the secret police come, when the torturers violate the innocent, there is nothing to be said to them of the form 'There is something within you which you are betraying. Though you embody the practices of a totalitarian society which will endure forever, there is something beyond those practices which condemns you.'"[79]

Against the background of Rorty's comments, let us ask: Should we – we who embrace the cause of human rights – abandon "human rights foundationalism?" Should we abandon the project of trying to ground, whether on religious or non-religious premises, the claim that each and every human being has inherent dignity and is inviolable? If we were to abandon the project of trying to ground that claim, what would we then be left with? Our sentiments and preferences?[80] ("When the secret police come...") How much weight these sentiments and preferences would be able to bear – and for how long – is an open question. Listen to the Polish poet and Nobel Laureate, Czeslaw Milosz:

> What has been surprising in the post-Cold War period are those beautiful and deeply moving words pronounced with veneration in places like Prague and Warsaw, words which pertain to the old repertory of the rights of man and the dignity of the person.

> I wonder at this phenomenon because maybe underneath there is an abyss. After all, those ideas had their foundation in religion, and I am not over-optimistic as to the survival of religion in a scientific-technological civilization. Notions that seemed buried forever have suddenly been resurrected. But how long can they stay afloat if the bottom is taken out?[81]

Perhaps some who have no ground – who find any religious ground implausible but can discern no plausible non-religious ground – are more confident about their conviction that every human being has inherent dignity and is inviolable than they would be about any possible ground for their conviction.

("I have reached bedrock and this is where my spade is turned.")[82] Perhaps some will say that they have no time to obsess about what the ground of their conviction might be because they are too busy doing the important work of "changing the world."[83] But, still, this question intrudes: If, as their (bedrock?) conviction holds, the Other, *even the Other*, truly does have inherent dignity and truly is inviolable, what *else* must be true; what *must be true for it to be true that the Other has inherent dignity and is inviolable?* This question brings us back to something I said in the Introduction to this book: The morality of human rights is deeply problematic for many secular thinkers, because that morality is difficult – perhaps to the point of being impossible – to align with one of their reigning intellectual convictions, what Bernard Williams called "Nietzsche's thought": "[T]here is, not only no God, but no metaphysical order of any kind..."[84]

As I emphasized earlier: The point is not that morality cannot survive the death of God. There is not just one morality; there are many (including, for example, David Gauthier's Nietzschean morality, which has no need of God[85]). The serious question is whether the morality of human rights can survive the death – or deconstruction – of God.[86] (Was it such a morality that Nietzsche saw in the coffin at God's funeral?) Nietzsche's thought ("not only no God, but no metaphysical order of any kind") and the morality of human rights (every human being has inherent dignity and is inviolable) are deeply antithetical to one another. Which will prevail?

PART TWO

∾

FROM MORALITY TO LAW

4

 ∽

From Morality to Law

> There remains an experience of incomparable value. We have for once learned to see the great events of world history from below, from the perspective of the outcast, the suspects, the maltreated, the powerless, the oppressed, the reviled – in short, from the perspective of those who suffer.
>
> Dietrich Bonhoeffer[1]

To affirm the morality of human rights is to affirm the twofold claim that each and every (born) human being has inherent dignity and is inviolable (not-to-be-violated). This is true no matter what ground one has, or thinks one has, for affirming the morality of human rights. Indeed, this is true even if one has no ground, religious or non-religious, for affirming the morality of human rights. ("I have reached bedrock and this is where my spade is turned.") We who affirm the morality of human rights, *because* we affirm it, should do what we can, all things considered – we have conclusive reason to do what we can, all things considered – to try to prevent human beings, including government offficials, from doing things (even if the doing is a not-doing) that "violate" human beings, in the sense of denying, implicitly if not explicitly, that one or more human beings lack inherent dignity.

Of course, the "all things considered" will be, in many contexts, indeterminate. What Amartya Sen, borrowing from Immanuel Kant, calls the distinction between "perfect" and "imperfect" duties is relevant here[2] – though I'd mark the distinction by different terms: "determinate" and "indeterminate" duties. As Sen remarks, "[t]he perfectly specified demand not to torture anyone is supplemented by the more general, and less easily specified, requirement to consider the ways and means through which torture can be prevented and then to decide what one should, thus, reasonably do."[3] Nonetheless, "[l]oosely

specified obligations must not be confused with no obligations at all."[4] Sen
elaborates:

> Even though recognition of human rights (with their associated claims and obli-
> gations) are ethical affirmations, they need not, by themselves, deliver a complete
> blueprint for evaluative assessment. An agreement of human rights does involve a
> firm commitment, to wit, to give reasonable consideration to the duties that fol-
> low from that ethical endorsement. But even with agreement on these affirmations,
> there can still be serious debates, particularly in the case of imperfect obligations, on
> (i) the ways in which the attention that is owed to human rights should be best paid,
> (ii) how the different types of human rights should be weighed against each other
> and their respective demands integrated together, (iii) how the claims of human
> rights should be consolidated with other evaluative concerns that may also deserve
> ethical attention, and so on. A theory of human rights can leave room for further
> discussions, disputations and arguments. The approach of open public reason-
> ing . . . can definitively settle some disputes about coverage and content (including
> the identification of some clearly sustainable rights and others that would be hard
> to sustain), but may have to leave others, at least tentatively, unsettled. The admissi-
> bility of a domain of continued dispute is no embarrassment to a theory of human
> rights.[5]

We who affirm the morality of human rights, *because* we affirm it, have
conclusive reason to do what we can, all things considered, to do more than
prevent human beings from doing things that violate human beings: We have
conclusive reason to do what we can, all things considered, to prevent human
beings from doing things that, even if they do not violate human beings,
nonetheless cause unwarranted human suffering. (I'm referring here to significant human suffering or other harm, not trivial human suffering. In Germany during World War II, Dietrich Bonhoeffer observed, in the passage at
the beginning of this chapter, that "[w]e have for once learned to see the great
events of world history from below, from the perspective of the outcast, the
suspects, the maltreated, the powerless, the oppressed, the reviled – in short,
from the perspective of those who suffer.") If we decline to do what we can
(all things considered) to prevent human beings from violating human beings
or otherwise causing unwarranted human suffering – and by "we" I mean
here primarily the collective we, as in "We the People," acting though our
elected representatives – we decline to do what we can to protect the victims. We thereby fail to respect the inherent dignity of "those who suffer"; *we
violate them by existentially denying that they have inherent dignity.* Primo
Levi wrote that once we know how to alleviate torment and choose not to, we
become tormentors.[6] In the same spirit, Martin Luther King Jr. declared that
"[m]an's inhumanity to man is not only perpetrated by the vitriolic actions of

those who are bad. It is also perpetrated by the vitiating inaction of those who are good."[7] Sometimes we violate a human being not by doing something to hurt her but by declining to do something to protect her. "Sins against human rights are not only those of commission, but those of omission as well."[8]

To say, in the present context, that an instance of human suffering is "unwarranted" is to say that the act that causes the suffering – even if only by failing to intervene to diminish the suffering – is not warranted, that it is not justified. Not justified *from whose perspective?* It is scarcely surprising that the act, and therefore the suffering it causes or fails to intervene to diminish, may be justified from the perspective of those whose act is in question. But theirs is not the relevant perspective. The relevant perspective belongs to those of us who, in coming face to face with the suffering, must decide what, if anything, to do, or to try to do, about it; in making that decision, we must reach our own judgment about whether the suffering is warranted.

This, then, is the relationship of the morality of human rights to the law of human rights; this is how we get from the morality of human rights to the law – more precisely, to what we believe *should be* the law – of human rights: We who affirm the morality of human rights, *because* we affirm it, should press our elected representatives:

(1) to enact and enforce laws and policies aimed at preventing human beings from violating human beings or otherwise causing unwarranted human suffering; and

(2) not to rely on any law or policy that violates (or would violate) human beings or otherwise causes unwarranted human suffering.

IN THE UNITED STATES, IT IS A MATTER OF GREAT CONTROVERSY (1) whether we citizens, through our elected representatives, should abolish capital punishment; (2) whether, and how, we should regulate abortion; and (3) whether we should recognize, by extending the benefit of law to, same-sex unions. (If there are larger controversies in the "culture wars" that presently afflict American politics, I am unaware of them.) In the next three chapters, I inquire whether we who affirm the morality of human rights – who affirm that each and every (born) human being has inherent dignity and is inviolable – should use the political freedom we enjoy as citizens of a liberal democracy to press our elected representatives to abolish capital punishment (Chapter 5), to ban at least some abortions (Chapter 6), and/or to recognize same-sex unions (Chapter 7).

Not everyone affirms the morality of human rights. Although my arguments in the next three chapters are addressed principally to those who *do* affirm that every human being has inherent dignity and is inviolable, much of what I say in the chapters will, I hope, be of interest even to readers who are agnostic about, or who reject, the morality of human rights.

5

~

Capital Punishment

Again, we who affirm the morality of human rights, because we affirm it, should press our government – our elected representatives – not to rely on any policy that violates human beings or otherwise causes unwarranted human suffering. Is capital punishment such a policy? Many countries have abolished capital punishment – indeed, most have abolished it[1] – but if we live in a country that has not done so, should we press our government to abandon reliance on capital punishment?[2]

THE TRAJECTORY OF THE INTERNATIONAL LAW OF HUMAN RIGHTS WITH RESPECT TO CAPITAL PUNISHMENT[3]

As I noted in Chapter 1, the International Bill of Rights is the informal name for three documents, including the Universal Declaration of Human Rights and the International Covenant on Civil and Political Rights (ICCPR). (The third document – the International Covenant on Economic, Social and Cultural Rights (ICESCR) – is not relevant to the issue of capital punishment.) Neither the Universal Declaration nor the ICCPR (i.e., the ICCPR as it was adopted in 1966 and entered into force in 1976) bans capital punishment. (The ICCPR does state, in Article 6(2), that "[i]n countries which have not abolished the death penalty, sentence of death may be imposed only for the most serious crimes in accordance with the law in force at the time of the commission of the crime . . ." It also states, in Article 6(5), that "[s]entence of death shall not be imposed for crimes committed by persons below eighteen years of age and shall not be carried out on pregnant women.") In 1989, however, the U.N. General Assembly adopted the Second Optional Protocol to the ICCPR, Article 1 of which provides:

1. No one within the jurisdiction of a State Party to the present Protocol shall be executed.
2. Each State Party shall take all necessary measures to abolish the death penalty within its jurisdiction.

Article 2 of the Second Optional Protocol permits a State, at the time it ratifies or accedes to the Protocol, to reserve for itself the right to apply "the death penalty in time of war pursuant to a conviction for a most serious crime of a military nature performed during wartime."[4]

The European Convention for the Protection of Human Rights and Fundamental Freedoms, when it took effect in 1950, did not ban capital punishment; to the contrary, Article 2(1) of the European Convention stated that "[n]o one shall be deprived of his life intentionally save in the execution of a sentence of a court following his conviction for a crime for which this penalty is provided by law." In 1982, however, the Council of Europe adopted Protocol No. 6 to the European Convention, Article 1 of which provides:

> The death penalty shall be abolished. No one shall be subjected to such penalty or executed.

Article 2 provides:

> A State may make provision in its law for the death penalty in respect of acts committed in time of war or of imminent threat of war . . .[5]

Then, in 2002, the Council of Europe went even further by adopting Protocol No. 13 to the European Convention, which provides in relevant part:

> Noting that Protocol No. 6 to the Convention . . . does not exclude the death penalty in respect of acts committed in time of war or of imminent threat of war;

> Being resolved to take the final step in order to abolish the death penalty in all circumstances . . .

> **Article 1 – Abolition of the death penalty**
> The death penalty shall be abolished. No one shall be condemned to such penalty or executed.[6]

Two years earlier – on Dec. 7, 2000 – the European Union adopted the Charter of Fundamental Rights, Article 2 of which proclaims:

1. Everyone has the right to life.
2. No one shall be condemned to the death penalty, or executed.

Should we who affirm the morality of human rights also affirm the trajectory marked by the Second Optional Protocol to the ICCPR (1989), Article 2 of the EU Charter of Fundamental Rights (2000), and Protocol No. 13 to the European

Convention (2002)?[27] In particular, should we press our government to abolish capital punishment (if it has not already done so)?

Many who oppose capital punishment do so at least in part because of the way the system of capital punishment – "the machinery of death," as U.S. Supreme Court Justice Harry Blackmun famously called it[8] – functions, or malfunctions, in their society: In the United States, for example, some innocent persons are likely to be executed,[9] the poor are more likely to be executed than the rich for the same kind of crime, and those whose victims are white are more likely to be executed than those whose victims are black.[10] But for those of us who affirm the morality of human rights, no question about capital punishment is more fundamental than this: Even if a system of capital punishment functioned perfectly,[11] and even if the death penalty were reserved only for the most depraved crimes, would capital punishment nonetheless violate human beings or otherwise cause *unwarranted* human suffering?[12]

There is no doubt that we who affirm the morality of human rights may punish duly convicted criminals (some more severely than others, depending mainly on the gravity of the crime and/or on the culpability of the criminal). To say this, however, is not to say what punishment we may impose. Presumably torture – torture as punishment – crosses the line, as does lengthy imprisonment for stealing a loaf of bread. Does capital punishment cross the line? That is, would it cross the line even if the system of capital punishment were perfectly functioning and the death penalty were reserved only for the most depraved crimes?

CAN ONE FORFEIT ONE'S INHERENT DIGNITY?

If one can forfeit one's dignity by acting in a sufficiently depraved way, presumably one could get it back by acting in a sufficiently repentant way. Presumably even a depraved criminal can be "born again" – even, perhaps, to the point of becoming a saint. So even if one can forfeit one's dignity, how does this support the case for capital punishment? "As I live – declares the Lord Yahweh – I do not take pleasure in the death of the wicked but in the conversion of the wicked who changes his ways and saves his life." (Ezekiel 33:11.)[13] Let's assume, however, that if one can forfeit one's dignity, this somehow supports the case for capital punishment. Can human beings, by acting in a sufficiently depraved way, forfeit – can they alienate themselves from – their inherent dignity?

Although the International Bill of Rights is silent about the ground of inherent dignity, it says nothing to suggest that one can forfeit one's dignity. In Chapter 2, I reported what Sarah believes to be the ground of inherent dignity, and what she believes leaves no room for the possibility that one can forfeit one's dignity: According to Sarah, we human beings have inherent dignity not because of anything we have done or have failed to do, but because of who we are, namely, beloved children of God and sisters/brothers to one another; moreover, God's love for us is unconditional; God's love is not contingent on our not acting in a depraved way.

During the papacy of John Paul II, the Roman Catholic Church became one of the most insistent and influential voices in support of the abolition of capital punishment. Yet until recently, the Church taught that one can forfeit one's dignity. As E. Christian Brugger explains in his book *Capital Punishment and Roman Catholic Moral Tradition*:

> Though the Catholic tradition has always affirmed the absolute immunity of *innocent* life from intentional attacks and destruction, moral culpability for gravely wrong acts has traditionally been understood to forfeit that status. The tradition is quite clear that the lives of those who deliberately commit serious crimes are *not inviolable*... [Thomas] Aquinas says that a grave sinner "falls" from human dignity and may be treated as a beast, Pius XII that a dangerous criminal, "by his crime,... has already disposed himself of his *right* to live." In both cases, the life of the malefactor through the malefactor's own deliberate act(s) *becomes* violable.[14]

Brugger goes on to note that "[t]his is not the teaching of the 1997 *Catechism* [*of the Catholic Church*] or of [the pope's 1995 encyclical] *Evangelium Vitae*. In fact, John Paul II emphatically states in the latter that '*Not even a murderer loses his personal dignity*' (no. 9)."[15] The Church's new position is that we human beings cannot forfeit our dignity. Our dignity is inalienable. In a recent statement calling for an end to use of the death penalty in the United States, the United States Conference of Catholic Bishops wrote:

> Each of us is called to respect the life and dignity of every human being. Even when people deny the dignity of others, we must still recognize that their dignity is a gift from God and is not something that is earned or lost through their behavior. Respect for life applies to all, even the perpetrators of terrible acts. Punishment should be consistent with the demands of justice *and* with respect for human life and dignity.[16]

Sarah, quoting Australian philosopher Raimond Gaita, insists that "the language of love...compels us to affirm that even...the most radical evildoers...are fully our fellow human beings."[17]

☙

THE MORALITY OF HUMAN RIGHTS HOLDS THAT EACH AND EVERY (born) human being has inherent dignity. There is no exception for depraved criminals. From the perspective of the morality of human rights, then, the question is not whether "even the vilest criminal remains a human being possessed of common human dignity."[18] For those of us who affirm the morality of human rights, the fundamental question is whether capital punishment crosses the line marked out by the morality of human rights – whether capital punishment violates human beings or otherwise causes unwarranted human suffering.[19]

THE "UNCONDITIONALIST" PRINCIPLE

The Catholic Church now teaches that every human being, innocent or not, has inherent dignity – a dignity that cannot be forfeited and is therefore inalienable. And John Paul II taught that to punish a human being by executing him is to fail to respect "the inalienable dignity of human life"; it is to treat him as if he lacks inherent dignity.[20] But is it true that punishment-by-execution necessarily treats a human being as if he lacks inherent dignity, thereby violating him?

The Church has long taught that it is always morally forbidden to kill an innocent human being intentionally.[21] As Brugger explains, however, the Church has also long taught the doctrine of "double effect," according to which it is morally permissible to choose to do something that will have a good effect, in order to achieve that effect, even if one foresees that one's choice will also have the bad effect of killing someone, so long as one does not intend one's choice to have the bad effect.[22] (However, the Church's doctrine of double effect contains this important proviso: "The fact that the [bad] effect...is unintended...does not by itself guarantee a morally good act....[O]ne's acceptance of [bad] side effects is subject to another moral principle, namely, the principle of proportionality: an unintended lethal act of self-defense is still wrong 'if it is not proportionate to its end' (i.e., if more violence than necessary is used to bring about the good end of rendering the aggressor incapable of committing harm).")[23] For example, assuming that the objective is sufficiently important and that no adequate alternative is available, a bomber pilot may blow up a munitions factory even though he foresees that this will surely result in killing innocent bystanders, so long as his intention is not to kill the bystanders but only to destroy the factory.

Again, the Church has long taught that it is always morally forbidden to kill an innocent human being intentionally. Why did John Paul II go further and teach that it is always morally forbidden to kill *any* human being, innocent or not, intentionally? Brugger explains: To kill someone intentionally is necessarily to want to kill him[24] (though it is *not* necessarily to want to be in the situation in which one feels constrained to want to kill him), and to want to kill a human being, no matter what "beneficial states of affairs [killing him] promises, . . . is *contrary to the charity we are bound to have for all*."[25] By contrast, to kill someone with foresight but not intent is not necessarily to want to kill him; indeed, it may be that one would rejoice if one's action did not result in killing anyone, even if it is virtually inevitable that one's action will yield death.[26]

So, according to John Paul II, as interpreted by Brugger, one may never kill any human being intentionally: To do so is to want to kill him; to want to kill him is "contrary to the charity we are bound to have for all," it is to fail to treat the victim lovingly; and to fail to treat him lovingly is to fail to respect his inherent dignity (thereby violating him). ("[W]hereas 'Thou shalt love thy neighbor as thyself' represents the Greek of the Septuagint (Leviticus 19:18) and of the New Testament, the Hebrew from which the former is derived means rather 'You shall treat your neighbor lovingly, for he is like yourself.'")[27] Like Sarah, John Paul II believes that one respects the inalienable dignity of a human being – one treats a human being as if he *has* inherent dignity, not as if he *lacks* it – by, and only by, treating him lovingly; if one fails to treat a human being lovingly, one fails to respect his inherent dignity. For John Paul II, to respect someone's inherent dignity *means* to treat him lovingly; to fail to treat him lovingly – to act "contrary to the charity we are bound to have for all" – is to fail to respect his inherent dignity.

According to John Paul II's "unconditionalist" principle, there are *no* conditions in which it is morally permissible to punish-by-executing a human being – or, more generally, to kill a human being intentionally. The moral impermissibility of such action is unconditional: No matter what conditions obtain – even if, for example, in a particular society capital punishment has been shown to have a significant deterrent effect – to kill a human being intentionally is beyond the moral pale.[28]

TESTING THE UNCONDITIONALIST PRINCIPLE

Should we who affirm the morality of human rights accept John Paul II's unconditionalist principle? I want to test the principle by means of three hypotheticals.

Hypothetical No. 1. I am a human rights activist in a country in the grip of a brutal dictator. My five-year-old daughter and I have been kidnapped by a paramilitary squad that is doing the dictator's bidding. I know that tomorrow morning, as I'm forced to watch, my child will be tortured and murdered, and then I'll be tortured and murdered. The only way I can spare my child, who is now sleeping beside me, this horrific fate is by killing her tonight, quickly and painlessly. If I choose to kill her, would I be failing to treat my child lovingly – and, so, treating her as if she lacks inherent dignity? Of course not. If I choose to kill my daughter, I'd be doing so *because* she is infinitely precious to me; I love my daughter more than life itself. To insist that if I choose to kill my daughter, I'd be treating her as if she lacks inherent dignity is, in a word, ridiculous. Therefore, the claim that to kill a human being intentionally is always to treat him as if he lacks inherent dignity – and thereby to violate her – is implausible.

To say that in killing my daughter intentionally I wouldn't be treating her as if she lacks inherent dignity is not to say that in choosing not to kill her, I'd be treating her as if she lacks inherent dignity, or even that, all things considered, I should kill her. It is just to say that in killing her intentionally so as to spare her the hideous fate that awaits her in the morning, I wouldn't be failing to treat her lovingly; I wouldn't be failing to respect her inherent dignity and thereby violating her.

Hypothetical no. 1, which is a counterexample to the unconditionalist claim that to kill a human being intentionally is always to treat him as if he lacks inherent dignity, may lead one to revise the claim, so that it now states: To kill a human being intentionally, *not for his own sake but for the sake of another,* is always to treat him as if he lacks inherent dignity. This revised claim is not only more plausible than the original claim. (It is one thing to use someone as a means – an instrument – to an end that is good for someone else; it is another thing to use someone as a means to an end that is good *for him.*) The revised claim is also sufficient to vindicate the position on the death penalty that Brugger attributes to John Paul II, because to punish a human being by executing him is not to kill him for his own sake. (Even if the criminal *wants* to die – as many do; they're called "volunteers"[29] – that's not why he's being executed.) Should we accept the revised claim? This brings us to the second hypothetical.

Hypothetical No. 2. I am the commander of a military force fighting a just war against the brutal dictator in hypothetical no. 1. It is imperative that we destroy the enemy's principal munitions factory, which is heavily fortified; if we succeed, the end of the war will be in sight. I face a choice. A new, more powerful bomb has just been added to our arsenal; I can order my pilots to drop this bomb on the factory. However, the dictator has arranged for about 1,000 people – mainly the factory workers, almost all of whom are coerced into working in the factory, and their families – to live in close proximity to the factory, so as to deter us from bombing it. I foresee (but do not intend) that if we drop the bomb on the factory, the bomb and the secondary explosions will kill virtually all 1,000 people, including the factory manager, his wife, and their children. Alternatively, I can send a special operations unit to infiltrate and destroy the factory. I'm attracted to this option, even though it is more risky, because if all goes as planned, as few as 100 of the 1,000 people would be killed, whereas under the first option, virtually all 1,000 would be killed. For various reasons, however, the only plan that stands a realistic chance of succeeding involves invading the factory manager's home, which is located just outside the factory, while he and his family are sleeping, threatening to kill the members of his family one by one unless he cooperates, and, if necessary, actually killing a member of his family to demonstrate that the threat is real. (Pretending to kill a member of his family won't work.) According to the revised claim, in killing a member of the factory manager's family intentionally, I'd be treating the victim – his wife, for example – as if she lacks inherent dignity, because I wouldn't be killing her for her own sake. But is it plausible to think that in killing her intentionally, I'd be treating her as if she lacks inherent dignity?

> It is easy to see that making a person die rather than live so that you can achieve some goal, however worthy, is using him as a means to your end. But it is extremely difficult to see how causing a person to die by one means rather than causing him to die by another, *in cases where it is permissible to cause the death by the first means* . . . , is using him as a means, or failing to respect him as an end.[30]

After reflection, I choose the second option; I choose, that is, intentionally causing the death of the factory manager's wife rather than merely foreseeably causing her death, in a context in which (1) the foreseeably-killing-her option is morally legitimate, and (2) the intentionally-killing-her option is better than the foreseeably-killing-her option in terms of minimizing the loss of human life.

This second hypothetical – which, like the first one, is a counterexample to the claim that to kill a human being intentionally is necessarily to treat him as if he lacks inherent dignity – may, like the first one, lead one to further revise the claim, so that it now states: To kill a human being intentionally, not for his own sake but for the sake of another, is always to treat him as if he lacks inherent dignity, *unless, first, there is a morally permissible foreseeably-killing-him option as well as an intentionally-killing-him option and, second, the latter option is better than the former in terms of minimizing the loss of human life or of achieving another morally compelling goal.* (Indeed, there is no discernible reason not to take this further revised claim another step: To kill a human being intentionally, not for his own sake but for the sake of another, is always to treat him as if he lacks inherent dignity, *unless he will die in any case – whether or not I kill him – and my killing him will save other human life.*)[31] This further revised claim is not only more plausible than the original claim; it is also sufficient to vindicate the position on the death penalty that Brugger attributes to John Paul II: To execute a human being is not to choose intentionally-killing-him over foreseeably-killing-him in a context in which he is going to be killed no matter which option is chosen. Should we accept the further revised claim? This brings us to the third/final hypothetical.

Hypothetical No. 3. I am the president of the United States, and I've just been informed that a group of terrorists has planted a nuclear bomb in the middle of New York City, and only they know where the bomb is located. The bomb will explode in two hours, killing millions of people, unless I (through those who will obey my orders) kill, within the next hour, someone, X, in the protective custody of the United States whom the terrorists desperately want dead. (X is being held in a secret location thousands of miles from New York City.) There is no way to fool the terrorists, and every reason to believe that they will keep their word. According to the further revised claim, in acceding to the terrorists' demand, I'd be treating X as if he lacks inherent dignity, because I'd neither be killing X for his own sake nor choosing intentionally-killing-X over foreseeably-killing-X in a context in which X is going to be killed no matter which option I choose. But is it plausible to think that in acceding to the terrorists' demand, I'd be treating X as if he lacks inherent dignity?

Now we have arrived at the heart of the matter. Let's assume that in the pursuit of a particular objective – saving the lives of millions of people, for example – Y may, if necessary, act in such a way that he foreseeably (but not intentionally) kills Z. That is, let's assume that in doing so, Y does not treat Z as if Z lacks inherent dignity. Now, a different scenario: If Y is to achieve the same objective, Y must kill Z intentionally. Why should we believe that in the second scenario, but not in the first, Y, in killing Z, would be treating Z as if Z lacks inherent dignity? The only possibly relevant difference I can discern is this: In the first scenario, in which Y foreseeably (but not intentionally) kills Z, Y does not want to kill Z, whereas in the second scenario, in which Y intentionally kills Z, Y necessarily wants to kill Z (because, again, to intend to bring about a state of affairs is necessarily to want to bring it about). But why should this difference, in and of itself, be determinative? After all, (1) Y wants to achieve the same compelling objective in each scenario, and it is no less true in the second scenario than in the first that (2) if Y chooses to act to achieve the objective, Y's act kills Z and (3) Y does not desire Z's death as an end in itself but only because the objective cannot be achieved without killing

Z; indeed, Y passionately desires that the objective be achieved without Z's having to die.[32]

Recall John Paul II's claim, per Brugger, that intentionally killing a human being, no matter what "beneficial states of affairs it promises, is in itself wrong, because, as the intentional destruction of a person's life, it is contrary to the charity we are bound to have for all."[33] It is far from clear, however, why in the second scenario, but not in the first, for Y to kill Z in the course of acting to achieve the objective would be for Y to act "contrary to the charity that we are bound to have for all" – why it would be for Y treat Z as if Z lacks inherent dignity. Y is caught in the unbreakable grip of a tragic conflict; he has an opportunity to prevent a disaster of truly catastrophic proportions. To insist that in the second scenario, but not in the first, we know that for Y to kill Z is for Y to treat Z as if Z lacks inherent dignity is implausible: What if Y would choose to kill Z even if Z were someone Y loves dearly? What if Y would readily kill himself rather than Z if doing so would achieve the objective?

∾

THE FUNDAMENTAL QUESTION, FOR THOSE OF US WHO AFFIRM THE morality of human rights, is whether (even a perfectly functioning system of) capital punishment violates human beings or otherwise causes unwarranted human suffering. For some, John Paul II's unconditionalist principle is a persuasive basis for answering this question in the affirmative. For others, however, including myself, the unconditionalist principle – even if amended in the two ways I suggested in my discussion of hypotheticals no. 1 and no. 2 – is problematic.[34] I therefore want to pursue a different approach – a "conditionalist" approach – to the question.

BEYOND UNCONDITIONALISM: A "CONDITIONALIST" APPROACH

The legitimate aims of punishment are generally understood to be retribution, deterrence, and rehabilitation.[35] Rehabilitation is beside the point in this context; capital punishment is not about rehabilitation. According to the retributive justification for punishment, "persons who culpably commit or attempt acts and omissions that are morally wrong deserve punishment."[36] But that a criminal deserves to be *punished* for his crime, even punished severely, does not entail that he deserves to be *executed* for his crime, any more than it entails that he deserves to be tortured for his crime. "It does not follow from the acceptance of retributive punishment that we must accept the death penalty. How much and what kind of punishment a person deserves don't automatically fall out of a retributive system."[37] (Indeed, there are retributivist arguments *against* capital punishment.)[38] Albert Camus wrote that "[w]e know enough to say that this or that major criminal deserves hard labor for life. But we do not know enough to decree that he should be shorn of his future – in other words, of the chance we all have of making amends."[39] Does any criminal deserve to be executed?

The point of departure, in answering this question, is the morality of human rights, which holds that every (born) human being has inherent dignity. There is no exception for depraved criminals. The inherent dignity that every human being has is inalienable, according to the morality of human rights; one cannot forfeit one's inherent dignity, no matter how depraved an act one commits.

It cannot be the case that any criminal deserves – *morally* deserves – to be executed if it is the case that we ought not – *morally* ought not – to execute any criminal. Given that every human being, and therefore every criminal, has inherent dignity, we ought not to execute any criminal unless there is a sufficiently weighty justification for doing so. In the absence of a sufficiently weighty justification, to opt for capital punishment over non-lethal forms of punishment – non-lethal forms that offer the possibility of rehabilitation[40] – would be to treat those who are executed as if they lack inherent dignity, as if they are what Thomas Aquinas believed some criminals to be: "fall[en] away from *human dignity*, . . . fall[en] somehow into the slavery of the beasts, so that [they] may be disposed of according to what is useful to others."[41]

Is there a sufficiently weighty justification for executing some criminals? According to the Catholic Church, no modern society need execute a convicted criminal in order to protect itself from him; section 2267 of the 1997 *Catechism of the Catholic Church* states, in relevant part: "Today, . . . as a consequence of the possibilities which the state has for effectively preventing crime, by rendering one who has committed an offense incapable of doing harm – without definitively taking away from him the possibility of redeeming himself – the cases in which the execution of the offender is an absolute necessity 'are . . . practically non-existent.'" (The words "are practically non-existent" are borrowed from John Paul II's 1995 encyclical *Evangelium Vitae*.)[42] The Church's position on this point seems right.[43] But, still, even a modern society may need to execute some convicted criminals in order to protect itself, not from *those* criminals, but from some *other* criminals, or from some would-be criminals. That is, capital punishment might have a deterrent effect; at least, it might have a deterrent effect in *some* societies.[44]

And, indeed, some recent economic studies suggest that in the United States, capital punishment has a deterrent effect.[45] But it remains a matter of great controversy, to say the least, whether capital punishment in the United States does in fact have a deterrent effect.[46] Indeed, one recent economic study – by my colleague, economist Joanna Shepherd – concludes that in several states, capital punishment not only has no deterrent effect but, perversely, has what she calls a "brutalization effect," increasing the number of murders: "[A] rough total estimate is that, in the many states where executions induce murders rather than deter them, executions cause an additional 250 murders a year."[47] Nonetheless, let's assume, for the sake of discussion, that in the United States – that is, in those states in those jurisdictions in the United States that still maintain a system of capital punishment – capital punishment does have a deterrent effect. Making this assumption brings to the fore a fundamental question about the legitimacy of capital punishment. There is surely no more compelling warrant for maintaining a system of capital punishment than the system's deterrent effect: If a deterrent effect does not warrant maintaining a system of capital punishment, then nothing can warrant maintaining a system of capital punishment.[48] Does a deterrent effect warrant maintaining a system of capital punishment?

I can only answer that question indirectly. Consider two questions:

1. In hypothetical no. 3, would saving the lives not of millions of people but, say, of eighteen hostages[49] warrant the president's killing X?
2. Does a deterrent effect of about eighteen fewer murders warrant imposition of the death penalty?

There is no algorithm – at least, I know of none – for determining what number of savable lives is large enough to warrant the intentional killing of a human being, but if we answer, or are inclined to answer, "No" to the first question, why wouldn't we answer, or be inclined to answer, "No" to the second question as well?[50] In June 2001, at an international conference on the death penalty, the Holy See of the Catholic Church stated that "[i]t is surely more necessary than ever that the inalienable dignity of human life be universally respected and recognized for its immeasurable value."[51] If one answers "No" to the first question and "Yes" to the second, is it plausible to claim that one recognizes "for its immeasurable value", and respects, "the inalienable dignity" of those who will be executed under a system of capital punishment?

As Carol Steiker has recently reminded us, "preventing murders is only one way in which the state protects the lives of its citizens. It does so also through public health policies, environmental protection, workplace safety regulations, and the like."[52] The U.S. Congress has authorized, at least partly for deterrent purposes, the execution of some convicted criminals even as it declines to make other choices that would save lives – the choice, for example, to impose stricter automobile safety regulations, which would save the lives of tens of thousands of people. Is it plausible, then, to claim that the Congress is treating those who will be executed as if they possess "the inalienable dignity" of which the Holy See, following the lead of John Paul II, spoke?[53] We can ask much the same question about any state legislature that maintains a system of capital punishment even as it declines to make other life-saving choices – for example, to ban secondhand smoke in public places, which research suggests would save many lives.[54]

Again, there is no algorithm for determining what number of savable lives is large enough to warrant the intentional killing of a human being. There is, however, a crucial question – a counterfactual question – for anyone who affirms that every human being has inherent dignity and who must decide whether intentionally to kill one human being, A, or whether to authorize someone else to kill A, in order to save the lives of a number of others: "If someone I love dearly – my child, for example – were in the position that A is in, would I want my child to be killed in order to save those lives?" (A may be a convicted murderer under a sentence of death, for example, or A may be the person that the terrorists in hypothetical no. 3 want the president of the United States to kill.) If the answer is "No," it seems fair to suspect that intentionally killing A would be a failure of love, but if the answer is "Yes," it seems doubtful that intentionally killing A would be a failure of love, that it would treat A as if he lacks inherent dignity. Of course, to allow that intentionally killing A would not be a failure of love, that it would not treat A as if he lacks inherent dignity, is not to deny that killing A would be, all things considered, tragic – even, perhaps, tragically misguided.

THIS IS THE QUESTION WITH WHICH WE BEGAN THIS CHAPTER: Should we who affirm the morality of human rights, because we affirm it, press our government to abandon reliance on capital punishment (if it has not already done so)? The answer to this question depends on whether capital punishment violates human beings or otherwise causes unwarranted human suffering. Those who, like John Paul II, accept the unconditionalist principle that to kill someone intentionally is necessarily to treat him as if he lacks inherent dignity, thereby violating him, have a simple, straightforward reason to press government to abolish capital punishment. As do those who accept to the unconditionalist principle as amended in the two ways I suggested in my discussion of Hypotheticals no. 1 and no. 2.

However, some of us who affirm the morality of human rights – who affirm
the radical, outlandish, subversive teaching that every human being, even the
most depraved criminal, has inherent dignity[55] – find ourselves unable to
accept the unconditionalist principle, even as amended. For those of us who
fit that profile, the matter is more complicated: What reason(s) do *we* have
to press our government to abolish (even a perfectly functioning system of)
capital punishment?

Recall that notwithstanding the recent economic studies to which I referred,
the claim that capital punishment has a deterrent effect remains extremely
controversial.[56] Indeed, the claim is controversial even among economists;
for example, the recent, important Donohue/Wolfers study cited in note 46
concludes that

> the existing evidence for deterrence is surprisingly fragile . . . Our key insight is that
> the death penalty – at least as it has been implemented in the United States [in
> the last thirty years] – is applied so rarely that the number of homicides it can
> plausibly have caused or deterred cannot be reliably disentangled from the large
> year-to-year changes in the homicide rate caused by other factors. Our estimates
> suggest not just "reasonable doubt" about whether there is any deterrent effect of
> the death penalty, but profound uncertainty. We are confident that the effects are
> not large, but we remain unsure even of whether they are positive or negative. The
> difficulty is not just one of statistical significance: whether one measures positive
> or negative effects of the death penalty is extremely sensitive to very small changes
> in econometric specifications. Moreover, we are pessimistic that existing data can
> resolve this uncertainty.[57]

Clearly, one may reasonably conclude that capital punishment either has no
deterrent effect or has only a small deterrent effect – too small a deterrent effect
to warrant maintaining a system of capital punishment. Strikingly, "even those
on the front line of crime are skeptical about the deterrent effect of capital
punishment. In a 1995 study of 386 randomly selected police chiefs, two-
thirds of them said the death penalty didn't significantly reduce the number
of homicides."[58] Moreover, "[a] 1996 survey of criminology experts – past and
current presidents of three criminology associations – also rejected the notion
that executions deter. More than 87 percent believed that the death penalty
had no deterrent effect . . ."[59]

Consider this: The world's liberal democracies are committed to doing what
they can to protect innocent human life, yet the vast majority of them have
abandoned reliance on capital punishment. (I give the statistics in chapter 9.)[60]
Why have they done so? We may safely infer that they have concluded that
capital punishment either has no deterrent effect or has too small a deterrent

effect to warrant maintaining a system of capital punishment. If we "conditionalists" concur in that conclusion, it follows, on the basis of the argument I've presented in this chapter, that we should press our government to abolish capital punishment in favor of nonlethal punishment.

∾

I ASKED WHAT REASON(S) WE WHO FIT A CERTAIN PROFILE (WE AFFIRM the morality of human rights but are unable to accept the unconditionalist principle, even as amended) have to press our government to abolish even a perfectly functioning system of capital punishment. But what system of capital punishment is perfectly functioning? In 1995, in a case in which the Constitutional Court of the Republic of South Africa declared capital punishment unconstitutional, the president of the court wrote:

> The differences that exist between rich and poor, between good and bad prosecutions, between good and bad defence, between severe and lenient Judges, between Judges who favour capital punishment and those who do not, and the subjective attitudes that might be brought into play by factors such as race and class, may . . . affect any case that comes before the courts, and is almost certainly present to some degree in all court systems. . . . Imperfection inherent in criminal trials means that error cannot be excluded; it also means that persons similarly placed may not necessarily receive similar punishment.[61]

As this passage makes clear, systems of capital punishment do not function even close to perfectly,[62] and, moreover, it is difficult to see how they could be made – reformed – to do so. This is an additional, reinforcing reason to press our government, if it has not already abolished capital punishment, to follow the lead of most countries in the world[63] – and of virtually all the liberal democracies – and abandon reliance on capital punishment.[64]

6

ॐ

Abortion

[T]he murder of new-born infants was a practice allowed of in almost all the
states of Greece, even among the polite and civilized Athenians; and whenever the circumstance of the parent rendered it inconvenient to bring up
the child, to abandon it to hunger, or to wild beasts, was regarded without
blame or censure.... Uninterrupted custom had by this time so thoroughly
authorized the practice, that not only the loose maxims of the world tol-
erated this barbarous prerogative, but even the doctrine of philosophers,
who ought to have been more just and accurate, was led away by the established custom, and upon this, as upon many other occasions, instead of
censuring, supported the horrible abuse, by far-fetched consideration of
public utility. Aristotle talks of it as what magistrates ought upon many
occasions to encourage. Plato is of the same opinion, and, with all that love
of mankind which seems to animate all his writings, no where marks this
practice with disapprobation.

Adam Smith[1]

INTRODUCTION

In Chapter 4, I explained that we who affirm the morality of human rights,
because we affirm it, should press our elected representatives:

(1) to enact and enforce laws and policies aimed at preventing human beings
from violating human beings or otherwise causing unwarranted human
suffering; and

(2) not to rely on any law or policy that violates (or would violate) human
beings or otherwise causes unwarranted human suffering.

In Chapter 5, I pursued the implications of (2) for capital punishment.
In this chapter, I pursue the implications of (1) for abortion. To violate

someone – someone who has been born and therefore, according to the moral-ity of human rights, has inherent dignity – is to deny that she has, or to treat her as if she lacks, inherent dignity. Do we who affirm the morality of human rights – who affirm that every born human being has inherent dignity – have any good reason to deny that at least some, and perhaps all, *unborn* human beings have inherent dignity? If not, should we conclude that when a woman has an abortion, she and those who help her to have the abortion violate a human being? If so, should we press our government – our elected representatives – to outlaw abortion?[2]

Let's move quickly past a non-issue: Although, as H. Tristram Engelhardt has observed, "many describe the status of the embryo imprecisely by asking when human life begins or whether the embryo is a human being . . . no one seriously denies that the human zygote is a human life. The zygote is not dead. It is also not simian, porcine, or canine."[3] Philosopher Peter Singer, who is famously and enthusiatically pro-choice, has acknowledged that "the early embryo is a 'human life.' Embryos formed from the sperm and eggs of human beings are certainly human, no matter how early in their development they may be. They are of the species *Homo sapiens*, and not of any other species. We can tell when they are alive, and when they have died. So long as they are alive, they are human life."[4] Similarly, constitutional scholar Laurence Tribe, a staunch pro-choice advocate, has written that "the fetus is alive. It belongs to the human species. It elicits sympathy and even love, in part because it is so dependent and helpless."[5] The serious issue, then, for those of us who affirm the morality of human rights, is not about the biological status of unborn human life but about its moral status: At what point, if any, does unborn human life acquire inherent dignity?

Whereas the issue of capital punishment leads us to think about when, if ever, human beings *forfeit* inherent dignity, the issue of abortion leads us to think about when human beings – when members of the species homo sapiens sapiens, unborn as well as born – *acquire* inherent dignity. To affirm, as some supporters of capital punishment do, that only some born human beings have inherent dignity – namely, human beings who have not acted in such a way that they have forfeited their inherent dignity – is not to affirm the morality of human rights, which holds that every born human being, even the most depraved criminal, has inherent dignity; it is to affirm *less than* the morality of human rights. But to affirm that only born human beings have inherent dignity is not to affirm less than the morality of human rights, because the morality of human rights does not hold that all or even some unborn human beings have inherent dignity. To affirm not only that every born human being has inherent dignity but also that every unborn human being has it, or even to affirm that some unborn human beings have inherent dignity – namely, those that have reached a certain stage of fetal development – is to affirm *more than* the morality of human rights.

The morality of human rights does not hold (though it does not deny either) that every human being has inherent dignity but only that every born human being has it. At the beginning of the human rights era, Article 1 of the Universal Declaration of Human Rights (1948) affirmed that "[a]ll human beings are *born* free and equal in dignity and rights" (emphasis added). More than forty years later – well after abortion had emerged as an issue on the political-legal agenda of many liberal democracies, including the United States – the drafters of the International Convention on the Rights of the Child, which entered into force in 1990,[6] specifically declined to use language that would have required state parties to the Convention to ban abortion.[7] So, whereas important international human rights documents – the International Covenant on Civil and Political Rights (ICCPR) and the European Convention for the Protection of Human Rights and Fundamental Freedoms – now speak loudly and clearly on the issue of capital punishment,[8] the international law of human rights remains silent on the issue of abortion.[9]

The fundamental question in Chapter 5 was whether we who affirm the morality of human rights should affirm the trajectory of the international law of human rights with respect to capital punishment – whether, that is, we should press our government to abolish capital punishment. But given what the morality of human rights holds, the inquiry in this chapter is more complex: First, should we who affirm the morality of human rights also affirm that all unborn human beings have inherent dignity, or that only some unborn human beings have inherent dignity – namely, those that have reached a certain stage of fetal development – or that no unborn human beings have inherent dignity? Second, what abortions (if any) should we press our government to ban?

DO UNBORN HUMAN BEINGS HAVE INHERENT DIGNITY?

Not everyone affirms the morality of human rights; not everyone affirms, that is, that all born human beings have inherent dignity (and are inviolable). Many of us, however, do affirm the morality of human rights, and in thinking about abortion as a human rights issue, the question arises for us whether we should also affirm that some unborn human beings – even, perhaps, all unborn human beings – have inherent dignity.

What sense would it make to affirm that all born human beings have inherent dignity but that no unborn human beings have it? Some babies are born after a gestation period of nine months; some are born after a shorter gestation period. (Some babies are born after a shorter gestation period because they are removed from their mother's womb prematurely in order to protect the baby and/or its mother.) It seems quite arbitrary to hold that although a baby born, say, seven months after fertilization acquired inherent dignity the moment it was born, an eight-month-old fetus, because it has not yet been born, has not yet acquired inherent dignity. As Chapters 2 and 3 made clear, we who affirm that every born human being has inherent dignity do not all agree about why – in virtue of what – every human being has inherent dignity; we don't all agree about the ground of the inherent dignity that (we believe) every human being has. But whatever the ground, it seems fair to say that the acquisition of inherent dignity does not depend on the happenstance of whether or not one *has* yet been born, if one could be born – that is, born as a viable infant, an infant *capable of survival outside the mother's womb*. Therefore, unless we want to be arbitrary – and it is surely arbitrary to suggest that whether one has inherent dignity depends on *where* one is located: inside the mother's womb? outside it? – we who affirm that every born human being has inherent dignity should also affirm that at least every unborn human being beyond the stage of fetal development known as "viability" has inherent dignity. In January 1998, *The New York Times* reported that because of advances "in neonatology, most experts place the point of fetal viability at 23 or 24 weeks."[10] The serious question, then, for those of us who affirm that every born human being has inherent dignity, is not whether we should also affirm that every unborn human being beyond viability has inherent dignity. We should so affirm: There is no good reason – no non-arbitrary reason – for us not to do so. The serious question is whether we should affirm that every unborn human being has inherent dignity from an even earlier point in pregnancy than viability – and if so, from what point?

Many opponents of abortion claim that the basic moral status that all born human beings have begins at the moment of fertilization, or at least from the moment of implantation. (The latter event – implantation – is often, but mistakenly, referred to as "conception.")[11] According to the morality of human rights, the basic moral status that all born human beings have is inherent dignity. Should we who affirm that all born human beings have inherent dignity also affirm that all born human beings have had this moral status from the moment of fertilization? Should we affirm, that is, that every unborn human being has inherent dignity from the moment of fertilization?

Assume that you believe that the basis for one's inherent dignity is that one is created in the image of God,[12] or is a beloved child of God,[13] or is ensouled by God. (Sarah is wary of talk about "souls." She prefers "metaphysics-light." But

Sarah thinks, correctly in my view, that each of these three propositions – that one is created in the image of God, is a beloved child of God, and is ensouled by God – is an effort to mediate in words substantially the same transcendent reality, a reality that cannot be captured or contained or domesticated by any particular formula or vocabulary. The best we can do, says Sarah, is speak analogically.)[14] Assume, too, that you also believe that one is created in the image of God (or is a beloved child of God, etc.) from the moment of fertilization. Then you should affirm that every unborn human being has inherent dignity from the moment of fertilization.

But many who believe that the ground of one's inherent dignity is that one is created in the image of God (etc.) do not have a confident view about precisely when, during pregnancy, a human fetus achieves the relevant status. One can be a person of deep religious faith without believing that humans can by dint of "reason" penetrate such mysteries as precisely when a human fetus is ensouled by God. ("Even St. Thomas Aquinas, who thought that a soul was infused into the body, could only guess at when that infusion took place (and he did not guess 'at fertilization').")[15] Some religious believers may be tempted to invoke "revelation" at this point, but revelation does not disclose when a fetus is ensouled. ("[Saint] Augustine was [not] certain when the soul was infused. . . . On the whole subject of the origins of life, [Augustine] said: 'When a thing obscure in itself defeats our capacity, and nothing in Scripture comes to our aid, it is not safe for humans to presume that they can pronounce on it.'")[16] So even if you are a theist, you might not have a confident view about when a fetus is ensouled by God, or becomes in the image of God, or becomes a beloved child of God. Or you might not be a theist at all.

Even if you fit one of those two profiles – theist without a confident view, non-theist – you might nonetheless conclude not only that there is no good (non-arbitrary) reason for singling out any point between fertilization and viability as the moment when the fetus acquires inherent dignity, but also that there is no good reason for selecting viability over fertilization as the moment when the fetus acquires inherent dignity. In that case, you should accept, by default, that every unborn human being has inherent dignity from the moment of fertilization. But is it true that there is no good reason for singling out any point between fertilization and viability, or viability over fertilization, as the moment when the fetus acquires moral status – that is, the moral status that every born human being has? In his important book *A Defense of Abortion*, philosopher David Boonin argues – persuasively, in my judgment – that several of the stages after fertilization but before birth that some have identified as the moment when the fetus acquires moral status – implantation (generally six to eight days after fertilization); actual fetal movement (between five and six weeks after fertilization); perceived fetal movement, or quickening (approximately sixteen to seventeen weeks after fertlization); and viability – are not plausible candidates for the moment when the fetus acquires moral status.[17] In Boonin's judgment, however, which he defends in an interesting, complex argument, there is a moment after fertilization but before birth when the fetus acquires moral status: the moment when the fetus begins to display "organized cortical brain activity."[18]

Boonin reports that "there is no evidence to suggest that [organized cortical brain activity] occurs prior to approximately the 25th week of gestation, and ample evidence to suggest that it does begin to occur sometime between the 25th and 32nd week."[19] This means that the point when organized cortical brain activity begins to occur is not a point *between* fertilization and viability; it is a point *after* viability: Again, fetal viability occurs at 23 or 24 weeks. Boonin's argument supports the proposition that if we want to be cautious, we should assume that every fetus that has reached the 25th week of pregnancy has moral status. But I've aready explained why we who affirm that every born human being has inherent dignity should affirm that at least every fetus that has reached the 23rd week of pregnancy – viability – has inherent dignity. Therefore, we should not select the emergence of "organized cortical brain activity" (OCBA) over viability as the moment when the fetus acquires inherent dignity. Imagine two post-viable fetuses whose OCBA has not yet emerged; they are of the same gestational age; the first has been born, the second has not. It seems quite arbitrary for we who affirm that every born human being has inherent dignity to hold that although the first fetus has inherent dignity, the second lacks it.

In any event, there is a second, independent reason why Boonin's selection of the emergence of OCBA as the point at which the fetus achieves moral status is problematic. In Boonin's argument, "desires" – albeit "ideal" (v. "actual"), "dispositional" (v. "occurent") desires – play the fundamental role: According to the argument Boonin develops, one human being is the moral equal of another human being at least partly in virtue of having desires, and to respect another human being as a moral equal is to respect her (ideal, dispositional) desires.[20] But, as Boonin explains, a fetus has no desires – in the relevant sense of "desires" – before the emergence of OCBA. However, according to a different argument that many would judge to be at least as plausible as Boonin's, to respect another human being as a moral equal is to respect not her *desires*, not even her ideal, dispositional desires, but her (authentic) *well-being* – or, as it is sometimes put, her *welfare*.[21] And even before the emergence of OCBA, a fetus has well-being, even if the fetus's well-being happens to be compromised in one or more respects.[22]

I said that we who affirm that every born human being has inherent dignity should affirm that at least every fetus that has reached the 23rd week of pregnancy – viability – has inherent dignity. Notice the "at least." If we affirm that every born human being and every post-viable fetus has inherent dignity, and if we can discern no good reason for singling out any point between fertilization and viability, or viability over fertilization, as the moment when the fetus acquires inherent dignity, then we should accept, by default, that every unborn human being has inherent dignity from the moment of fertilization. Boonin is right, in my judgment, that there is no good reason for singling out any point between fertilization and the emergence of "organized cortical brain activity" as the moment when the fetus achieves moral status.[23] A fortiori, there is no good reason for singling out any point between fertilization and viability, or viability over fertilization, as the moment when the fetus acquires inherent dignity. So, we who affirm that every born human being has inherent dignity should also affirm not only that every post-viability fetus has inherent dignity, but also that every pre-viable fetus has inherent dignity too.

Sometimes conclusions are counterintuitive; this one, however, is not: Why should we think that the fact a fetus is viable – that it is capable of survival outside the mother's womb – is relevant to the question of whether the fetus has inherent dignity? Why should we think that a six-month-old fetus, because it is capable of surviving outside its mother's womb, has inherent dignity, but that a five-month-old fetus, because it is not yet capable of surviving outside its mother's womb, does not have inherent dignity? Why should we think that one lacks inherent dignity just because one cannot yet survive outside the womb in which one has been gestating?[24] I can't discern a satisfactory answer.[25] Readers who think they can should take a look at the note accompanying this sentence.[26]

It bears emphasis, then, that some of us who affirm that human fetuses, pre-viable as well as post-viable, have inherent dignity do so simply because we can discern no good reason – no non-arbitrary reason – not to affirm it, given that we *already* affirm that all born human beings have inherent dignity. ("The strongest case for personhood *ab initio* I have heard argues from the fact that there is no stage of nascent development that is so significant that it points to a major qualitative change: not implantation, not quickening, not viability, not birth.")[27] Now, one can certainly inquire, as I did in Chapters 2 and 3, as to *why* one should affirm – *on what basis* one should affirm – that all born human beings have inherent dignity. But the fact of the matter is that many of us *do* affirm it; for whatever reason, or for no articulable reason, we *do* affirm the morality of human rights. And the question for us is that *given* that we affirm that all born human beings have inherent dignity, is there any good reason not to affirm that all human beings, unborn as well as born, have it too?

What philosopher Michael Wreen has written recently about what he calls the Abortion Argument applies, with slight terminological modification, to the argument I am making here – that it is an indirect argument for its conclusion, one that simply piggybacks on the claim that every born human being – for example, a two-year-old – has inherent dignity. The fundamental grounds for possession of this moral status, "inherent dignity," are not mentioned, much less explored, in the argument. What this means is that it's a secondary, indirect argument, one that attempts to carry the day without itself tackling any of the weightier issues, both metaphysical and moral, that surround humanity and moral status.[28] "It could be that such an argument is the best that can be done as far as the issue of foetal status and the morality of abortion is concerned . . . "[29]

WHAT PRE-VIABILITY ABORTIONS SHOULD WE PRESS GOVERNMENT TO BAN?

So let's assume, at least for the sake of discussion, that we who affirm the morality of human rights – who affirm that every born human being has inherent dignity – should also affirm that every unborn human being has inherent dignity. It doesn't take much to explain why we should want the law to ban *post-viability* abortions, as distinct from premature (but post-viability) deliveries.[30] (Hereafter in this chapter, when I say "we," I mean we who affirm that every human bieng, unborn as well as born, has inherent dignity.) A post-viability termination of a pregnancy – for example, to save the life of the mother – need not result in the death of the fetus, because a viable fetus is by definition capable of survival outside the mother's womb. If we should want the law to ban infanticide, as I assume we should, we should also want it to ban post-viability abortions, understood as post-viability terminations of pregnancy of a *particular sort*: post-viability terminations of pregnancy in which someone intentionally kills the fetus or withholds care from the fetus so that it will not survive. With respect to the post-viability terminations of pregnancy that the law chooses to permit (for example, to save the life of the mother), "the law could mandate that the technique used . . . be the one most likely to produce a living fetus. Since there is sturdy consensus in our society that live-born infants are vested with full legal status, adequate procedures should be instituted to protect the best interests of those infants whose 'birth' is a late-term abortion."[31]

The serious question is what *pre-viability* abortions we should want the law to ban (if any). Our level of confidence that pre-viable fetuses have inherent dignity might not be sufficiently high that we are comfortable forbidding those who disagree with us to have pre-viability abortions. Or we might be wary about "imposing" our religious beliefs on others.[32] But let's assume, for the sake of discussion, that our confidence level is sufficiently high and that we have concluded, as indeed I've argued elsewhere,[33] that with respect to this issue we need not be wary about bringing our religious beliefs to bear.

There is at least one category of pre-viability abortion that most agree the law should not ban and that no liberal-democratic polity would choose to ban. (That X, a human being, has inherent dignity does not entail that one may not kill X – in self-defense, for example. As I noted in Chapter 5, even the Roman Catholic Church holds that one may sometimes make a choice that foreseeably, but not intentionally, kills a human being.)

> If Ann continues with her pregnancy, she will, or is very likely to, die. Betty's pregnancy poses a serious threat of grave and irreparable damage to her *physical* health. Ann and Betty each choose, therefore, to end their pregnancies; each chooses to sever the connection between herself and her pre-viable fetus, foreseeing that her fetus, because it is pre-viable, will die. It seems clear that, notwithstanding our affirmation that every human being, unborn as well as born, has inherent dignity, we would not want and in any event should not want the law to ban either Ann's or Betty's choice, which is an act of self-defense that each foresees will (but does not intend to) kill the fetus.[34] [MJP]

There is a second category of pre-viability abortion that we should not want the law to ban – a category that, in any event, few if any liberal-democratic polities would choose to ban. The reason that we should not want the law to ban – and that few if any liberal-democratic polities would choose to ban – abortions in this category is that, as Catholic legal scholar and theologian Cathleen Kaveny of the University of Notre Dame has explained, pursuing a line of argument developed by Thomas Aquinas, "the limits of the criminal law are the limits of ordinary virtue"; with respect to abortions in the following category, this fact "weighs against the institution of penal sanctions."[35]

> If Carla carries her fetus to term, her baby, because of a grave defect, will be "born into what is certain to be a brief life of grievous suffering..."[36] So Carla chooses to end her pregnancy; she chooses to sever the connection between herself and her fetus, foreseeing that her fetus, because it is pre-viable, will die. Unlike Ann's and Betty's abortions, Carla's abortion is not an act of self-defense. Nonetheless,

it is difficult to discern why we should want the law to ban Carla's choice: Even if Carla chose, heroically, to carry her fetus to term and give birth, her baby would die within at most a few days after birth. One might think such heroism admirable, but still there is no discernible reason why we should want the law to *require* Carla to continue to endure the physical and especially emotional burdens of such a pregnancy, given the inevitable outcome. No matter what Carla chooses – to carry her fetus to term or to have an abortion – the fetus is destined to die soon after it departs Carla's body.[37] [MJP]

∽

I've just identified two categories of pre-viability abortion that even we who affirm that every unborn human being has inherent dignity do not have good reason to want the law to ban. There are two other categories of pre-viability abortion that few liberal democracies will ban: abortion where the unwanted pregnancy is due to rape and abortion where the fetus has a serious genetic abnormality. Jesuit theologian John Langan has written that

> pro-life advocates . . . are extremely unlikely to persuade the general public to accept an absolute and universal ban on abortion. Hard cases (conception as a result of rape or incest, fetuses with grave mental or physical handicaps, the likelihood of very negative consequences for the mother) will make a universal ban impossible to achieve. For that reason, some sort of compromise on the details of any prohibition of abortion is necessary if the prohibition is to be sustainable in a democratic society. Pro-life advocates may well regard compromise on this matter as regrettable; but we all have to live with many things we deplore.[38]

Let's now focus on the abortions that do not fall into any of the four categories just identified. As a practical matter, most liberal democracies, including most states in the United States, will not ban early abortions: abortions during the first two months of pregancy,[39] say, or during the first term – the first three months – of pregnancy.[40] There are three basic reasons why this is so.

1. There is in virtually all liberal democratic societies, including the United States, a deep and widespread dissensus about the moral status of the human fetus in its earliest stages of development. Moreover, there is little if any reason to doubt that this dissensus will be enduring. Referring to "philosophy, neurobiology, psychology, [and] medicine," Garry Wills has noted that "[t]he evidence from natural sources of knowledge has been interpreted in various ways, by people of good intentions and good information. If natural law teaching were clear on the matter, a consensus would have been formed by those with natural reason."[41] As John Langan has observed, "continuing and intense public disagreement [underlines] how far we are from having a broad public

consensus against the practice [of abortion] and of how difficult it would be
to enact and enforce a legal prohibition against it."[42]

2. The enduring dissensus about the fetus's moral status during early pregnancy means that even if government did enact a ban on early abortions, there
would be "serious problems of enforcement, patterns of passionate resistance
to the prohibition, failures to convict offenders and further threats to public
order."[43] Moreover, these "problems of enforcement, patterns of passionate
resistance to the prohibition, failures to convict offenders and further threats
to public order" would be especially acute, because, as "pro-life advocates
must recognize[,] the pro-choice position . . . is held by many of its advocates
as a matter of conscience."[44] So there is widespread skepticism about how
effective a ban on early abortions would be.

In the United States, it is predictable that many non-poor women who
are determined to have an abortion – and some poor women, too, with
the help of a kind of underground railroad – would travel from their own
abortion-restrictive jurisdiction to another, abortion-permissive jurisdiction.
(In the United States, even if the Supreme Court were to overrule *Roe v. Wade*,
"California, New York and at least 20 other states would almost certainly keep
abortion legal . . .".)[45] Many other, mainly poor women determined to have an
abortion would simply resort to illegal abortions. (Too often, illegal abortions
are also unsafe abortions, which the World Health Organization defines as
"a procedure for terminating an unwanted pregnany either by persons lacking the necessary skills or in an environment lacking the minimal medical
standards, or both.")[46] Professor Kaveny concurs: "The ready availability of
illegal abortions means that laws against [early abortions] are likely to be
ineffective."[47] "Ineffective" may be an overstatement, but "much less effective" is not – much less efffective than proponents of a ban on early abortions
hope the ban would be.

3. Given the first two reasons, there is in liberal democracies a much
more widespread appetite for alternatives to criminalization of early abortions than for criminalization itself – alternatives that both government and
civil society can provide to minimize the number of early abortions that
women with problem pregnancies will otherwise choose to have. (To paraphrase something Professor Kaveny has written, one can insist that the law
not be indifferent to the well-being of the unborn without supposing that
stringent criminal penalties for abortion are the only way, or even the best
way, for the law to express its concern.)[48] What alternatives? "What sort of legislative response to abortion would manifest proper sensitivity to [abortion's]
moral dimension?"[49] Drawing on the thinking of Thomas Aquinas about the

proper relationship between morality and law, and referring specifically to early abortions, Professor Kaveny sketches an agenda of several related public policies:

> [I]nformed consent requirements conjoined with a short mandatory waiting and reflection period could be instituted. The state's concern for both unborn life and vulnerable pregnant women could be manifested in stress on information not about anatomical details and abortion procedures but about practical alternatives to abortion. In short, counselors could be trained to put together a "pro-life package," attempting to show a woman how she could feasibly carry her child to term while getting on with her own life.
>
> For such a package to be more than a pathetic and half-hearted stab at a pervasive social problem, intense effort and imagination will be needed. First, a concerted attempt must be made effectively to hold fathers equally responsible with mothers for the well-being of their offspring. For Aquinas, this would not be a discretionary matter but a question of justice, going to the heart of a pro-life legal policy's legitimacy. In the face of any gross unfairness, the mere fact that a given policy was designed to further a virtuous societal response to the unborn would not be sufficient to insure its moral acceptability. Of situations "when burdens are imposed unequally on the community, although with a view to the common good," Aquinas declares, "the like are acts of violence rather than laws; because as Augustine says, 'a law that is not just, seems to be no law at all.'"
>
> Secondly, we need to restructure our adoption laws so that deciding not to mother a baby after it is born does not seem to be such a draconian option. Worthy of serious consideration are recent experiences in less secretive adoption proceedings, where the birth mother has some influence upon the choice of adoptive parents and maintains some contact with the adoptive family as the child she bore grows to adulthood.
>
> Thirdly, we need to insist that both public and private institutions dealing with young women provide easily available help so that those who find themselves pregnant can carry their fetuses to term while continuing with their own lives. For example, how many Catholic colleges have on their staffs an advocate specifically designated for women with problem pregnancies, someone who will facilitate the arrangement of alternative housing and medical care, run interference with professors and deans, organize a support network, and provide financial counseling?[50]

Policies like these should appeal even to those who cannot bring themselves to affirm that pre-viable fetuses have inherent dignity – or who are skeptical of talk about "inherent dignity" – as long as they affirm that the life of pre-viable human fetuses is precious.[51] Indeed, policies like these – which are aimed, after all, at giving a woman with a problem pregnancy a more meaningful choice about whether to continue with her pregnancy – may appeal even to some who identify themselves as pro-choice.

☙

The foregoing three reasons help explain why most liberal democracies will not criminalize early abortions; they help to explain why it is politically futile to press the citizens and policymakers of most liberal democracies – including most states in the United States – to do so.[52] However, the citizens and policymakers of some, perhaps many, liberal democracies may be willing to consider seriously a ban on mid-term abortions (that is, mid-term abortions that do not fall into any of the four categories identified here). Consider, in that regard, that although a majority of citizens in the United States *opposes* the criminalization of early abortions, a significant majority *supports* stricter limits on later pre-viability abortions.[53] Consider too that a discussion has recently emerged in Britain about whether a 1990 law permitting abortions up to twenty-four weeks was now "outdated" and should be amended to permit abortions only up to twelve weeks.[54] There is no reason to assume that it is politically futile to seek a ban on mid-term abortions.[55]

For those of us who affirm the morality of human rights, as well as for many others, no questions are more important than those that concern the intentional killing of human beings.[56] I explained in Chapter 5 the circumstances in which we who affirm that every born human being has inherent dignity should press our elected representatives to abandon reliance on capital punishment. In this chapter, I've argued that we who affirm that every human being, unborn as well as born, has inherent dignity should press – we have good reason to press – our elected representatives both to ban mid-term abortions (that do not fall into any of the four categories) and, at the same time, to adopt policies like those proposed by Professor Kaveny.

> In the words of the Roman Catholic Bishops' pastoral letter on warfare, "When we accept violence in any form as commonplace, our sensitivities become dulled.... Violence has many faces: oppression of the poor, deprivation of basic human rights, economic exploitation, sexual exploitation and pornography, neglect or abuse of the aged and the helpless, and innumerable other acts of inhumanity." A lenient attitude toward abortion, then, should finally be viewed as a prismatic and poignant example of a callousness toward life in general, a callousness that must be eradicated in all its forms.[57]

7

cﾚ

Same-Sex Unions

The evil of our times consists in the first place in a kind of degradation,
indeed in a pulverization, of the fundamental uniqueness of each person.

John Paul II[1]

INTRODUCTION

Now we come to the final of the three political-moral controversies addressed
in this book: same-sex unions. I explained in Chapter 4 that we who affirm the
morality of human rights, because we affirm it, should press our government
to enact and enforce laws and policies aimed at preventing human beings from
violating human beings or otherwise causing unwarranted human suffering.
Some of the laws we should support are directed to government itself – say, a
law that forbids legislators and other government officials from discriminating
on certain bases. The Constitution of the Republic of South Africa, which
entered into force in 1996, provides us, in subsection 9(3), with a relatively
recent example of such a law:

> The state may not unfairly discriminate directly or indirectly against anyone on one
> or more grounds, including race, gender, sex, pregnancy, marital status, ethnic or
> social origin, colour, sexual orientation, age, disability, religion, conscience, belief,
> culture, language and birth.

In this chapter, I articulate a general non-discrimination ideal and explain
why we who affirm the morality of human rights should be committed to this
ideal – in particular, why we should want this ideal to be embodied in our
law as a limitation on governmental power. I then pursue the implications of
the ideal (and so of law that embodies the ideal) for government's refusal to
recognize same-sex unions. In refusing to extend the benefit of law to same-sex

unions, is government acting consistently with the non-discrimination ideal to which we who affirm the morality of human rights should be committed?[2]

Here is the general non-discrimination ideal: *Government may not discriminate against anyone – it may not treat one human being less well than another – on the basis either of (a) a demeaning view about one or another aspect of (what we may call) one's "particularity" – about one's race, for example, or one's sex, or of (b) a negative generalization about one or another aspect of one's particularity, if government can, without serious cost, avoid reliance on the generalization.* By a "demeaning" view about an aspect of one's particularity, I mean a view that *implausibly* attributes a deficit of some kind – a lack, an inferiority – to one because of that aspect.[3] An example: Women are, as such (that is, because they are women), less fit than men for the practice of law. By a negative generalization about an aspect of one's particularity, I mean a generalization – an "in general" premise – that *plausibly* attributes a deficit/lack/inferiority to the group that is the object of the generalization. An example: Women are, in general, weaker than men.[4]

DISCRIMINATION ON THE BASIS OF A DEMEANING VIEW ABOUT ONE'S PARTICULARITY

We all know that governments have sometimes discriminated against the members of a racial or ethnic group on the basis of a demeaning view about their race/ethnicity. (To say that a government action or policy is based, even partly, on a view is to say that government would not have taken the action or adopted the policy but for the view.) The paradigmatic example of such a view holds that some persons, because of their race/ethnicity, are not truly, fully human and therefore lack the moral status that those who are truly, fully human have. History, recent as well as distant, is brimming with instances of such views – racist views.[5] Nazi ideology famously – notoriously – held that Jews were not truly, fully human.[6] An instance closer to home should be painfully familiar to us Americans: "the straightforward assertion that the Negro is not really a human being at all, not part of . . . the 'Adamic family' that originated in the Garden of Eden."[7]

The most common way to deny what the morality of human rights affirms – that every human being (or, as the Preamble to Universal Declaration of Human Rights puts it, "all members of the human family") has inherent dignity; the most common way, that is, other than straightforwardly denying that every human being has inherent dignity – is to claim that not all who are *apparently* human beings are really human beings, that although some who are apparently human beings are really human beings, some are not, some are merely pseudohumans. "The texts of Western moral philosophy and theology are littered with less-than-fully-human 'others.' ... In 1933, Carl Schmitt, a distinguished political theorist and avid Hitler supporter, paraphrased a slogan used often in Nazi circles when he denounced the idea of universal human rights, saying: Not every being with a human face is human. This belief expressed the bedrock of Nazi morality."[8] Understood as a variation on the claim that only some human beings have inherent dignity, the claim that only some who are apparently human beings are really human beings contradicts the morality of human rights. For government to discriminate on the basis of the view that those against whom it is discriminating are less than truly, fully human is for government to violate those against whom it is discriminating.

Although the most demeaning view about one or another aspect of one's particularity – about one's race, for example – is that because of that aspect, one is not human at all, one is merely pseudohuman, not all discrimination that we rightly regard as unjust is based on a view that denies that every human being is truly, fully human. (Indeed, some who supported the institution of race slavery in the American South did not believe that the slaves were less than truly, fully human.)[9] The problem with much discrimination against women, for example, is that even though it does not deny that women are truly, fully human,[10] it is nonetheless based on a demeaning view – an implausible, deficit-attributing view – about women (that is, about women as such).

Consider the American experience. In 1873, in the course of his now-notorious opinion in *Bradwell v. Illinois*, in which the U.S. Supreme Court ruled that Illinois could exclude women from admission to the bar, Justice Joseph Bradley declared: "The natural and proper timidity and delicacy which belongs to the female sex evidently unfits it for many of the occupations of civil life.... The paramount mission and destiny of woman are to fulfill the noble and benign offices of wife and mother. This is the law of the Creator."[11] Such sentiments were not confined to the judiciary. As the U.S. Supreme Court stated in a 1996 opinion:

> Dr. Edward H. Clarke of Harvard Medical School, whose influential book, Sex in Education, went through 17 editions, was perhaps the most well-known speaker from the medical community opposing higher education for women. He maintained that the physiological effects of hard study and academic competition with boys would interfere with the development of girls' reproductive organs. See E. Clarke, Sex in Education 38–39, 62–63 (1873); id. at 127 ("identical education of the two sexes is a crime before God and humanity, that physiology protests against, and that experience weeps over"); see also H. Maudsley, Sex in Mind and in

Education 17 (1874) ("It is not that girls have not ambition, nor that they fail generally to run the intellectual race [in coeducational settings], but it is asserted that they do it at a cost to their strength and health which entails life-long suffering, and even incapacitates them for the adequate performance of the natural functions of their sex."); C. Meigs, Females and Their Diseases 350 (1848) (after five or six weeks of "mental and educational discipline," a healthy woman would "lose ... the habit of menstruation" and suffer numerous ills as a result of depriving her body for the sake of the mind.)[12]

Why should we who affirm the morality of human rights want our law to embody a non-discrimination ideal that forbids government to discriminate against anyone on the basis of a demeaning view about an aspect of one's particularity – for example, about one's being a woman? There are places in the world where the members of one or more racial/ethnic groups are systematically disadvantaged on the basis of demeaning views about their race/ethnicity; there are also many places where women are systematically disadvantaged on the basis of demeaning views about their being women.[13] For any human beings to be systematically disadvantaged on the basis of demeaning views about an aspect of their particularity is for them to be ensnared by what John Paul II described, in a passage I've used as the epigraph for this chapter, as "the evil of our times[:] ... a kind of degradation, indeed ... a pulverization, of the fundamental uniqueness in each person."[14] As our historical experience powerfully attests, such systematic discrimination has often constituted a regime of social and political subordination and, as such, has caused great and widespread – and unwarranted – human suffering. As I explained in Chapter 4, we who affirm the morality of human rights should press our government to avoid reliance on any law or policy that violates (or would violate) human beings *or otherwise causes unwarranted human suffering.*

DISCRIMINATION ON THE BASIS OF A NEGATIVE
GENERALIZATION ABOUT ONE'S PARTICULARITY

Recall something I said at the beginning of this chapter: By a demeaning view about an aspect of one's particularity, I mean a view that implausibly attributes a deficit/lack/inferiority to one because of that aspect of one's particularity. By a negative generalization about an aspect of one's particularity, I mean a generalization – an "in general" premise – that *plausibly* attributes a deficit/lack/inferiority to the group that is the object of the generalization. Therefore, to rely on a negative generalization about an aspect of one's particularity is not to rely on a demeaning view about that aspect of one's particularity. For example, to rely on the negative (deficit-attributing) premise that in the

United States at this time, African-American high school students are "in general" less well prepared for college than are Asian-American high school students is *not* to rely on the demeaning view that African-American high school students are, as such, less well prepared for college than Asian-American high school students. Nonetheless, we who affirm the morality of human rights should be skeptical about political reliance on negative generalizations about an aspect of one's particularity. Again, our historical experience is illuminating; it attests that political reliance on such generalizations – negative generalizations about race, sex, and so on – has often served to buttress a regime of social/political subordination.

The point is not that government should never generalize about any aspect of one's particularity. The point rather is that government should avoid reliance on a negative generalization about an aspect of one's particularity *if government can do so without serious cost.* Government often disadvantages the members of a group on the basis of a negative generalization about the group; for example, government denies a driver's license to everyone under sixteen years of age on the basis of a negative generalization about those who are not yet sixteen. Given the practical necessity of governing – of regulating – on the basis of such generalizations, it is unrealistic to think that each and every time government disadvantages someone on the basis of a negative generalization that is implausible *with respect to her*, government acts improperly.[15] But it is not unrealistic to think that government acts improperly when it disadvantages the members of a group, especially a group that historically has been socially/politically subordinated, on the basis of a negative generalization about an aspect of their particularity *if government can, without serious cost, avoid reliance on the generalization* – if it can, for example, rely instead on individualized determinations.[16] (Imagine, for example, that government refuses even to consider hiring women as firefighters because "in general" women are less strong than men and therefore less fit to serve as firefighters.)[17] We who affirm the morality of human rights have good reason to insist that government avoid reliance on such generalizations if government can, without serious cost, do so. History shows us needless political reliance on such generalizations causes needless and therefore unwarranted human suffering.[18]

GOVERNMENT'S REFUSAL TO EXTEND THE BENEFIT OF LAW TO SAME-SEX UNIONS[19]

[In its refusal to recognize same-sex unions,] the law effectively excludes [same-sex partners] from a broad array of legal benefits and protections incident to the marital relation, including access to a spouse's medical,

life, and disability insurance, hosptial visitation and other medical decisionmaking privileges, spousal support, intestate succession, homestead
protections, and many other stautory protections.[20]

Again, we who affirm the morality of human rights, because we affirm it,
should press our government – our elected representatives – not to rely on
any law or policy that violates, or would violate, human beings (or otherwise causes unwarranted human suffering). Recall that a law/policy violates
a human being, according to the morality of human rights, if the rationale
for the law/policy denies, implicitly if not explicitly, that the human being
has inherent dignity. Does (the rationale for) government's refusal to extend
the benefit of law to same-sex unions violate homosexuals? Does it deny that
homosexuals have inherent dignity – or, equivalently, that homosexuals are
truly, fully human? It is understandable that some believe that – just as a policy that refuses to recognize interracial marriages is rooted in and expresses,
and is finally inexplicable apart from, the racism in a culture – a policy that
refuses to recognize same-sex unions is rooted in and expresses, and is finally
inexplicable apart from, the "irrational fear and loathing of" homosexuals,
who, like the Jews with whom they "were frequently bracketed in medieval
persecutions[,] . . . are despised more for who they are than for what they
do . . ."[21]

> [T]he judge's famous speech at Oscar Wilde's sentencing for sodomy, one of the
> most prominent legal texts in the history of homosexuality, "treats the prisoners as
> objects of disgust, vile contaminants who are not really people, and who therefore
> need not be addressed as if they were people." From this it is not very far to Hein-
> rich Himmler's speech to his SS generals, in which he explained that the medieval
> German practice of drowning gay men in bogs "was no punishment, merely the
> exterminatiion of an abnormal life. It had to be removed just as we [now] pull up
> stinging nettles, toss them on a heap, and burn them."[22]

In most if not all contemporary liberal democracies, however, including
the United States, such "irrational fear and loathing" has generally receded
to the point where it is no longer plausible to claim that opposition to extending
the benefit of law to same-sex unions is based on the view that homosexuals
are not truly, fully human. One of the foremost opponents of government's
recognizing same-sex unions is the magisterium – the pope and the bishops –
of the Roman Catholic Church.[23] The magisterium's "teaching about the
dignity of homosexual persons is clear. They must be accepted with respect,
compassion, and sensitivity. Our respect for them means that we condemn
all forms of unjust discrimination, harrassment or abuse."[24] Hate the sin, but
love the sinner.

However, that a policy does not deny that the members of a group (for example, women) are truly, fully human does not entail the notion that the policy is not based on a demeaning view – an implausible, deficit-attributing view – about the members of the group. If based on such a view, a policy is contrary to the non-discrimination ideal defended in this chapter – and, so, causes unwarranted human suffering. Is government's refusal to extend the benefit of law to same-sex unions based on a demeaning view about homosexuals?

Assume, for the sake of discussion, that government may criminalize all non-marital sex: all sexual (genital) contact between persons who are not married to one another.[25] This does not mean that government may outlaw all non-marital sex *between two persons of the same sex* while leaving unregulated all non-marital sex *between two persons of different sexes*, any more than it means that government may outlaw all non-marital sex between two persons of different races while leaving unregulated all non-marital sex between two persons of the same race. Of course, that proposition A does not entail proposition B, does not entail that B is false; A and B may both be true even though A does not entail B. May government single out for criminal prohibition non-marital sex between two persons of different races? It may not; in so doing, government would be discriminating against some couples – it would be treating some couples less well than others couples – on the basis of a demeaning view about the racial identity of one member of the couple.[26] May government target – may it single out for criminal prohibition – non-marital sex between two persons of the same sex? Not if in so doing, government would be proceeding on the basis of a demeaning view about one's being homosexual. Does it make sense to conclude that in targeting non-marital sex between two persons of the same sex, government would be proceeding on the basis of a demeaning view about one's being homosexual?

In 1993, the Supreme Court of Kentucky ruled that a Kentucky statute targeting homosexual sexual conduct violated the Kentucky constitution's antidiscrimination provision. In explaining its ruling, the Court said that "[c]ertainly, the practice of [sodomy] violates traditional morality. But so does the same act between heterosexuals, which activity is decriminalized. Going one step further, *all* sexual activity between consenting adults outside of marriage violates our traditional morality."[27] The Court then put the central constitutional question: "The issue here is not whether sexual activity traditionally viewed as immoral can be punished by society, *but whether it can be punished solely on the basis of sexual preference*. . . . The question is whether a society that no longer criminalizes adultery, fornication, or [sodomy] between heterosexuals, has a rational basis to single out homosexual acts for different treatment."[28] The Court concluded – correctly, in my view – that although "[t]he Commonwealth [of Kentucky] has tried hard to demonstrate a legitimate government interest justifying a distinction [between homosexuals and heterosexuals], . . . it has failed."[29] As the Court saw it,

> Many of the claimed justifications are simply outrageous: that "homosexuals are more promiscuous than heterosexuals, . . . that homosexuals enjoy the company of children, and that homosexuals are more prone to engage in sex acts in public." The only proffered justification with superficial validity is that "infectious diseases are more readily transmitted by anal sodomy than by other forms of sexual copulation." But this statute is not limited to anal copulation, and this reasoning would apply to male-female anal intercourse the same as it applies to male-male anal intercourse. . . .
>
> In the final analysis we can attribute no legislative purpose to this statute except to single out homosexuals for different treatment for indulging their sexual preference by engaging in the same activity heterosexuals are now at liberty to perform. . . . We need not sympathize, agree with, or even understand the sexual preference of homosexuals in order to recognize their right to equal treatment before the bar of criminal justice.[30]

Kentucky failed to persuade the Kentucky Supreme Court that any of the proffered reasons for the law – any of the proffered premises about homosexuals (homosexuals are "more promiscuous than heterosexuals," and so on) – was *not* a demeaning (implausible, deficit-attributing) view about homosexuals.[31]

It is not surpising that Kentucky failed. It is genuinely difficult to discern a plausible non-demeaning rationale – that is, a *plausible* rationale – for tolerating non-marital sex between two persons of different sexes but not between two persons of the same sex. Catholic theologian Rosemary Ruether has explained that for anyone who rejects the Catholic Church's official teaching (that is, the teaching of the magisterium of the Church) on sex and procreation – the teaching that it is immoral for anyone, male or female, to choose (a) to engage in any species of sex act that of its nature ("inherently") cannot be procreative (for example, oral sex), or (b) to prevent any particular sex act from being procreative (for example, by using a contraceptive device) –

> it is no longer possible to argue that sex/love between two persons of the same sex cannot be a valid embrace of bodily selves expressing love. If sex/love is centered primarily on communion between two selves *rather than on biologistic concepts of procreative complementarity*, then the love of two persons of the same sex need be no less than that of two persons of the opposite sex. Nor need their experience of ecstatic bodily communion be less valuable.[32]

In any event, today few if any liberal democracies have an appetite for targeting homosexual sex for criminal prohibition.[33] Nonetheless, policymakers in the United States and in many other liberal democracies have refused to extend the benefit of law to same-sex unions.[34] (Some states in the United States have gone so far as to erect a state constitutional ban on recognizing same-sex unions.)[35] That a same-sex union is not – that by definition it *cannot* be – a marriage *in the traditional sense* does not mean that government may, consistent with the non-discrimination ideal defended in this chapter, refuse to extend the benefit of law to such unions. In any society, the vast majority of whose citizens reject – indeed, the vast majority of whose *Catholic* citizens reject – the official Catholic position on sex and procreation, it is extremely difficult to discern a non-demeaning (plausible) rationale for government's refusal to extend the benefit of law to same-sex unions.

For some Christians, this – or something like this – may be a credible and therefore non-demeaning rationale: "According to the Bible, which discloses to us the will of God, same-sex unions are contrary to the will of God. Government should not affirm, by extending the benefit of law to, relationships that are contrary to the will of God." In my book *Under God? Religious Faith and Liberal Democracy*, I've explained why such an argument is a legitimate basis for political decision-making in a liberal democracy – even a liberal democracy that, like the United States, is constitutionally committed to the nonestablishment of religion.[36] I've also explained there, however, why Christians, *as Christians*, have good reason to be wary about relying on this biblically based argument as a ground for opposing the legal recognition of same-sex unions. The interested reader may want to take a look at the relevant portions of *Under God?*[37] For our present purposes, suffice it to say that for many of us – including many of us who self-identify as Christian, even as evangelical Christian – a biblically based argument that same-sex unions are contrary to the will of God is not credible.[38]

Again, one of the foremost opponents of government's extending the benefit of law to same-sex unions is the magisterium of the Catholic Church. The magisterium of the Church argues against the legal recognition of same-sex unions on non-religious grounds: grounds that presuppose the authority neither of Catholicism nor of Christianity nor, indeed, of any religious belief. So the magisterium's grounds for opposing the legal recognition of same-sex unions – unlike, for example, grounds that presuppose the authority of the Bible – are especially fit for critical evaluation in the public political discourse of a pluralistic liberal democracy.

In September 2003, the Administrative Committee of the United States Conference of Catholic Bishops (USCCB), in a statement titled "Promote, Preserve,

Protect Marriage," argued: "What are called 'homosexual unions,' . . . *because they are inherently nonprocreative*, cannot be given the status of marriage."[39] This argument is grounded in the Church's official teaching that it is immoral for anyone, male or female, to choose (a) to engage in any species of sex act that of its nature ("inherently") cannot be procreative (for example, oral sex), or (b) to prevent any particular sex act from being procreative (for example, by using a contraceptive device). For most citizens of liberal democracies, this teaching is not credible; indeed, for most Catholics in liberal democracies, this teaching has long since ceased to be credible. So it is fanciful to suppose that the Church's teaching on sex and procreation underlies, say, Georgia's refusal to extend the benefit of law to same-sex unions.

British philosopher Roger Scruton has presented a non-religious rationale for opposing the legal recognition of same-sex unions that does not presuppose the Catholic Church's official teaching on sex and procreation. Here is Scruton's argument, as summarized by Roderick Hills:

> [O]ne might reasonably believe that men and women have different and complementary sexual "temperaments" such that sexual relationships between members of different sexes will be more psychologically satisfactory than relationships between members of the same sex. Scruton argues that men tend to be more sexually predatory and promiscuous than women; while women seek permanence in their sexual relationships, men tend to seek adventure. Therefore, if men form sexual relationships with other men rather than with women, those relationships will tend to have shorter duration and a greater concentration on physical self-gratification than heterosexual relationships. If one assumes that these characteristics are undesirable, then one might conclude that at least male homosexuality is undesirable.[40]

Even if we credit his controversial empirical generalizations,[41] Scruton's argument fails as a rationale for refusing to extend the benefit of law to same-sex unions. First, the argument doesn't explain why government should refuse to extend the benefit of law to woman-woman unions. Second, the argument doesn't explain why, even if in general man-woman unions might be "more psychologically satisfactory" than man-man unions, government should refuse to extend the benefit of law to man-man unions if those who form such unions are incapable of forming man-woman unions. Third, the argument doesn't explain why, even if in general man-man sexual relationships are more transitory than man-woman sexual relationships, government should refuse to extend the benefit of law to the man-man sexual relationships of those who are committed to, and seek public affirmation of, their relationships *as lifelong unions of faithful love*.[42] There is no reason to think that legal recognition of such relationships would do the relationships harm – and no reason to doubt that legal recognition would do the relationships good.[43] Scruton's rationale for opposing the legal recognition of same-sex unions is unavailing.

In "Promote, Preserve, Protect Marriage," the Administrative Committee of the United States Conference of Catholic Bishops advanced a second non-religious argument – one that does not presuppose the Church's official teaching on sex and procreation – for its "[strong opposition to] any legislative and judicial attempts, both at state and federal levels, to grant same-sex unions the equivalent status and rights of marriage – by naming them marriage, civil unions or by other means": Extending the benefit of law to same-sex unions would have, *in the long run*, subversive consequences for marriage as we have known it.[44]

> The magisterium fears that a purely non-procreative, contractualized notion of marriage might lead to the elimination of the family and to anarchy in child-rearing practices. They believe that even conservative gays who want to have the monogamous commitments receive the social support that comes from legal validation are, unwittingly or not, pursuing a Trojan horse policy in which entry into the institution will eventually lead to its demise. Instead of helping matters, contractualism would leave them on their own and make it easier for fathers routinely to abandon their children.[45]

As it happens, this seems to be the principal non-religious argument advanced in public political debate by activists opposed to the legal recognition of same-sex unions. This, to me and many others, is a deeply counterinutive argument.[46] But counterintuitive or not, little if any empirical data supports the argument.[47] For a careful presentation and vigorous rebuttal of the argument, one should read this important paper, published in 2004: William N. Eskridge Jr., Darren R. Spedale, and Hans Ytterberg, *Nordic Bliss? Scandinavian Registered Partnerships and the Same-Sex Marriage Debate.*[48]

For those of us who join Eskridge et al. in rejecting the "subverts marriage" argument, and who find wanting the other arguments rehearsed or referenced here, it follows that there is no non-demeaning rationale for government's refusal to extend the benefit of law to same-sex unions. Indeed, even for those who accept the Catholic Church's official teaching on sex and procreation, it is difficult to discern a non-demeaning rationale for insisting that *none* of the benefits of law should be extended to same-sex unions. Significantly, some Catholic bishops in the United States have recently expressed a willingness to consider supporting, as a matter of distributive justice, the extension of *some* of the benefits of law to same-sex unions.[49]

CONCLUSION

I expect that within the next generation or two – within the lifetime of our children or our children's children – the understanding will come to be widely shared, in the world's liberal democracies, that refusing to recognize same-sex unions, if not morally akin to outlawing interracial unions,[50] is nonetheless bereft of any non-demeaning rationale.[51] Meanwhile, for those of us who have already concluded that there is no non-demeaning rationale for withholding legal recognition from same-sex unions, this is the answer to the question I posed at the beginning of the chapter: Government's refusal to recognize – its refusal to extend the benefit of law to – same-sex unions betrays the non-discrimination ideal to which we who affirm the morality of human rights should be committed.[52]

APPENDIX A: NON-DISCRIMINATION IDEAL, ANTIDISCRIMINATION LAW

To what extent do existing human rights laws – international, transnational (regional), and national – conform to the non-discrimination ideal advocated in this chapter?

Article 2 of the Universal Declaration of Human Rights specifically condemns, with respect to "all the rights and freedoms set forth in this Declaration," any discrimination based on "race, colour, sex, language, religion, political or other opinion, national or social origin, property, birth or other status." Article 2 of the International Covenant on Civil and Political Rights (ICCPR) requires that "Each State Party . . . undertake[] to respect and to ensure to all individuals within its territory and subject to its jurisdiction the rights recognized in the present Covenant, without distinction of any kind, such as race, colour, sex, language, religion, political or other opinion, national or social origin, property, birth or other status." Article 2 of the International Covenant on Economic, Social, and Cultural Rights (ICE-SCR) contains much the same language: "The State Parties . . . undertake[] to guarantee that the rights enunciated in the present Covenant will be exercised without discrimination of any kind as to race, colour, sex, language, religion, political or other opinion, national or social origin, property, birth or other status." Moreover, Article 26 of the ICCPR states: "All persons are equal before the law and are entitled without any discrimination to the equal protection of the law. In this respect, the law shall prohibit any discrimination and guarantee to all persons equal and effective protection against discrimination on any ground such as race, colour, sex, language, religion, political or other opinion, national or social origin, property, birth or other status."

The International Convention on the Elimination of All Forms of Racial Discrimination, which took effect in 1969 and as of June 2004 had 169 state parties, and the International Convention on the Elimination of All Forms of Discrimination Against Women, which became effective in 1981 and as of June 2004 had 177 state parties, provide further, more elaborate and robust protection from discrimination – albeit, from discrimination defined more narrowly ("all forms of racial discrimination" and "discrimination against women").

Clearly, the non-discrimination ideal defended in this chapter looms large in international human rights law.

It also looms large in transnational (regional) human rights law. The three principal transnational human rights treaties are the European Convention for the Protection of Human Rights and Fundamental Freedoms, the American Convention on Human Rights, and the African Charter on Human and Peoples' Rights. Article 14 of the European Convention states: "The enjoyment of the rights and freedoms set forth in this Convention shall be secured without discrimination based on any ground such as sex, race, colour, language, religion, political or other opinion, national or social origin, association with a national minority, property, birth or other status." According to Article 21 of the Charter of Fundamental Rights of the European Union, "[a]ny discrimination based on any ground such as race, colour, ethnic or social origin, genetic features, language, religion or belief, political or other opinion, membership of a national minority, property, birth, disability, age or sexual orientation shall be prohibited." Article 1 of the American Convention and Article 2 of the African Charter are substantially similar (except that neither contains an explicit reference to sexual orientation). Article 1 of the American Convention states:

> The States Parties to this Convention undertake to respect the rights and freedoms recognized herein and to ensure to all persons subject to their jurisdiction the free and full exercise of those rights and freedoms, without any discrimination for reasons of race, color, sex, language, religion, political or other opinion, national or social origin, economic status, birth, or any other social condition.

Article 2 of the African Charter states:

> Every individual shall be entitled to the enjoyment of the rights and freedoms recognized and guaranteed in the present Charter without distinction of any kind such as race, ethnic group, color, sex, language, religion, political or any other opinion, national or social origin, fortune, birth or other status.

What about national human rights law? Liberal democracies, in their constitutional and other law, generally provide no less protection from discrimination than that provided by international and transnational human rights
law. A few prominent examples: The United Kingdom, which is a party to
the European Convention for the Protection of Human Rights and Fundamental Freedoms, has recently made the rights and freedoms set forth in the
European Convention a part of its national (domestic) law. (I comment on
this development in the Appendix to Chapter 8.) The Canadian Charter of
Rights and Freedoms, which is part of the Canadian Constitution, states in
subsection 15(1): "Every individual is equal before the law and has the right
to the equal protection and equal benefit of the law without discrimination
and, in particular, without discrimination based on race, national or ethnic
origin, colour, religion, sex, age or mental or physical disability." The Constitution of the Republic of South Africa, which took effect in 1996, states in
subsection 9(3): "The state may not unfairly discriminate directly or indirectly against anyone on one or more grounds, including race, gender, sex,
pregnancy, marital status, ethnic or social origin, colour, sexual orientation,
age, disability, religion, conscience, belief, culture, language and birth." Note
the word "unfairly" in subsection 9(3). Clearly, for government to discriminate on the basis of a demeaning view about one particularity – about one's
race, sex, and so on – is for government "unfairly" to discriminate; similarly,
for government to discriminate on the basis of a negative generalization about
one's particularity, if government need not rely on the generalization, is for
government "unfairly" to discriminate.[53]

APPENDIX B: GOVERNMENT'S RELIANCE ON RACE- OR
ETHNICITY-BASED AFFIRMATIVE ACTION

I will say a few words here about the implications of the non-discrimination
ideal advocated in this chapter for another greatly controversial political-moral
issue: government's reliance on race- or ethnicity-based affirmative action. By
race- or ethnicity-based affirmative action, I mean

1. a policy designed to increase the number of *qualified* persons from
   a racial (or enthnic) group who succeed in gaining access to a scarce
   opportunity – for example, a position in a university class – by giving the
   members of the racial group, or some of them, a competitive advantage
   in the process that governs access to the scarce opportunity;
2. a policy that is aimed at achieving a state of affairs in which

(a) the marginalization of the racial group – whether that marginalization is social, political, and/or economic – is diminished and

(b) a healthier society – in particular, a society that is more widely
perceived as legitimate and is therefore more stable and productive –
is thereby achieved.[54]

Government reliance on policies that fit the foregoing profile is greatly
controversial wherever it exists – for example, in the United States, Brazil,
India, and Malaysia.[55] Some people object to (government reliance on) one
or another program of race-based (or ethnicity-based) affirmative action on
the ground that the program in question hurts the very group(s) it is meant to
help. Some object to one or another program of race-based affirmative action –
or perhaps to all such programs – on the ground that, all things considered,
the program or programs hurt society more than they help it (for example, by
fomenting divisive racial resentment). Some object to all programs of race-
based affirmative action on the ground that – whatever the costs and benefits
of such programs – it is unjust for government to classify persons by race no
matter what the reason for doing so – and, therefore, even if the reason is
"benign" rather than "invidious." Some object to all programs of race-based
affirmative action on the ground that – no matter what the costs and benefits
of such programs, and even assuming for the sake of that such programs
are not unjust – the relevant law forbids government to classify persons by
race.

1. I am interested here in the last sort of objection: objections grounded
on a legal claim. I want to make two points here. First: That government is
relying on (a program of) race-based affirmative action does not mean that
government is acting contrary to the non-discrimination ideal defended in this
chapter. Undeniably, in relying on race-based affirmative action, government
is treating some persons – namely, those who are not members of the racial
group (or a racial group) that gets the competitive advantage – less well than
some other persons; in favoring (and, in that sense, discriminating *for*) some
persons on the basis of race, government necessarily disfavors (and, in that
sense, discriminates *against*) some other persons on the basis of race. But,
clearly, that government is relying on race-based affirmative action does not
mean that government is relying on a demeaning view – an implausible, deficit-
attributing view – about any aspect of the particularity (for example, the race)
of those who are *disfavored* by the affirmative action. Even some critics of race-
based affirmative action are admirably quick to concede this point and move
on. Jeremy Rabkin is a recent example: "It is perfectly true – and pointless

to deny – that affirmative action does not injure whites in the same way that the old discrimination injured minorities. Reverse discrimination does not stamp disappointed white candidates with a stigma of inferiority or signal that minority individuals cannot bear to mix with them."[56]

True, that government is relying on race-based affirmative action does mean that government is relying on a negative generalization about an aspect of the particularity (the race or ethnicity) of those who are *favored* by the affirmative action – namely, the premise that the members of the group favored by the affirmative action are *in general* at a disadvantage in the competition to gain access to the scarce opportunity. (Recall: By a negative generalization about an aspect of one's particularity, I mean a generalization – an "in general" premise – that *plausibly* attributes a deficit/lack/inferiority to the group that is the object of the generalization.) But this does not mean that government is relying on a negative generalization about any aspect of the particularity of those who are *disfavored* by the affirmative action.

So the non-discrimination ideal advocated in this chapter does not forbid government to rely on race-based affirmative action.

2. Now, the second point I want to make: As a general matter, existing human rights law does not forbid government to rely on race-based affirmative action. As U.S. Supreme Court Justice Ruth Bader Ginsburg has emphasized: "Contemporary human rights documents . . . distinguish between policies of oppression and measures designed to accelerate *de facto* equality."[57] Ginsburg gives this important example: "The International Convention on the Elimination of All Forms of Racial Discrimination, ratified by the United States in 1994, . . . endorses 'special and concrete measures to ensure the adequate development and protection of certain racial groups or individuals belonging to them, for the purpose of guaranteeing them the full and equal enjoyment of human rights and fundamental freedoms.'"[58]

The Constitution of India, which took effect in 1949, is another example. Several provisions of the Indian Constitution ban racial and other sorts of discrimination. Article 14 declares: "The State shall not deny to any person equality before the law or the equal protection of the laws within the territory of India." Article 15(1) forbids government to "discriminate against any citizen on grounds only of religion, race, caste, sex, place of birth or any of them." Article 16(1) states that "[t]here shall be equality of opportunity for all citizens in matters relating to employment or appointment to any office under the State."

At the same time, however, the Indian Constitution recognizes that there is a world of difference between discrimination that is hostile to a socially/politically/economically subordinated group and discrimination that is friendly to such a group. Article 15(4) specifically provides that "[n]othing in this article...shall prevent the State from making any special provision for the advancement of any socially and educationally backward classes of citizens or for the Scheduled Castes and the Scheduled Tribes." Similarly, paragraphs (4) and (4A) of Article 16 allow government to engage in "compensatory discrimination" with respect to appointments to, or promotions in, public employment. Indeed, Article 46 requires that "[t]he State promote with special care the educational and economic interests of the weaker sections of the people, and in particular, of the Scheduled Castes and the Scheduled Tribes..." These provisions were meant to "recognize[] and encourage[] compensatory discrimination in favor of socially and educationally backward classes of citizens..."[59] Marc Galanter has noted that Indian constitutional provisions authorizing such compensatory discrimination "do not merely carve out an area in which the general principle of equality is inapplicable. Rather, they are specifically designed to implement and fulfill the general principle."[60] Galanter quotes an Indian judge: "Social justice...cannot be reached if we overemphasize the 'merit theory.'"[61]

The same judge sought to explain, however, that using compensatory discrimination (among other strategies) to ameliorate the social/political/economic subordination of some social groups is important not just as a matter of implementing and fulfilling the general principle of equality; it is important, that is, not just as a matter of achieving "social justice." It is also important – in fact it is no less important – as a way of promoting both the "stability" and "real progress" of the nation:

> [T]here can be neither stability nor real progress if predominant sections of an awakened Nation live in primitive conditions, confined to unremunerative occupations and having no share in the good things of life, while power and wealth are confined in the hands of only a few and the same is used for the benefit of the sections of the community to which they belong.... Unaided many sections of the people...cannot compete with the advanced sections of the people, who today have a monopoly of education and consequently have predominant representation in the Government services as well as in other important walks of life. It is cynical to suggest that the interest of the Nation is best served if a barber's son continues to be a barber and a shepherd's son continues to be a shepherd.[62]

Consider next the Canadian Constitution (1982), which states, in subsection 15(1) of the Charter of Rights and Freedoms:

Every individual is equal before and under the law and has the right to the equal protection and equal benefit of the law without discrimination and, in particular, without discrimination based on race, national or ethnic origin, colour, religion, sex, age, or mental or physical disability.

Subsection 15(2) then makes clear that the antidiscrimination right protected by subsection 15(1) does not forbid government from relying on race-based affirmative action (or on other sorts of affirmative action):

[Section 15(1)] does not preclude any law, program or activity that has as its object the amelioration of conditions of disadvantaged individuals or groups including those that are disadvantaged because of race, national or ethnic origin, colour, religion, sex, age or mental or physical disability.

Finally, consider the Constitution of the Republic of South Africa, which took effect in 1996. Subsection 9(1) declares: "Everyone is equal before the law and has the right to equal protection and benefit of the law." Subsection 9(3) elaborates:

The state may not unfairly discriminate directly or indirectly against anyone on one or more grounds, including race, gender, sex, pregnancy, marital status, ethnic or social origin, colour, sexual orientation, age, disability, religion, conscience, belief, culture, language or birth.

Subsection 9(2) makes clear, however, that the commitment of the South African Constitution to racial (and other sorts of) equality not only does not forbid government from relying on race-based affirmative action, but can justify such reliance:

Equality includes the full and equal enjoyment of all rights and freedoms. To promote the achievement of equality, legislative and other measures designed to protect or advance persons, or categories of persons, disadvantaged by unfair discrimination may be taken.

As South African legal scholar Saras Jagwanth has explained, subsection 9(2) "explicitly recognizes that affirmative action and other remedial measures are not an exception or a limitation to equality but a means to promote and achieve it. These measures do not constitute a diminution of the right; rather they buttress and reinforce it."[63]

3. Whether, all things considered, it is *prudent* for government – prudent as a matter of sound public policy – to rely on one or another, or indeed on any, program of race-based affirmative action is distinct from the question of whether it is *legal* for government – legal according to the governing

antidiscrimination law – to do so. The two questions should not be conflated. I've argued here that in relying on a program of race-based affirmative action, government is acting contrary *neither* to the non-discrimination ideal advocated in this chapter *nor* to existing human rights law. But this does not mean that, all things considered, it is prudent for government to rely on one or another, or on any, program of race-based affirmative action.[64] That's a different question – and one I've not addressed here.[65]

PART THREE

FROM LAW TO COURTS

8

༨

Protecting Human Rights in a Democracy: What Role for the Courts?

Preliminary clarification. In the Introduction to this book, I confessed to a bias against *moral*-rights-talk. So it bears emphasizing that when I refer to "human rights" in this chapter and the next one, I am referring to legal rights.[1] Put another way, I am referring to human rights *laws* – in particular, to human rights laws *directed at government*. Such laws – for example, a law forbidding government to deny the freedom of speech, or one requiring government to provide due process of law – are my principal concern in this chapter.

INTRODUCTION

In the preceding three chapters, I inquired as to whether we who affirm the morality of human rights – who affirm that each and every (born) human being has inherent dignity and is inviolable – should use the political freedom we enjoy as citizens of a liberal democracy to press our elected representatives to abolish capital punishment (Chapter 5), to ban at least some abortions (Chapter 6), and/or to extend the benefit of law to same-sex unions (Chapter 7). In this chapter, I inquire into what role we should want the courts to play, if any, in determining public policy with respect to capital punishment, abortion, same-sex unions, and other morally controversial practices.

In liberal democracies with judicially enforceable constitutions – meaning most liberal democracies – questions about public policy often become entwined with questions about constitutionality. Although the Constitution of the Republic of South Africa does not explicitly ban capital punishment, the South African Constitutional Court has nonetheless interpreted the constitution to ban capital punishment.[2] Many people in the United States think that the United States Supreme Court should interpret the Eighth Amendment to the United States Constitution – which bans "cruel and unusual punishments" – to mean ban capital punishment. (The Court has already interpreted the cruel and unusual punishment clause to ban the death penalty for persons who were seventeen or younger when they committed the crime and for persons who are retarded.)[3] In one of the most controversial judicial rulings in American history, the Court interpreted the Fourteenth Amendment to mean forbiding government to outlaw pre-viability abortions. Many Americans, fearful that the Court might be tempted to interpret the Fourteenth Amendment as requiring government to recognize, by extending the benefit of law to, same-sex unions, want to amend the Constitution to prevent the Court from doing so. (In the next chapter, I inquire as to how the Court should rule on constitutional challenges to capital punishment, restrictive abortion legislation, and government's refusal to recognize same-sex unions.)

What role should we who affirm the morality of human rights want our country's courts to play in protecting the human rights provisions of our country's constitution?[4] What role should we want the courts to play in adjudicating disputed questions about such provisions, such as the question of whether the general antidiscrimination provision of the constitution requires government to recognize, by extending the benefit of law to, same-sex unions? This subject – the courts' proper role in protecting (what we may call) the constitutional law of human rights – has been, and remains, greatly contested, not least in the United States, where the courts, especially the Supreme Court, have sometimes played a large role in adjudicating disputed questions about the constitutional law of human rights.

Not least in the United States, but certainly not only in the United States. In the period since the end of World War II, most liberal democracies have followed the lead of the United States in empowering their judiciaries to enforce their constitutional law of human rights.[5] (For an important recent example of such judicial empowerment, see the South African Constitution, which took effect in 1996.)[6] This "global expansion of judicial power"[7] – which has been called "one of the most significant trends in late-twentieth and early-twenty-first-century government"[8] – has led, in the view of some commentators, to "the judicialization of politics."[9]

In most liberal democracies, some human rights laws are both (1) superior (lexically prior) to ordinary laws and policies, and (2) entrenched: *exceedingly difficult, sometimes to the point of practically impossible, to amend or repeal.* It is relatively easy for legislators to overrule a judicial decision with which they strongly disagree, if the decision is based on a law that is relatively easy for them to amend or repeal: They simply amend or repeal the law on which the decision is based. But some laws are exceedingly difficult to amend or repeal. A conspicuous example: The United States Constitution, which by its own terms can be amended only by a complex, supermajoritarian political act:

In the [United States, a constitutional] amendment is permitted only upon completion of supermajority requirements both in Congress and in the states: an amendment must be proposed, either by 2/3 of each House of Congress or by a convention called at the request of the legislatures of 2/3 of the states, and then the proposed amendment must be approved by the legislatures of or conventions in 3/4 of the states. This makes the U.S. Constitution one of the most deeply entrenched [in the world].[10]

It is precisely because it is so difficult to amend or repeal an entrenched law that entrenching certain human rights makes sense: A liberal democracy's commitment to certain human rights – the right to freedom of speech, for example – is the principal political-moral foundation of any genuinely liberal democracy, any democracy truly committed to the inherent dignity of every human being. (A commentator on the transition to democracy in South Africa observed that an entrenched "bill of rights was crucial . . . to the whole question of legitimacy of a post-apartheid regime. For its powerful symbolism would establish an arena not just for law, but would also be a definition of what is, and is not, legitimate in politics.")[11] This is not to deny that in liberal democracies, laws that are not entrenched have an important role to play in securing human rights – especially human rights of the "welfare" sort.[12] But most liberal democracies understandably entrench certain human rights – typically by means of constitutional law.[13]

However, that it makes sense in a liberal democracy to entrench certain human rights does not mean that it also makes sense to empower courts to protect (enforce) the entrenched rights; whether it makes sense to do the latter is a separate question. ("One can have a constitution of entrenched rules but leave the interpretation of those rules to democratic decision making, and many countries do just that.")[14] The problem with ceding to politically independent courts[15] the power to protect entrenched rights is this: If a court rules against a government law or policy on the basis of an entrenched right, legislators who strongly disagree with the court and support the law/policy cannot simply amend or repeal the law on which the court relied. Because the law is entrenched, it will be exceedingly difficult – if not, as a practical matter, impossible – for legislators who support the law/policy to amend or repeal the law. Two important questions therefore arise:

Is it appropriate – is it a good idea, all things considered – for the citizens of a liberal democracy to cede to their courts the power to oppose, in the name of constitutionally entrenched human rights, laws and policies of their government?[16]

If such a power is to be ceded to the courts, how great should the power be; in particular, should it be the power to have the last word when the judge(s) concludes that government has violated the human right at issue (the last word, i.e., short of an extremely improbable event: a successful, supermajoritarian effort to amend or repeal the entrenched provision on which the court based its decision)? [MJP]

THE INDETERMINACY OF ENTRENCHED HUMAN RIGHTS

Whether it is a good idea for the citizens of a liberal democracy to cede to their courts the power to protect entrenched human rights is a difficult question principally for this reason: *Most entrenched human rights are indeterminate in the context of many of the cases in which they are invoked, and many are indeterminate in the context of most of the cases in which they are invoked. Consequently, in protecting entrenched human rights, courts are often in the position of "making" law rather than simply "applying" it.* I will elaborate.

As articulated in a legal text, a right is *determinate* in the context of a case in which the right is invoked – a case in which, let's assume, the relevant facts are clear and beyond controversy – if there is no room for a reasonable difference of judgment about what the right forbids or requires in the case.[17] Some human rights are highly determinate, in the sense that it is difficult to imagine any case (in which the relevant facts are clear and beyond controversy) in which there is room for a reasonable difference of judgment about what the right forbids (or requires) – that is, it is difficult to imagine any real as distinct from hypothetical case. Let's look at the European Convention for the Protection of Human Rights and Fundamental Freedoms, a legal text whose provisions articulating rights and freedoms have been incorporated into the domestic law of several European democracies, including, most recently, the United Kingdom.[18] (The vehicle of incorporation in the United Kingdom was the UK Human Rights Act of 1998, which I discuss in the Appendix to this chapter.) Consider, for example, Article 1 of Protocol No. 6 to the European Convention: "The death penalty shall be abolished. No one shall be condemned to such penalty or executed." Some other examples from the European Convention include Article 4 ("Prohibition of slavery and forced labour"), Article 1 of Protocol No. 4 ("Prohibition of imprisonment for debt"), and Article 3 of Protocol No. 4 ("Prohibition of expulsion of nationals"). It is relatively unproblematic to empower courts to protect provisions like these, because there is little, if any, room for a reasonable difference of judgment about what such a provision forbids in any imaginable case. At the same time, it is not likely that judicial enforcement of provisions like these will be necessary, at least in a contemporary, well-functioning liberal democracy, because it is not likely that such a democracy will violate such provisions: Again, there is little if any room for a reasonable difference of judgment about what such a provision forbids in any imaginable case. In any event, the serious question is not whether it is a good idea, all things considered, for the citizens of a liberal democracy to cede to their courts the power to protect human rights that, as articulated in entrenched legal texts, are highly determinate. The serious question concerns human rights that are indeterminate.

As articulated in a legal text, a right is *indeterminate* in the context of a case in which it is invoked – a case in which the relevant facts are clear and beyond controversy – if there is room for a reasonable difference of judgment about what the right forbids in the case.[19] As it happens, most human rights are indeterminate in the context of many of the cases, and many are indeterminate in the context of most of the cases, in which they are likely to be invoked. Consider, for example, Article 9 of the European Convention:

1. Everyone has the right to freedom of thought, conscience and religion; this right includes freedom to change his religion or belief and freedom, either alone or in community with others and in public or private, to manifest his religion or belief, in worship, teaching, practice, and observance.

2. Freedom to manifest one's religion or beliefs shall be subject only to such limitations as are prescribed by law and are necessary in a democratic society in the interests of public safety, for the protection of public order, health or morals, or for the protection of the rights and freedoms of others.

Similarly indeterminate provisions include Article 8 ("Right to respect for private and family life"), Article 10 ("Freedom of expression"), and Article 11 ("Freedom of assembly and association"). Some other provisions, though less indeterminate, are nonetheless indeterminate. (The indeterminacy of a legal right is a matter of degree.) Consider, for example, Article 3: "No one shall be subjected to torture or to inhuman or degrading treatment." (Precisely when does "treatment" cross the line and become "inhuman or degrading"?) Consider, too, Article 5(3), which provides, in part: "Everyone arrested or detained in accordance with the provisions of paragraph 1.c of this article shall be brought promptly before a judge or other officer authorised by law to exercise judicial power and shall be entitled to a trial within a reasonable time or to release pending trial. . . . " (Given the complexities and exigencies of a particular case, what is a "reasonable" time?) I could give many other examples, but there is no need to do so because the point is clear and undeniable: Most human rights are indeterminate in the context of many of the cases in which they are likely to be invoked; with respect to most human rights, there is room for a reasonable difference of judgment, in many, if not most, cases about what the right at issue forbids, even if the relevant facts are clear and beyond controversy.[20] Indeed, in Canada, all the rights and freedoms articulated in the Charter of Rights and Freedoms (which is a part of the Canadian Constitution) are indeterminate in many if not most cases, because all the rights and freedoms are defined (in section 1 of the Charter) as subject "to such reasonable limits prescribed by law as can be demonstrably justified in a free and democratic society." Similarly, in South Africa, all the rights articulated in the Bill of Rights (Chapter 2) of the South African Constitution are indeterminate in many if not most cases, because all the rights are defined as subject to the limits articulated in section 36 of the Bill of Rights:

> (1) The rights in the Bill of Rights may be limited only in terms of law of general application to the extent that the limitation is reasonable and justifiable in an open and demcratic society based on human dignity, equality and freedom, taking into account all the relevant factors, including –
> a. the nature of the right;
> b. the importance of the purpose of the limitation;
> c. the nature and extent of the limitation;
> d. the relation between the limitation and its purpose; and
> e. less restrictive means to achieve the purpose.

To protect a right that, as articulated in a legal text, is indeterminate in the particular context in which it is invoked, the person or persons doing the protecting must reach a judgment about what the right shall mean – about what it shall forbid – in that context, all things considered. In that sense, the person(s) doing the protecting must *specify* the contextual meaning of the right. For example, to protect, in a particular case, the right to freedom of religion articulated by Article 9 of the European Convention, the European Court of Human Rights must reach a judgment about whether, all things considered, the challenged limitation on the right is "prescribed by law" and, if so, is "necessary in a democratic society in the interests of public safety, for the protection of public order, health or morals, or for the protection of the rights and freedoms of others." With respect to the rights and freedoms articulated in the Charter of Rights and Freedoms, the Canadian Supreme Court must decide whether challenged limitations "can be demonstrably justified in a free and democratic society" (Charter, section 1). With respect to the rights articulated in the South African Bill of Rights, the South African Supreme Court must decide whether challenged limitations are "reasonable and justifiable in an open and democratic society . . . taking into account all the relevant factors . . . " (section 36).

This need for specification – the need to specify the concrete meaning of an indeterminate legal norm in the particular context in which it is invoked – is familiar. In *The Federalist Papers*, James Madison commented on the need, in adjudication, for such specification: "All new laws, though penned with the greatest technical skill and passed on the fullest and most mature deliberation, are considered as more or less obscure and equivocal, until their meaning be liquidated and ascertained by a series of particular discussions and adjudications."[21] Whereas the process of applying a determinate norm is essentially deductive, the process of specifying an indeterminate norm is essentially non-deductive.[22] A specification "of a principle for a specific class of cases is not a deduction from it, nor a discovery of some implicit meaning; it is the act of setting a more concrete and categorical requirement in the spirit of the principle, and guided both by a sense of what is practically realizable (or enforceable), and by a recognition of the risk of conflict with other principles or values. . . . "[23] The challenge of specifying an indeterminate human right, then, is the challenge of deciding how best to achieve, how best to "instantiate," in the particular context at hand, the political-moral value (or values) at the heart of the right;[24] it is the challenge of discerning, in the context at hand, what way of achieving that value, what way of embodying it, best reconciles all the various and sometimes competing interests at stake in the context at hand.

∾

THE SERIOUS QUESTION, THEN, IS WHETHER IT IS A GOOD IDEA, ALL things considered, for the citizens of a liberal democracy to cede to their courts the power to protect *entrenched, indeterminate* human rights – human rights that, as articulated in entrenched legal texts, are indeterminate in many, if not most, of the cases in which they are likely to be invoked. To empower politically independent courts to protect such rights is necessarily to empower them to specify the concrete meaning of the rights in the various contexts in which they are likely to be invoked; in that sense, it is to empower them to "make" law rather than simply to "apply" it. But such a power – a power, as Richard Posner has described it, to make "a creative decision, involving discretion, the weighing of consequences, and, in short, a kind of legislative judgment"[25] – arguably belongs in the hands of the the politically dependent, because electorally accountable, policymaking officials of the legislative and/or executive branches of government.

In the remainder of this chapter, when I refer to human rights I mean human rights that, as articulated in entrenched legal texts, are indeterminate in many, if not most, of the contexts in which they are likely to be invoked.

THE ESSENTIAL CASE FOR EMPOWERING COURTS
TO PROTECT HUMAN RIGHTS

I now want to sketch the principal argument for empowering courts to protect (entrenched, indeterminate) human rights. (Such rights are, for the most part, rights *against government*.)[26] A sketch will suffice; the argument is familiar.[27] It bears emphasis that the argument I am about to recite neither discounts the importance of non-judicial protections of human rights[28] nor denies the fact that legislators or other government officials are sometimes more protective than judges of some human rights.[29] The choice liberal democracies face is not either-or: The argument for empowering courts to protect human rights is not a case against empowering non-judicial governmental institutions and officials to protect human rights too – though it is an argument against empowering only non-judicial governmental institutions and officials to protect human rights. Beware the beguiling either-or.[30]

We should be wary about generalizing across different liberal democracies, with their different histories, cultures, and trajectories,[31] but the particular generalizations on which the argument relies – the argument for empowering courts to protect human rights – are not controversial. The argument begins with the premise that incumbency is a cardinal value – not the only value, but nonetheless a cardinal one – for electorally accountable government officials: Such officials typically want to preserve their own incumbency and/or the incumbency of as many other members of their party as possible.[32] Therefore, such officials want to make popular decisions; at a minimum, they want to avoid making unpopular decisions. But the best (optimal) resolution of a human rights controversy – a controversy about what a right means (that is, should be understood to mean), about what it requires, in a particular context in which it is invoked – may well be unpopular. Such officials also want to make decisions that will please their most powerful constituencies; at a minimum, they want to avoid making decisions that will displease those constituencies.[33] But the best resolution of a human rights controversy may well displease some of their most powerful constituencies. Moreover, such officials want to be identified with – and therefore want to spend time dealing with – high-profile issues, issues that concern the well-being of a large number of citizens. But a human rights issue may well be low-profile; it may well concern the well-being only of a relatively few, marginal – and perhaps marginalized – citizens; indeed, it may well concern the well-being only of non-citizens.[34] Therefore, many human rights are not likely to be optimally protected in a democracy unless politically independent courts play a significant role in protecting them. The non-judicial, electorally accountable branches of government – the legislative and executive branches – frequently have insufficient political or institutional (bureaucratic) incentives to attend to a claim – or, if they do attend to it, to take seriously the claim – that government has violated, or is violating, an entrenched right. Indeed, they sometimes have powerful incentives – above all, incumbency – to ignore, or at least to discount, such a claim.[35]

The observations recited in the preceding paragraph are grounded in the historical experience of, and are widely endorsed in, liberal democracies. Speaking from a British perspective, Lord Scarman, in 1984, wrote: "[I]f you are going to protect people who will never have political power, at any rate in the foreseeable future (not only individuals but minority groups with their own treasured and properly treasured social customs, religion and ways of life), if they are going to be protected it won't be done in Parliament – they will never muster a majority. It's got to be done by the Courts and the Courts can do it only if they've got the proper guidelines."[36] More recently, and speaking from a broader perspective, Mac Darrow and Philip Alston wrote that "there are ample grounds, based on experience in countries with constitutional human rights protections, to suggest that entrenchment of bills of rights can contribute significantly to the empowerment of disadvantaged groups, providing a judicial forum in which they can be heard and seek redress, in circumstances where the political process could not have been successfully mobilized to assist them."[37] Statements such as this are quite common. For example, in a case in which the eleven justices of the Constitutional Court of the Republic of South Africa ruled unanimously that imposition of the death penalty was unconstitutional under the transitional 1993 constitution, the President of the Court wrote:

> The very reason for establishing the new legal order, and for vesting the power of judicial review of all legislation in the courts, was to protect the rights of minorities and others who cannot protect their rights adequately through the democratic process. Those who are entitled to claim this protection include the social outcasts and marginalized people of our society. It is only if there is a willingness to protect the worst and the weakest amongst us, that all of us can be secure that our own rights will be protected.[38]

The American experience is relevant here too, in particular the American experience with the federal judiciary in the post-World War II era, which is, of course, the era in which human rights discourse has emerged and flourished. This experience confirms that politically independent judges – precisely because they are politically independent – are often more likely than electorally accountable officials to address a human rights controversy in a way that is both impartial and (relatively) detached: impartial between (or among) the parties to, and detached as to the proper outcome of, the controversy. This is especially true when the controversy pits, as many human rights controversies do, a political majority against an unpopular political minority – or a large, insensitive if not hostile bureaucracy against marginalized persons. Even in the pre-World War II era, many Americans understood the importance of entrusting the protection of basic rights to a politically independent judiciary. "As a writer in the Jesuit publication America observed in November 1924, 'Any citizen whose life, liberty and property were in jeopardy would rather have his case tried before nine lawyer-judges whom he could look in the eye, than before that vast, miscellaneous, political throng at Congress, responding or not to the roll call as they saw fit.'"[39]

The basic argument for empowering courts to protect human rights – the argument I've just sketched – is both familiar and, as the emergence of constitutional courts in the second half of the twentieth century attests, powerful.[40] As Rick Pildes has observed, "all new democratic systems are being formed as constitutional democracies, with courts operating under fairly indeterminate constitutional texts" and "embracing constitutional courts as means of settling controversial and profound moral questions."[41] Consider, for example, that when South Africa adopted its new constitution in 1996 it specifically provided for a judicial power to protect the rights articulated in the constitution.[42] (If you, dear reader, had been a citizen of South Africa in the 1990s, would you have opposed this development?) Even more recently, no less a champion of parliamentary supremacy than the United Kingdom adopted the Human Rights Act of 1998, which empowers courts to protect the rights articulated in the European Convention for the Protection of Human Rights and Fundamental Freedoms. (I discuss the UK Human Rights Act in the Appendix to this chapter.) These developments have led Mark Tushnet to conclude that "[f]or all practical purposes the debate among constitution designers over parliamentary supremacy versus judicial review is over. Proponents of judicial review have carried the day..."[43] (Actually, the matter is more complicated than Tushnet suggests: As I explain later in this chapter, the choice in both Canada and the United Kingdom, has not been for judicial review *rather than* parliamentary supremacy, but for judicial review *within a system of parliamentary supremacy*.)

THE ESSENTIAL CASE AGAINST EMPOWERING COURTS TO PROTECT HUMAN RIGHTS: THE TWOFOLD ARGUMENT FROM DEMOCRACY

That the argument for empowering courts to protect (entrenched, indeterminate) human rights is both familiar and powerful – indeed, that it has "carried the day" – does not mean that there are no arguments *against* doing so. There are several such arguments, which are well rehearsed elsewhere.[44] But there is one important argument, which I want to sketch here. We may call it the "argument from democracy." According to the first part of the argument, it is undemocratic to give to politically independent courts – rather than to politically dependent, because electorally accountable, policymaking officials of the legislative and/or executive branches of government – the authoritative word as to what human rights forbid (or require) in particular contexts.[45] This passage by Jeremy Waldron dramatizes the point:

> If we are going to defend the idea of an entrenched Bill of Rights put effectively beyond revision by anyone other than the judges, we should try and think what we might say to some public-spirited citizen who wishes to launch a campaign or lobby her [representative] on some issue of rights about which she feels strongly and on which she has done her best to arrive at a considered and impartial view. She is not asking to be a dictator; she perfectly accepts that her voice should have no more power than that of anyone else who is prepared to participate in politics. But – like her suffragette forbears – she wants a vote; she wants her voice and her activity to count on matters of high political importance.
>
> In defending a Bill of Rights, we have to imagine ourselves saying to her: "You may write to the newspaper and get up a petition and organize a pressure group to lobby [the legislature]. But even if you succeed, beyond your wildest dreams, and orchestrate the support of a large number of like-minded men and women, and manage to prevail in the legislature, your measure may be challenged and struck down because your view of what rights we have does not accord with the judges' view. When their votes differ from yours, theirs are the votes that will prevail." It is my submission that saying this does not comport with the respect and honor normally accorded to ordinary men and women in the context of a theory of rights.[46]

According to the second part of the argument from democracy, it is hostile to the practice of democratic deliberation, and therefore subversive of the citizens as a community of judgment, to give to politically independent courts the last word as to what a right forbids government to do .[47] By imposing on government their own judgments about what human rights forbid government to do in particular contexts, courts necessarily discourage citizens and their electorally accountable representatives from themselves deliberating about what the human rights forbid in those contexts.[48] Listen, in that regard, to James Bradley Thayer, who cautioned that "the exercise of judicial review . . . is always attended with a serious evil, namely, that the correction of legislative mistakes comes from the outside, and the people thus lose the political experience, and the moral education and stimulus that comes from fighting the question out in the ordinary way, and correcting their own errors. The tendency of a common and easy resort to this great function, now lamentably too common, is to dwarf the political capacity of the people, and to deaden its sense of moral responsibility."[49] Listen, too, to Alexander Bickel: "The search must be for a [judicial] function . . . whose discharge by the courts will not lower the quality of the other departments' performance *by denuding them of the dignity and burden of their own responsibility.*"[50]

SPLITTING THE DIFFERENCE

The argument against empowering courts to protect human rights is undeniably strong. But so is the argument for doing so: To choose not to empower courts to protect such rights is unattractive, because, again, such rights are not likely to be optimally protected in a democracy unless politically independent courts are empowered to protect them. (Or, if that generalization is too broad, let us say that some such rights are not likely to be optimally protected in most democracies unless politically independent courts are empowered to protect them.[51] This, though, is the position widely accepted in most liberal democracies, because in most liberal democracies, some human rights are both constitutionally entrenched and judicially protected.)[52] If the citizens of a liberal democracy had to choose between (a) giving courts no power to protect human rights, and (b) giving them the kind of power exercised by the United States Supreme Court – "judicial supremacy" – they would be in a bind. Choice (a) is extreme, because it in effect denies the truth of the case for empowering politically independent courts to protect human rights. But choice (b) is extreme too – it is at the other extreme from choice (a) – because it in effect denies the truth of the case against empowering politically independent courts to protect human rights. Happily, (a) and (b) are *not* the only choices; there are other, more moderate choices.

Assume that, persuaded by the argument for doing so, the citizens of a liberal democracy have decided to empower politically independent courts to protect the human rights that are entrenched in their constitution. It is an entirely distinct question as to *how much power* to give to the courts. For example, should the judiciary's opinion about what a right means in the context of the case at hand – its opinion about what the right forbids (or requires) government to do in that context – be invulnerable to overruling by ordinary political means; should it be subject to overruling only by an extraordinary political act, like the act of amending the constitution? Or should the judiciary's opinion be subject to overruling by ordinary political means? Or should the judiciary's opinion not be binding at all but only hortatory? There are different ways of structuring the relationship between the power of the judiciary to protect human rights and the power of the legislative and/or executive branches to respond to the exercise of that power.

In the United States, the Supreme Court exercises the power of judicial review: the power to determine, in an appropriate case, in an opinion binding not just on the parties to the case but also on all the other branches and agencies of government, whether – and, therefore, *that* – a particular law, policy, or other governmental act (or failure to act) violates the Constitution.[53] How great is this power of judicial review? According to the doctrine of judicial supremacy, a decision by the Supreme Court that a law (policy, act) is unconstitutional may be overruled not by ordinary political means but only by extraordinary political means, such as constitutional amendment; Congress, for example, may not overrule the opinion by enacting legislation rejecting the opinion.[54] As I said, ceding to the judiciary this degree of power to protect human rights is extreme, because doing so in effect denies the truth of the argument against empowering politically independent courts to protect human rights; it denies the truth of the twofold argument from democracy.

But not every choice to empower the courts to protect human rights is so extreme. I now want to discuss a more moderate choice, one that accepts the truth of the argument for empowering courts to protect human rights without denying the truth of the countervailing argument from democracy.

THE CANADIAN SYSTEM

The Canadian Charter of Rights and Freedoms is Part 1 of Canada's Constitution Act of 1982. As its name suggests, the Charter articulates several fundamental rights and freedoms, which it organizes into seven categories. The rights and freedoms in four categories ("Democratic Rights," "Mobility Rights," "Official Languages of Canada," and "Minority Language Educational Rights") are highly determinate. By contrast, the rights and freedoms in the other three categories ("Fundamental Freedoms," "Legal Rights," and "Equality Rights") are relatively indeterminate. Assume that the Supreme Court of Canada rules that a law enacted by the Canadian Parliament, or by a provincial legislature, violates one of the indeterminate rights or freedoms – the right to "freedom of association" (section 2(d)), for example, or "the right to the equal protection and equal benefit of the law . . . without discrimination based on . . . sex" (section 15(1)). According to section 33 of the Charter, the Parliament, or the provincial legislature, may override that ruling by reenacting the law with an express declaration that the law "shall operate notwithstanding" the right or freedom the law is claimed to violate:

(1) Parliament or the legislature of a province may expressly declare in an Act of Parliament or of the legislature, as the case may be, that the Act or a provision thereof shall operate notwithstanding a provision included in section 2 ["Fundamental Freedoms"] or sections 7 to 15 ["Legal Rights" and "Equality Rights"] of this Charter.

(2) An Act or a provision of an Act in respect of which a declaration made under this section is in effect shall have such operation as it would have but for the provision of the Charter referred to in the declaration.

(3) A declaration made under subsection (1) shall cease to have effect five years after it comes into force or on such earlier date as may be specified in the declaration.

(4) Parliament or a legislature of a province may re-enact a declaration made under subsection (1).

(5) Subsection (3) applies in respect of a re-enactment made under subsection (4).

Because of section 33, the Canadian Supreme Court's judgment that a particular law violates one of the (indeterminate) rights articulated in section 2 or sections 7 to 15 of the Charter is subject to overruling by ordinary political means.[55]

The contrast between the degree of judicial power to protect human rights represented by American doctrine of judicial supremacy and the degree represented by section 33 of the Charter is striking. Like the American practice of judicial review, section 33 acknowledges the importance of empowering courts to protect human rights, but unlike the American doctrine of judicial supremacy, section 33 also acknowledges the power of the argument from democracy. Section 33 represents an imaginative way of accommodating *both* the argument for empowering courts to protect human rights *and* the argument from democracy; as Walter Murphy put it, section 33 represents an "elegant compromise."[56] Listen to Paul Weiler, who was an architect of section 33:[57]

> One cannot choose...between formal [constitutional] amendment and legislative override as the preferred method for revising judge-made constitutional policy simply by a priori reasoning about rights and democracy. One must make a practical judgment about the relative competence of two imperfect institutions in the context of a particular nation. The premise of the Charter is that the optimal

arrangement for Canada is a new partnership between court and legislature. Under this approach judges will be on the front lines; they will possess both the responsibility and the legal clout necessary to tackle "rights" issues as they arise. At the same time, however, the Charter reserves for the legislature the final say to be used sparingly in the exceptional case where the judiciary has gone awry. This institutional division of labor rests on the assumption that the chief threat to rights in Canada comes from legislative thoughtlessness about particular intrusions, a fault that can be cured by thoroughly airing the issues of principle in a judicial forum. The Charter contemplates no serious danger of outright legislative oppression; certainly none sufficient to concede ultimate authority to Canadian judges and lawyers.[58]

THE CASE FOR JUDICIAL "PENULTIMACY"

One issue a liberal democracy faces is whether to cede any power to politically independent courts to protect human rights. (If, as in many liberal democracies, politically independent courts already have this power, the issue is whether they should have it.) If a liberal democracy decides to empower courts to protect human rights, it must next decide what degree of power to give to the courts. (Or it must decide whether the courts should have the degree of power they already have.) Should they be given, as in the United States, the power of judicial supremacy – the power to have the *ultimate* say when the judge(s) concludes that government has violated the right at issue? (The ultimate say, that is, short of an extremely improbable event: a successful, supermajoritarian effort to amend or repeal the entrenched provision on which the court based its decision.) Or, instead, should they be given, as in Canada, the power to have only the *penultimate* say?[59] Which choice makes more sense – which is more appropriate – for a liberal democracy: judicial ultimacy or judicial penultimacy?[60]

As the Canadian model illustrates, judicial penultimacy is consistent with the proposition, which is part of the argument from democracy, that electorally accountable legislators should have the last word – the *ultimate* word – even if their last word is to accept the court's judgment. The Canadian Charter is "premised on the idea that it is possible to have... judicial protection of fundamental rights *and* the legislature retaining the right to have the last word on what is the law of the land."[61] The Charter thus provides for the judicial protection of human rights without compromising the ideal of parliamentary supremacy.[62]

Recall the second part of the argument from democracy – that it is hostile to the practice of democratic deliberation, and therefore subversive of the citizens as a community of judgment, to give to politically independent courts the last word as to what an entrenched right forbids (or requires) government to do. By leaving the last word with the electorally accountable representatives of the people, judicial penultimacy is not hostile but congenial to the practice of democratic deliberation; judicial penultimacy does not subvert but maintains the citizens and their representatives as a community of judgment – though the courts, too, have a crucial role to play in the ongoing process of deliberation. Something I said many years ago about American-style judicial review now seems to me substantially false, given that such review is part and parcel of a system of judicial supremacy/ultimacy. Applied to a liberal democracy with a well-functioning system of judicial penultimacy, however, what I said portrays a realistic ideal: In the dialogue between the politically independent courts and the other, electorally accountable parts of government, a dialogue about the concrete meaning of indeterminate human rights in particular contexts in which they are invoked, "what emerges is a far more self-critical political morality than would otherwise appear, and therefore likely a moral mature political morality as well – a morality that is moving... toward, even though it has not always and everywhere arrived at, right answers, rather than a stagnant or even regressive morality."[63]

WHAT ROLE FOR THE COURTS, THEN, IN PROTECTING HUMAN RIGHTS? So far I've addressed two main questions in this chapter. These are my conclusions:

1. It is appropriate – it *is* a good idea, all things considered – for the citizens of a liberal democracy to cede to their courts the power to oppose, in the name of constitutionally entrenched human rights, laws and policies of their government.
2. The power that should be ceded to the courts, however, is not the power of judicial ultimacy – the power to have the last word when the judge(s) concludes that government has violated the human right at issue – but the power of judicial penultimacy.

JUDICIAL "ULTIMACY" AND THE THAYERIAN PLEA FOR JUDICIAL DEFERENCE

In the United States, however, the federal judiciary, atop which sits the Supreme Court of the United States, exercises the power of judicial ultimacy (supremacy). This state of affairs gives rise to a third important question:

If in a liberal democracy the courts have the power of judicial ultimacy, should they exercise this great power deferentially? That is, should the courts defer to some degree to the judgment of the members of the legislative and/or executive branches of government whose law/policy is in question and who presumably have concluded that the law/policy does not violate the human right at issue? [MJP]

The choice here is best understood as a choice between two different judicial attitudes or orientations. For a judge to adopt a deferential attitude – for her to be oriented deferentially – is for her to be prepared to rule that a challenged law/policy does not violate a human rights norm if there is a "not unreasonable" specification of the norm according to which the challenged law/policy does not violate the norm. For a judge to adopt a non-deferential attitude is for her to be prepared to rule that a challenged law/policy violates a human rights norm if according to the judge's preferred specification of the norm, the law/policy violates the norm – even if there is another, "not unreasonable" specification according to which the law/policy does not violate the norm. The difference between these two attitudes, or orientations, is a matter of degree: A judge can be *more or less* deferential, or *more or less* non-deferential. More-over, not every judge will draw the boundaries of the "not unreasonable" in the same place. An arrogant judge will not draw them at all. ("Be reasonable. Think like I do!" Thus reads the mocking sign my wife has hung in my office. Better in my office, I suppose, than around my neck.) Still, the difference between the two attitudes is recognizable and not inconsequential: It is easy to imagine human rights cases in which the difference will make a difference to the outcome of the case.

Recall again the second part of the argument from democracy, according to which a system of judicial ultimacy is not only undemocratic, but hostile to the practice of democratic deliberation and therefore subversive of the citizens as a community of political-moral judgment. In a system of judicial ultimacy, the courts can mitigate this defect by proceeding deferentially.[64] From the standpoint of the argument from democracy, and crediting the argument for empowering courts to protect human rights, a system of judicial penultimacy is best, a system of judicial ultimacy in which courts exercise their power nondeferentially is worst, and a system of judicial ultimacy in which courts exercise their power deferentially is somewhere in between.

In the United States, a system of judicial ultimacy has long been in place; it is not surprising, therefore, that arguments for judicial deference have long been made in the United States. The most famous and influential such argument was made by James Bradley Thayer in an essay published in the October 1893 issue of the Harvard *Law Review*: "The Origin and Scope of the American Doctrine of Constitutional Law."[65] Even now, over a hundred years later, Thayer's essay remains the locus classicus of the argument that in enforcing constitutional norms, the courts – including the Supreme Court – should proceed deferentially:

> [The court] can only disregard the [challenged] Act when those who have the right to make laws have not merely made a mistake, but have made a very clear one – so clear that it is not open to rational question. That is the standard of duty to which the courts bring legislative Acts; that is the test which they apply – not merely their own judgment as to constitutionality, but their conclusion as to what judgment is permissible to another department which the constitution has charged with the duty of making it. This rule recognizes that, having regard to the great, complex, ever unfolding exigencies of government, much which will seem unconstitutional to one man, or body of men, may reasonably not seem so to another; that the constitution often admits of different interpretations; that there is often a range of choice and judgment; that in such cases the constitution does not impose upon the legislature any one specific opinion, but leaves open this range of choice; and that whatever choice is rational is constitutional.
>
> . . .
>
> [A] court cannot always . . . say that there is but one right and permissible way of construing the constitution. When a court is interpreting a writing merely to ascertain or apply its true meaning, then, indeed, there is but one meaning allowable; namely, what the court adjudges to be its true meaning. But when the ultimate question is not that, but whether certain acts of another department, officer, or individual are legal or permissible, then this is not true. In the class of cases which we have been considering, *the ultimate question is not what is the true meaning of the constitution, but whether legislation is sustainable or not.*[66]

Thayer's plea for judicial deference – his plea for "the rule of the clear mistake," as Alexander Bickel called it[67] – was not rooted in a faith in the capacity of the other, non-judicial departments of government – the legislative and executive departments – to resolve constitutional questions responsibly; nor was it rooted in a belief that the legislative and executive departments are truly representative of the people.[68] Thayer's position was rooted, instead, in his conviction that because in the United States, which is a democracy, the citizens are the ultimate political sovereign, they and not the judiciary should have final responsibility for resolving, through their elected representatives, contested constitutional questions – unless there is no room for a reasonable difference in judgments about how such a question should be resolved.[69] Thayer's argument for judicial deference has always had great appeal in the context of American-style judicial supremacy, as evidenced by the fact that in the United States, in one or another version, the argument is always being mounted anew.[70] But does the Thayerian argument for judicial deference have much power – does it makes much sense – in the context of a system of judicial penultimacy? Does the argument make much sense, for example, in Canada?

The Thayerian argument derives its power from the fact that the deference for which Thayer contended is a way of mitigating the principal defect of the American system of judicial ultimacy: The courts have the final say when they conclude that government has violated the right at issue. (Again, by "final" I mean final short of a successful, supermajoritarian effort to amend or repeal the entrenched provision on which the court based its decision.)[71] This state of affairs – judicial supremacy – is not only undemocratic, but hostile to the practice of democratic deliberation and therefore subversive of the citizens as a community of political-moral judgment. A system of judicial penultimacy, however, avoids that difficulty (and is attractive for just that reason): The courts do not have the final say.

At least, as a formal matter they do not have the final say. In a system of judicial penultimacy like Canada's, the burden of legislative inertia falls on those who would negate a judicial decision, with the consequence that, as Mark Tushnet has observed, "even majorities may find themselves unable to displace the Court's decision, at least if what the Court has done has the support of a substantial minority."[72] In a system of judicial penultimacy that is not well functioning – a system in which determined political majorities are rarely, if ever, able to overcome the burden of legislative inertia – one might want to say, with Tushnet, that "the invention of weak-form judicial review [i.e., judicial penultimacy] may not displace the long-standing controversy in strong-form systems over judicial activism and restraint."[73] But a system of judicial penultimacy need not be one in which determined political majorities are almost always unable to overcome the burden of legislative inertia. (Of course, even in a well-functioning system of judicial penultimacy, a determined political majority will sometimes be unable to overcome the burden of legislative inertia, especially "if what the Court has done has the support of a substantial minority.") Moreover, one should not confuse a system of judicial penultimacy in which political majorities rarely even want to override their supreme court's human rights decisions with a system in which they want to do so but are almost always unable to overcome the burden of legislative inertia. Jeffrey Goldsworthy argues that in Canada "the most likely reason for legislators [habitually declining to use the override provision] is that the electorate is unlikely to trust their judgment about constitutional rights more than the judge's judgment. And surely that is the electorate's democratic prerogative ... "[74] Goldsworthy adds: "There is clearly a difference between relinquishing or disabling one's power to make certain kinds of decisions, and declining – even routinely – to exercise it. For example, in constitutional law there is a crucial difference between, on the one hand, a legislature irrevocably transferring its powers to another body, and, on the other, its delegating those powers while retaining its ability at any time to override its delegate or even cancel the delegation."[75] In any event, in a system of judicial penultimacy that is (like Canada's) well functioning, there is little if any need for Thayerian deference.

Indeed, in such a system, there is a need for courts to avoid such deference: Thayerian deference would deprive the political community of the court's own best judgment about the optimal specification of an indeterminate human rights norm in a particular context. There is a good reason for bearing this cost in a system of judicial ultimacy – namely, to mitigate the principal defect of such a system. But there is no good reason for bearing this cost in a well-functioning system of judicial penultimacy, because, again, that defect does not exist in such a system. On the contrary, there is a good reason for avoiding this cost in a system of judicial penultimacy. The argument for empowering courts to protect human rights, presented earlier, gives the citizens of a liberal democracy ample reason to place a high value on hearing the politically independent judiciary's own best judgment about the optimal specification of a human rights norm. (And that they have only the power of penultimacy gives courts reason to offer their own best judgment.)[76] Earlier I suggested that the citizens of a liberal democracy with a well-functioning system of judicial penultimacy can realistically hope that in "the dialogue between the politically independent courts and the other, electorally accountable parts of government, a dialogue about the concrete meaning of indeterminate human rights in particular contexts in which they are invoked, 'what emerges is a far more self-critical political morality than would otherwise appear, and therefore likely a moral mature political morality as well – a morality that is moving ... toward, even though it has not always and everywhere arrived at, right answers, rather than a stagnant or even regressive morality.'"[77] For courts to exercise Thayerian deference in a system of judicial penultimacy would be for them to make impossible this inter-institutional dialogue, thereby impeding the emergence of a more self-critical and mature political morality.

But, again, the United States Supreme Court exercises the power of judicial ultimacy. It is extremely unlikely that the citizens of the United States, through their elected representatives, will do anything to alter this state of affairs in the foreseeable future. (There's no point in speculating about the unforeseeable future.) The question is nonetheless important, as a matter of democratic political theory, whether it would be a good idea, all things considered, for the citizens of the United States to disestablish the power of judicial ultimacy and to establish in its place the power of judicial penultimacy. Perhaps one or another version of Canada's "override" provision would be, for the United States, "an intrinsically sound solution to the dilemma of rights and courts".[78] Paul Weiler has raised this possibility:

> I suspect that this arrangement would not be unthinkable in the United States . . . if it were translated into a *congressional* override of the Supreme Court. Any measure that could be navigated through all the branches of the national legislative process, each reflecting a variety of constituencies and points of view, might well be considered a more sensible approach to the problem than would a verdict from a bare majority of five on the Supreme Court. But almost all American scholars would have grave qualms about conferring any such power on the state legislatures, both from general disenchantment with the deliberative capacities of state governments and because of the fear that certain state legislatures would respond to majorities that do not necessarily adhere to the values spelled out in the national constitution. For many people, reflection on what might have happened after *Brown v. Board of Education* had Mississippi had a legislative override on fourteenth amendment issues is sobering enough to discredit the entire notion.[79]

Alexander Bickel once suggested that "courts have certain capacities for dealing with matters of principle that legislatures and executives do not possess. Judges have, or should have, the leisure, the training, and the insulation to follow the ways of the scholar in pursuing the ends of government. This is crucial in sorting out the enduring values of a society, and it is not something that institutions can do well occasionally, while operating for the most part with a different set of gears. It calls for a habit of mind, and for undeviating institutional customs."[80] A system of judicial penultimacy, like Canada's, has this great advantage over the American system of judicial supremacy: A system of judicial penultimacy preserves an active, vigorous judicial role – a role that, at its best, is special, and perhaps even indispensable, in just the way Bickel suggested – in contentious discourse about the contextual meaning of indeterminate human rights imperative; at the same time, however, a system of judicial penultimacy does not so privilege the judicial voice in that discourse that there is, realistically, no opportunity for effective political response. A system of judicial penultimacy represents an effort to have the best of two worlds: an opportunity for a deliberative judicial consideration of a difficult and perhaps divisive human rights issue and an opportunity for electorally accountable officials to respond in an politically effective way.[81]

Recall Thayer's claim that "the exercise of judicial review, even when unavoidable, is always attended with a serious evil – namely, that the correction of legislative mistakes comes from the outside – and the people thus lose the political experience, and the moral education and stimulus that comes from fighting the question out in the ordinary way, and correcting their own errors. The tendency of a common and easy resort to this great function, now lamentably too common, is to dwarf the political capacity of the people, and to deaden its sense of moral responsibility."[82] Establishing a system of judicial penultimacy would significantly enhance, not diminish, the "political capacity" and "moral responsibility" of the people – it would encourage greater citizen participation in what Sandy Levinson has called "the conversation about constitutional meaning"[83] – and should therefore be an attractive goal for those who, like Levinson, Jeremy Waldron, Mark Tushnet, and others, want to deprivilege the judicial voice in constitutional discourse.[84]

However, because it is exceedingly unlikely that the citizens of the United States will disestablish the system of judicial ultimacy in any foreseeable future,[85] this question arises: Should we who are citizens of the United States want the Supreme Court to exercise its power of judicial ultimacy deferentially; should we want the the Court defer to the "not unreasonable" judgment of the members of the legislative and/or executive branches of government whose law/policy is in question and who presumably have concluded that the law/policy does not violate the human right at issue?

Mark Tushnet and Jeremy Waldron have suggested that American-style judicial review – judicial review cum judicial supremacy – is not only a bad idea, but that *it is worse than no judicial review at all.*[86] If one is inclined to concur in the Tushnet-Waldron judgment, one should be no less inclined to concur in the view that because American-style judicial review is a fact of life, Supreme Court justices, in the exercise of judicial review, should proceed in the deferential way that Thayer recommended; they should adopt a deferential attitude. But is it true that American-style judicial review is worse than no judicial review at all? In the United States, has the American system of judicial ultimacy *always* been worse than no judicial review at all? Has it been worse than no judicial review no matter what right has been at issue? What if the right concerned, say, religious liberty?[87] What if the right protected detainees, prisoners, and others from torture or other inhumane and degrading treatment? Are these questions not relevant?

Of course, we should be more concerned with the future of American-style judicial review than with its past. (In the United States, will the system of judicial ultimacy be worse than no judicial review at all thirty years from now? One hundred?) Nonetheless, we cannot reasonably speculate about

the future of American-style judicial review – if we can reasonably speculate about it at all – without first evaluating its past. "So far as the scene of
American judicial review is concerned, the question whether judicial review
has been on balance a good thing for America may be the only question
worth asking once the detritus of philosophers' arguments is swept off the
table."[88]

Whatever our view – and we may not have a confident view – about "whether
judicial review has on balance been a good thing for America," we are left
with this question: Which arrangement, for the United States, is better going
forward:[89]

> A system of judicial ultimacy in which the Supreme Court's is deferential (Thay-
> erian) in the exercise of its power to protect constitutionally entrenched human
> rights?
>
> Or a system of judicial ultimacy in which the Court exercises its power nondef-
> erentially?

One may want to answer this question on the basis of a prediction about the
likely long-run consequences of the Court's embracing Thayerian deference.[90]
But any such judgment will be highly speculative – and easily contestable.

For better or worse, I lack confidence in such judgments. (Should anyone
have confidence in such judgments?) So I am left to answer the question on the
basis of the same, straightforward premise that Thayer invoked: In the United
States, we citizens are the ultimate political sovereign; we, therefore, through
our elected representatives, should have final responsibility for resolving contested constitutional questions *unless there is no room for a reasonable difference
in judgments about how such a question should be resolved.*

POSTSCRIPT: HUMAN RIGHTS OF THE "WELFARE" SORT

The human rights that have been my principal concern in this chapter are
human rights *against government.* Such rights – like rights generally – can be
either "negative" or "positive." A right is "negative" if it imposes a duty *not*
to do something, a duty to *refrain from* doing something. A right not to be
executed, a right to freedom of speech, and a right to non-discrimination are
negative rights; each imposes on government a duty not to do something.
A right is "positive" if it imposes a duty *to do* something. A right to due
process of law in the context of a criminal prosecution is a positive right:
Government's duty under the right is not to refrain from doing something but
to do – to provide – something – namely, due process of law (an independent
judicial tribunal, assistance of counsel if one cannot afford counsel, and so

forth). Although it is a positive right, the right to due process, like many other positive rights, implements a negative right: the right to freedom from unfair or arbitrary prosecution, which imposes on government the duty to refrain from such prosecution. The principal aim of the right to due process is to prevent government from prosecuting unfairly or arbitrarily.

Many of the rights against government that we who affirm the morality of human rights should want the law to establish are positive rights. After all, government can violate human beings, or otherwise cause unwarranted human suffering, by omission (that is, by deciding not to do something for them) as well as by comission (doing something to them); government can violate human beings, or otherwise cause unwarranted human suffering, by means of policies of *not doing something for* as well as by policies of *doing something to*. So, just as we – we who affirm the morality of human rights – should support laws that (would) impose on government duties to refrain from relying on policies that violate human beings or otherwise cause unwarranted human suffering, we should also support laws that impose on government duties to adopt policies that fit a certain profile: policies such that government's failure to adopt them violates human beings or otherwise causes unwarranted human suffering.

The most prominent kind of positive right against government that we find in human rights law, whether international, transnational, or national, is a "welfare" right: a right that imposes on government a duty to adopt a policy (or policies) aimed at helping persons – persons who live where the government rules – get what they must have if they are to live minimally decent lives. "[A]mongst ... the most important [of these welfare rights] are the right to a minimum income, the right to housing, the right to health care, and the right to education."[91] The International Covenant on Economic, Social, and Cultural Rights – which, again, is a major component of the International Bill of Rights – is concerned mainly with welfare rights. Article 2(1) of the ICESCR states:

> Each State Party to the present Covenant undertakes to take steps, individually and through international assistance and cooperation, especially economic and technical, to the maximum of its available resources, with a view to achieving progressively the full realization of the rights recognized in the present Covenant by all appropriate means, including particularly the adoption of legislative measures.

The welfare rights to which Article 2(1) refers include "the right to work" (Article 6), "the right of everyone to social security, including social insurance" (Article 9), "the right of everyone to an adequate standard of living ... , including adequate food, clothing and housing" (Article 11), "the right of everyone to the enjoyment of the highest attainable standard of physical and mental health" (Article 12), and "the right of everyone to education" (Article 13).

Two major questions arise with respect to welfare rights. First: *Should we who affirm the morality of human rights – who affirm that each and every human being has inherent dignity and is inviolable – want our government to entrench (some) welfare rights against government?* We should – for the same reason we should want our government to entrench other rights against government: A liberal democracy's commitment to certain rights is a principal political-moral foundation of any genuinely liberal democracy – any democracy that truly respects the inherent dignity of every human being – and therefore should not be negotiable. But, asks the skeptic, why should we accept the proposition that a commitment to (some) welfare rights is foundational for any democracy that truly respects the inherent dignity of every human being? Recall the statement by Dietrich Bonhoeffer with which Part Two of this book begins: "We have for once learned to see the great events of world history from below, from the perspective of the outcast, the suspects, the maltreated, the powerless, the oppressed, the reviled – in short, from the perspective of those who suffer." Let me paraphrase something I said in the Introduction: For the citizens of a liberal democracy to commit themselves to, by entrenching, welfare rights is for them to commit themselves to do what they can, all things considered – acting collectively, through their government – to diminish the oppressive, demeaning suffering of cruel poverty. To decline to make such a commitment is to fail to respect the inherent dignity of – and, so, it is to violate – "the least of these brothers [and sisters] of mine."[92] Of course, for the citizens of a liberal democracy to entrench (some) welfare rights is not necessarily for them to agree among themselves about the optimal policies for diminishing poverty; citizens equally committed to diminishing poverty can and do disagree about the best way(s), all things considered, to do so. (Not that all citizens in a liberal democracy are equally committed, or committed at all, to diminishing poverty.)

However, to hold that welfare rights should be constitutionally entrenched is not necessarily to hold that they should also be judicially enforceable. As I noted earlier in this chapter, constitutional entrenchment is one thing, judicial enforcement another.[93] Both the Irish Constitution and the Indian Constitution entrench some welfare rights, but both also specifically disallow judicial enforcement of the rights. In a section titled "Directive Principles of Social Policy," the Irish Constitution introduces a list of welfare rights with this statement: "The principles of social policy set forth in this Article are intended for the general guidance of the [Parliament]. The application of those principles... shall not be cognisable by any Court under any of the provisions of this Constitution."[94] Similarly, the Indian Constitution, in a section titled "Directive Principles of State Policy," states that "the provisions contained in this Part shall not be enforceable by any court, but the principles therein laid down are nevertheless fundamental in the governance of the country and it shall be the duty of the State to apply these principles in making laws."[95] The South African Constitution, by contrast, provides for judicial enforcement of all the rights – including the welfare rights – set forth in the constitution's "Bill of Rights."[96]

The second major question, then, is this: *If the citizens of a liberal democracy decide to entrench (some) welfare rights against government, should they provide for judicial enforcement of the rights?* This is a difficult and much disputed question.[97] Although it is a traditional task for constitutional courts in liberal democracies to enforce entrenched negative rights and some entrenched positive rights – especially positive rights that, like the right to due process, implement negative rights – it is anything but a traditional task for constitutional courts to enforce entrenched welfare rights. Indeed,

> the judicial enforcement of [entrenched] welfare rights would radically reduce the reach of democratic decision. Henceforth, the judges would decide, and as cases accumulated, they would decide in increasing detail, what the scope and character of the welfare system should be and what sorts of redistribution it required. Such decisions would clearly involve significant judicial control of the state budget and, indirectly at least, of the level of taxation – the very issues over which the democratic revolution was originally fought.[98]

This passage by Michael Walzer states the conventional wisdom. (Surveying the American scene, Mark Tushnet has observed that "[l]ike the [United States] Supreme Court, most constitutional scholars in the United States shrink in horror at the idea of [judicially enforceable] constitutional social welfare rights.")[99] However, Cécile Fabre has mounted a powerful, illuminating counterargument; in *Social Rights under the Constitution: Government and the Decent Life*, Fabre has explained how courts can play – and has argued that they *should* play – an important role in protecting entrenched welfare rights.[100] For the reader interested in pursuing this issue, Fabre's book and the other pieces cited in the preceding note are a good place to start.

I've argued in this chapter that the citizens of a liberal democracy who cede to their judiciary the power to protect constitutionally entrenched human rights should cede only the power of judicial penultimacy. Even one who rejects my argument – perhaps because one is (understandably) skeptical about generalizing across all liberal democracies – should nonetheless accept this proposition: If the citizens of a liberal democracy, persuaded by Fabre's argument, decide to cede to their judiciary the power to protect constitution- ally entrenched human rights *of the welfare sort*, they should cede only the power of judicial penultimacy. Why should one accept that proposition? Look again at Walzer's statement.[101]

APPENDIX: THE UK HUMAN RIGHTS ACT OF 1998[102]

We examined in this chapter the Canadian system of judicial protection of human rights. I now want to examine the (new) system in place in the United Kingdom. The Human Rights Act (HRA) of 1998, which took effect in October 2000, is an attempt by the United Kingdom to take human rights more seriously – by protecting them judicially – but without compromis- ing the cherished ideal of parliamentary supremacy. Like Canada's section 33, the HRA represents an imaginative way of accommodating both the argu- ment for empowering courts to protect human rights and the argument from democracy. The HRA makes the principal rights provisions of the European Convention (to which the United Kingdom is a signatory) a part of the domes- tic law of the United Kingdom.[103] Before the HRA went into force, these rights provisions were not a part of the domestic law of the United Kingdom; there- fore, no such provision could serve as a basis of decision by a court of the United Kingdom. Nonetheless, even before the HRA went into force, the pro- visions the HRA makes a part of the domestic law of the United Kingdom were entrenched in the United Kingdom – though, unlike constitutional rights in the United States, they were not entrenched as a formal, legal matter. (In the United States, constitutional rights may be disestablished not by an ordinary political act but only by constitutional amendment.) Rather, they were – and are – entrenched as a practical, political matter: It is virtually inconceivable, as a practical, political matter, that in the foreseeable future the UK Parliament could (even if it wanted to, which is unlikely) renounce the United Kingdom's status as a signatory to the European Convention, which has come to have a quasi-constitutional status in the United Kingdom and throughout the rest of Europe.

How great a power to protect human rights does the HRA grant to the courts of the United Kingdom? Under the HRA, a court is to interpret challenged legislation, "[s]o far as it is possible to do so, . . . in a way which is compatible with the Convention rights." (HRA, section 3(1).)[104] What if a court concludes that such an interpretation is not possible? If a court is persuaded, in a case

before it, that (what the HRA calls) "primary legislation" (parliamentary legislation) "is incompatible with a Convention right, it may make a declaration
of that incompatibility." (HRA, section 4(2).) If a court is persuaded that
"secondary legislation" (legislation by a lawmaking body inferior to Parliament) is incompatible with a Convention right, the court may fashion relief
that removes the incompatibility unless primary legislation somehow prevents
the court from doing so, in which case the court can only make a declaration
of incompatibility. (Section 4(3) & 4(4).) If a court is persuaded that an "act
of public authority" (defined to include the courts) is incompatible with a
Convention right, the court may so rule in a decision binding on the parties
unless "(a) as a result of one or more provisions of primary legislation, the
authority could not have acted differently; or (b) in the case of one or more
provisions of, or made under, primary legislation which cannot be read or
given effect in a way that is compatible with Convention rights, the authority was acting so as to give effect to or enforce those provisions." (Section
6(2). If the court concludes that section 6(2)(a) or 6(2)(b) is applicable, presumably the challenge to the act of public authority should be understood
as a challenge to the "one or more provisions of, or made under, primary
legislation" to which 6(2) refers, in which case the court, under section 4,
should decide whether to make a declaration of incompatibility.) Thus, under
the HRA, a court does not have the power to overturn parliamentary legislation or even any secondary legislation or act of public authority that bears
the requisite relation to parliamentary legislation. All a court can do is make
a declaration of incompatibility, which, as the HRA specifically states, "(a)
does not affect the validity, continuing operation or enforcement of the provision in respect of which [the declaration] is given; and (b) is not binding
on the parties to the proceedings in which it is made." (Section 4(6).) If a
court makes a declaration of incompatibility that is not overturned on appeal
by a higher court, it is up to Parliament to decide whether to remove the
incompatibility.[105]

In both Canada and the United Kingdom, the courts have the penultimate
say, but whereas in Canada the Supreme Court's penultimate say is legally
authoritative unless/until rejected by Parliament or a provincial legislature,
in the United Kingdom the judiciary's penultimate say – its declaration of
incompatibility – is not legally authoritative; it is up to Parliament to decide
whether to fix the law to remove the incompatibility. On paper, judicial power
to protect human rights appears to be much weaker in the United Kingdom
than in Canada. (At least, *domestic* judicial power appears to be much weaker
in the United Kingdom than in Canada. But domestic judicial power is not all
the judicial power there is in the United Kingdom; there is also *transnational*

judicial power. More about this in a moment.) In Canada, those who want to override a Supreme Court ruling that a parliamentary or provincial law is unconstitutional bear the burden of overcoming legislative inertia, often not an easy burden to bear: The Supreme Court ruling stands unless/until the requisite majority can be mobilized in the Canadian Parliament, or in a provincial legislature, to invoke section 33 and override the Court's decision. In the United Kingdom, by contrast, those who want Parliament to accept a judicial declaration of incompatibility bear the burden of overcoming legislative interia: The primary legislation stands unless/until Parliament amends the legislation to remove the incompatibility.

But appearances, we know, can be deceiving. In the United Kingdom, Parliament has a powerful incentive to take very seriously a judicial declaration of incompatibility (assuming the declaration has been affirmed on appeal): If the courts *of* the United Kingdom have concluded that parliamentary legislation is incompatible with a Convention right, there is a serious possibility that a powerful court *outside* the United Kingdom whose rulings the United Kingdom is treaty-bound to respect – the European Court of Human Rights – would reach the same conclusion. So, unless Parliament wants to risk the considerable political embarassment of having the United Kingdom lose a case before the European Court of Human Rights, Parliament will amend the legislation in question to remove the incompatibility. It was in part to avoid such embarassment – the United Kingdom had lost a number of high-profile cases before the European Court[106] – that Parliament adopted the HRA in the first place. (The thought was that if the UK's own courts could protect "Convention rights," it would lessen the number of occasions the United Kingdom would be brought before the European Court and make it less likely, when the United Kingdom was brought before the European Court, that the United Kingdom would lose.) Indeed, in the period leading up to passage of the Human Rights Act, Prime Minister Blair's Labor Government "repeatedly stated its belief that the normal course of action would be that [a declaration of incompatibility] 'will almost certainly prompt Government [whichever party is in power] and Parliament to change the law.'"[107] Therefore, those who bear the burden of overcoming legislative inertia under the Human Rights Act do not bear such a heavy burden after all; their position is greatly strengthened by the serious possibility that in the end, the European Court of Human Rights would support their cause in the unlikely event the UK Parliament did not. Contrary to the appearance that judicial power to protect human rights is weaker in the United Kingdom under the HRA than in Canada under the Charter, judicial power to protect human rights is at least as strong in the United Kingdom as in Canada. If the United Kingdom were not treaty-bound to respect the rulings of the European Court, the situation might be otherwise.[108]

Furthermore, it is misleading to describe the judicial protection of Convention rights in the United Kingdom in terms of judicial penultimacy without noting the following complication. Although the domestic legal system of the United Kingdom is, with respect to Convention rights, a system of judicial penultimacy, the United Kingdom participates in a transnational legal system – the European Human Rights System – that is a system of judicial *ultimacy*. The United Kingdom is a signatory to the European Convention for the Protection of Human Rights and Fundamental Freedoms, and in that system, a judgment by the European Court of Human Rights that the United Kingdom has violated, or is violating, a particular Convention right is final. The United Kingdom is treaty-bound to respect – the UK Parliament may not overrule – such a judgment.[109] (One might be tempted to reply at this point that Convention rights are not entrenched in the United Kingdom. Though in the United Kingdom, Convention rights are not entrenched as a formal, legal matter, they are entrenched as a practical, political matter. As I noted earlier, it is virtually inconceivable, as a practical, political matter, that in the foreseeable future the UK Parliament could – even if it wanted to, which is unlikely – renounce the United Kingdom's status as a signatory to the European Convention, which has come to have a quasi-constitutional status in the United Kingdom and throughout the rest of Europe.) Moreover, because the right of individual petition exists in the European Human Rights System – because, in particular, citizens of the United Kingdom and others subject to its jurisdiction may, after exhausting domestic remedies, sue the United Kingdom before the European Court of Human Rights – the distinction between the domestic legal system of the United Kingdom and the transnational legal system in which the United Kingdom participates is, with respect to Convention rights, much less consequential than it would be if there were no right of individual petition.[110] It seems clear, therefore, that with respect to Convention rights, there is a dual legal system operative in the United Kingdom – a domestic system and a transnational system – and that unlike the domestic system, the transnational system is one of judicial ultimacy. Because in cases of conflict, the transnational system trumps the domestic system – because, that is, a judgment by the European Court of Human Rights that the United Kingdom has violated, or is violating, a Convention right, which judgment Parliament is treaty-bound to respect, takes precedence over a judgment to the contrary by a UK court – perhaps we should say that the overall legal system in the United Kingdom is, with respect to Convention rights, one of judicial ultimacy.

At first, it appeared that judicial power to protect human rights was weaker in the United Kingdom than in Canada. This is because in looking at the United Kingdom, we were focusing just on domestic judicial power. In broadening our focus to include transnational judicial power, it now seems that judicial power to protect human rights is not only stronger in the United Kingdom than in Canada, but that it may well be virtually as strong as it is in the United States. This is why I've chosen to feature in this chapter the sharp contrast between the United States, with its system of judicial ultimacy, and Canada, with its system of judicial penultimacy.

9

~

How Should the Supreme Court Rule?
Capital Punishment, Abortion, and Same-Sex Unions

I was concerned in Chapter 8 with the proper role of courts – their proper role, that is, in a liberal democracy – in protecting constitutionally entrenched human rights. I am concerned in this chapter with the proper role of one particular court: the Supreme Court of the United States. The point of departure for this chapter is a position I defended in Chapter 8: Because the power the Supreme Court exercises in protecting constitutionally entrenched human rights is the power of judicial ultimacy, the Court should exercise the power in a deferential (Thayerian) fashion. In this chapter, I pursue the implications of that position for three questions:

- Should the Supreme Court rule that capital punishment is "cruel and unusual" within the meaning of the Eighth Amendment to the United States Constitution?
- Should it rule that laws banning pre-viability abortions violate the Fourteenth Amendment?
- Should it rule that state refusals to recognize, by extending the benefit of law to, same-sex unions violates the Fourteenth Amendment?

In Part Two of this book, I began exploring the human rights dimensions of capital punishment (Chapter 5), abortion (Chapter 6), and same-sex unions (Chapter 7); in this chapter, I continue and conclude the exploration.

CAPITAL PUNISHMENT AND THE EIGHTH AMENDMENT

The Eighth Amendment to the Constitution, which limits both national (federal) and state power,[1] provides:

> Excessive bail shall not be required, nor excessive fines imposed, nor cruel and unusual punishments inflicted.

118

Is capital punishment "cruel and unusual" within the meaning of the Eighth Amendment? And if so, should the Supreme Court so rule?

The Preamble to the Constitution declares in part that "We the People of the United States . . . do ordain and establish this Constitution for the United States of America." The text of the Constitution is *We-the-People's* text; it is *their* text, *their* written communication of various imperatives. To whom does the Preamble's "We the People" refer? Neither to those who wrote (drafted) the constitutional text (or some part of it) nor even to those in the states who voted to ratify the text. Rather, "We the People" refers to the citizens of the United States *on whose behalf* the text was written and ratified. The constitutional text is primarily *their* text. The text of the Bill of Rights is the text of the People – the citizens – in 1789–91 who, through their elected representatives, ratified – who "ordain[ed] and establish[ed]" – the Bill of Rights. The text of the Fourteenth Amendment is the text of the People in 1866–68 who, through their elected representatives, ratified the Fourteenth Amendment. And so on.

So, the question of whether capital punishment is "cruel and unusual" within the meaning of the Eighth Amendment depends partly on what "cruel and unusual" meant to the People in 1789–91 who constitutionalized (that is, constitutionally entrenched) the imperative that "cruel and unusual" punishments [not be] inflicted. The cruel and unusual punishments clause of the Eighth Amendment is *their* text; it is *their* written communication of an imperative. And we cannot know whether imposition of the death penalty is consistent with *their* imperative not to inflict "cruel and unusual" punishment unless we know what "cruel and unusual" meant to them. The now-common name for the People's understanding of what their text meant is the "original" understanding or meaning.[2]

Unfortunately, nothing in the historical record discloses what the People in 1789–91 likely understood "cruel and unusual" to mean.[3] Nothing, that is, other than dictionaries of the time, which suggest the People in 1789-91 understood "cruel and unusual" to mean just what we would understand it to mean were we putting the cruel and unusual punishments clause into the Constitution today. In Samuel Johnson's *A Dictionary of the English Language,* first published in 1756, "cruel" is defined (in volume 1, at page 250) as: "1. Pleased with hurting others; inhuman; hard-hearted; barbarous. 2. [Of things.] Bloody; mischievous; destructive." "Unusual" is defined (in volume 2, at page 503) as: "Not common; not frequent; rare."

Few would deny that the Eighth Amendment forbids punishment that, like torture,[4] is *intrinsically* barbaric (and, in that sense, inhumane): barbaric *in and of itself,* no matter how heinous the crime, how culpable the criminal, or how effectively the punishment would deter. But the Eighth Amendment, which declares that *"excessive* bail shall not be required, nor *excessive* fines imposed" (emphasis added), forbids more than intrinsically barbaric punishment. Both individually and cumulatively, the emphasis in the Eighth Amendment on "excessive" and the ordinary meaning of "cruel" support the conclusion that a punishment is "cruel," within the meaning of the Eighth Amendment, if it goes well beyond what is necessary – if it is significantly harsher than necessary – to serve the legitimate aims of punishment.[5] All serious punishment is harsh; the question is whether a punishment is harsher than necessary – *significantly* harsher, not marginally or trivially harsher – and, in that sense, "cruel."[6]

What is the point, then, of adding "and unusual"? Wouldn't it have been enough to ban the imposition just of "cruel" punishments? One important way to test whether a punishment that one believes, or is inclined to believe, is cruel is in fact cruel – whether it is in fact intrinsically barbaric or, at least, significantly harsher than necessary to serve the legitimate aims of punishment – is to inquire whether the punishment is "unusual": not commonly used for any crime or, at least, for the sort of crime at issue, or for the sort of criminal (for example, a minor).[7] That a punishment is "unusual" in the sense of "not commonly used" is probative – not determinative, but probative – of whether the punishment is in fact "cruel." The thought here is that if a punishment is not "unusual" – if, to the contrary, the punishment is commonly used – it is less likely that the punishment is in fact either intrinsically barbaric or significantly harsher than necessary to serve the legitimate aims of punishment. According to the Eighth Amendment, then, a punishment is not unconstitutional unless it is both "cruel and unusual": either intrinsically barbaric or significantly harsher than necessary *and evidenced as such by the fact that the punishment is not commonly used.*

Why ban "cruel and unusual punishments," thus understood? Because such punishments are inhumane – they treat human beings inhumanely. In the vocabulary of the morality of human rights, "cruel and unusual punishments" violate human beings; they treat human beings as if they lack inherent dignity. To impose on a human being a punishment that, even if not intrinsically barbaric, is significantly harsher than necessary to serve the legitimate aims of punishment is to treat him inhumanely; it is to violate him. "The infliction of a severe punishment by the State cannot comport with human dignity . . . [i]f there is a significantly less severe punishment adequate to achieve the purposes for which the punishment is inflicted . . ."[8]

Given this construal of "cruel and unusual punishments," and even if capital punishment is not intrinsically barbaric, the Eighth Amendment forbids government to impose capital punishment for, say, the crime of stealing a loaf of bread.[9] In the last five years, the Supreme Court has ruled that the Eighth Amendment forbids government to impose capital punishment on anyone who is retarded[10] or was not yet eighteen when he committed the crime.[11] The question I address here is whether the Eighth Amendment's ban on "cruel and unusual punishments" forbids government to impose capital punishment on anyone for any crime, *even if capital punishment is not intrinsically barbaric.*

For Antonin Scalia and many others, the question is easy – and the answer is no. Like Robert Bork before him,[12] Justice Scalia argues that the People who constitutionalized the cruel and unusual punishments clause did not think they were thereby banning capital punishment. Therefore, argues Scalia, the Eighth Amendment as originally undertood does not ban capital punishment.[13] Scalia's "therefore" is a non sequitur.

Scalia is right that the People who constitutionalized the cruel and unusual punishments clause did not think they were thereby banning capital punishment. Indeed, the due process clause of the Fifth Amendment, which became a part of the Constitution at the same time the Eighth Amendment became a part (1791), and the due process clause of the Fourteenth Amendment, which became a part of the Constitution in 1868, both state that government may not deprive a person of life without due process of law. Moreover, the grand jury clause of the Fifth Amendment states that government may not prosecute a person for a "capital" crime – a crime for which the penalty of death may be imposed – unless a grand jury authorizes it to do so. Clearly, then, the People who made the Fifth and Eighth Amendments a part of the Constitution, like the People who made the Fourteenth Amendment a part of the Constitution, assumed that government may impose capital punishment (albeit subject to certain specified constraints).

However, that the People who made the Eighth Amendment a part of the Constitution did not think they were thereby banning capital punishment – indeed, that they expected capital punishment to continue into the foreseeable future – does not mean that capital punishment is consistent with the cruel and unusual punishments clause.[14] Even if it is not intrinsically barbaric, capital punishment is *not* consistent with the cruel and unusual punishments clause – the clause *as originally understood* – if:

no matter what the crime and who the criminal, capital punishment is significantly harsher than necessary to serve the legitimate aims of punishment; and

as evidence that it is significantly harsher than necessary, capital punishment is not commonly used for any crime.

That the People who made the Eighth Amendment a part of the Constitution did not think that in their day capital punishment was significantly harsher than necessary does not mean that in our day capital punishment is not significantly harsher than necessary. Perhaps today capital punishment is not significantly harsher than necessary to serve the legitimate aims of punishment, but if so, the reason is not that the People in 1789–91 did not think that in their day capital punishment was significantly harsher than necessary. Similarly, that capital punishment was not "unusual" in 1789–91 – that, to the contrary, capital punishment was *commonly* used in 1789–91 – does not mean that it is not unusual now. Perhaps capital punishment is not unusual now, but if so, the reason is not that capital punishment was not unusual in 1789–91.

Scalia confuses the imperative the People in 1789–91 constitutionalized – the imperative that "cruel and unusual punishments [not be] inflicted" – with what they thought, or would have thought, the implications of that imperative to be for capital punishment. It is the imperative that is a part of the Constitution, not the People's thoughts about the implications of the imperative. Consider the point in a different context. It's a safe bet that the People in 1866–68 who, through their elected representatives, ratified the Fourteenth Amendment did not think they were thereby banning either racially segregated public schooling or antimiscegenation legislation, each of which persisted into the middle of the twentieth century. But this does not mean that racially segregated public schooling and antimiscegenation legislation do not violate any of the imperatives the People constitutionalized in ratifying the Fourteenth Amendment. As Keith Whittington has put the point:

> [I]n a defensible version of originalism, authorial expectations about how the text will be applied are not the important measure of textual meaning. It is entirely possible for a text to embody principles or general rules, and much of the constitutional text does exactly that. The point for an originalist should be to understand [what] those original principles or rules [are], to understand what principle was entrenched in the Constitution.[15]

Now, this is not to deny what I have emphasized elsewhere: What the People thought, or would have thought, the implications of their constitutionalizing an imperative to be for one or another practice is probative of what they understood the meaning of their imperative to be.[16] Probative, but not determinative:

> The scope beliefs that particular drafters might have had about the application of [a] constitutional principle may be useful to understanding what principle they actually intended to convey with their language, but the textual principle should

not be reduced to the founders' scope beliefs about that principle. The founders could be wrong about the application and operation of the principles that they intended to adopt.[17]

Again, the most plausible candidate for the original meaning of the cruel and unusual punishments clause is this: *Do not inflict a punishment that is either intrinsically barbaric or significantly harsher than necessary to serve the legitimate aims of punishment, as evidenced by the fact that the punishment is not commonly used.* If we assume, at least for the sake of discussion, that capital punishment is not intrinsically barbaric, the question of whether capital punishment is "cruel and unusual" within the meaning – the *original* meaning – of the Eighth Amendment is the question of whether capital punishment is significantly harsher than necessary to serve the legitimate aims of punishment, as evidenced by the fact that the punishment is not commonly used.[18]

I explained in Chapter 4 why, *given the morality of human rights*, the only legitimate aim of capital punishment is deterrence.[19] But is the morality of human rights a "given" in the present context? Why assume that the morality of human rights bears on our analysis of the constitutionality of capital punishment under the Eighth Amendment? No interpretation of the Eighth Amendment that fails to affirm the morality of human rights – that fails to affirm that every human being has inherent dignity – is even plausible. As Chief Justice Earl Warren emphasized in 1958, in speaking for the Supreme Court, "[t]he basic concept underlying the Eighth Amendment is nothing less than the dignity of man."[20] Almost half a century later, the Supreme Court explained that "[b]y protecting even those convicted of heinous crimes, the Eighth Amendment reaffirms the duty of the government to respect the dignity of all persons."[21] ("All persons" includes even the most depraved criminal. Affirming the morality of human rights, Justice William Brennan once wrote that "even the vilest criminal remains a human being possessed of common human dignity.")[22] The morality of human rights is now a bedrock premise of the constitutional law of the United States, including the Eighth Amendment. In the present context, then, the question of whether capital punishment is significantly harsher than necessary to serve the legitimate aims of punishment is the question of whether in the United States, or in some part of it, it is more likely than not that capital punishment has a deterrent effect.

It remains a matter of great controversy, as I explained in Chapter 4, whether in the United States generally or in any state capital, punishment does in fact have a deterrent effect; one may reasonably doubt that capital punishment has a deterrent effect.[23] Suppose, however, that our doubt about the deterrent effect of capital punishment is less secure – our doubt is more tentative – than we would like. After all, the importance of reaching the most careful conclusion we possibly can is profound: Depending on the conclusion we reach, people may live who would otherwise die, or die who would otherwise live. How then might we test our suspicion that capital punishment is "cruel"?

Recall the point of adding "and unusual" to "cruel" in the Eighth Amendment: An important way to test whether a punishment that one believes, or is inclined to believe, is cruel is in fact cruel – whether it is in fact significantly harsher than necessary – is to inquire whether the punishment is "unusual": not commonly used for the sort of crime at issue, or perhaps for any crime, or for the sort of criminal (for example, a minor). That a punishment is "unusual" in the sense of "not commonly used" is probative of whether the punishment is in fact "cruel"; if a punishment is not "unusual" – if, to the contrary, the punishment is commonly used – it is less likely that the punishment is in fact significantly harsher than necessary to serve the legitimate aims of punishment. According to the Eighth Amendment, then, a punishment is not unconstitutional unless it is both "cruel and unusual": significantly harsher than necessary *and evidenced as such by the fact that the punishment is not commonly used.*

Is capital punishment "unusual" – is it "not commonly used" – in the United States at this time? Twelve states and the District of Columbia have abolished capital punishment. The abolitionist states include Massachusetts, Michigan, Minnesota, and Wisconsin. Thirty-eight states, the U.S. government, and the U.S. military still allow the death penalty (although in 2004 the death penalty was invalidated on the basis of the state constitution in both New York and Kansas).[24] To maintain the death penalty on the books is not necessarily to use the death penalty, or to use it very often.[25] Still, it is not plausible to say that in the United States at this time, capital punishment is "not commonly used."[26]

However, we need not – and indeed should not – confine our inquiry to the United States: Is capital punishment "unusual" among the liberal democracies of the world?[27] (I assume it needs no argument that the practice of liberal democracies – democracies that take seriously the claim that every human being has inherent dignity – is the relevant measure, not the practice of dictatorships and fundamentalist theocracies.) Given why we're asking the question ("Is capital punishment 'unusual'?") in the first place, it would make no sense at all to confine our inquiry to the United States. If every liberal democracy in the world except the United States had abolished capital punishment, wouldn't this be probative of whether the United States, in continuing to rely on capital punishment, was relying on a punishment significantly harsher than necessary to serve the legitimate aims of punishment? If so, confining our inquiry to the United States would deprive us of the very information we need to test our belief that capital punishment is significantly harsher than necessary. We should cast our net broadly, not because we think that the United States should follow the moral lead of other liberal democracies, but because what other liberal democracies are doing is probative – not determinative, but probative – of whether what the United States is doing is significantly harsher than necessary and therefore cruel (inhumane).[28]

Which liberal democracies have abolished the death penalty (for all crimes)? The list of abolitionist states, many of which we would recognize as genuine liberal democracies, contains eighty-five countries, including, in addition to our neighbors to the north (Canada) and south (Mexico), Australia, Austria, Belgium, the Czech Republic, Denmark, Finland, France, Germany, Hungary, Ireland, Italy, the Netherlands, New Zealand, Norway, Poland, Portugal, the Slovak Republic, South Africa, Spain, Sweden, Switzerland, Turkey, and the United Kingdom. Which liberal democracies have retained the death penalty? The list of retentionist states[29] contains seventy-six countries, a small minority of which are liberal democracies, including India, Japan, South Korea, and the United States of America. Undeniably, then, capital punishment is "unusual" – it is "not commonly used" – among the liberal democracies of the world.[30]

Perhaps the deterrent effect of capital punishment is significantly greater in the United States than it was in the liberal democracies that have abolished capital punishment. Perhaps the liberal democracies that have abolished capital punishment, or some significant number of them, have abolished it without regard to its deterrent effect. Unless there is a plausible argument that one or both of those possibilities is true, however – I'm aware of no such argument – the fact that capital punishment is unusual among the liberal democracies of the world strongly supports the claim that in the United States as well as in other liberal democracies, capital punishment is not necessary to serve the legitimate aims of punishment.

Assume, then, that in the United States generally and in every state, capital punishment is "cruel and unusual" within the meaning of the Eighth Amendment (and that therefore both the government of the United States and the government of every state in the United States that has not already done so should abandon reliance on capital punishment). Does it follow that the Supreme Court should so rule? I've explained here why we can reasonably conclude that even if it is not intrinsically barbaric, capital punishment now violates one of the principal human rights provisions of the Constitution of the United States – namely, the Eighth Amendment's ban on punishment that is *significantly harsher than necessary to serve the legitimate aims of punishment, as evidenced by the fact that the punishment is not commonly used.* I have not argued, however, that one cannot reasonably reject that conclusion. Whether one can reasonably reject it depends ultimately on whether one can reasonably affirm either of the two following propositions. (In the following propositions, "Texas" stands for whatever state it is whose system of capital punishment is at issue.)[31]

1. In "Texas" (or in the United States, if the federal system is at issue), capital punishment has, or probably has, a deterrent effect.
2. Although it is not clear whether in "Texas" capital punishment has a deterrent effect, "Texas" legislators may resolve the benefit of the doubt in favor of the assumption that it *does* have a deterrent effect; that is, they may resolve the benefit of the doubt in favor of protecting the lives of the innocent rather than the lives of those who are guilty of a heinous crime. The legislators must choose, and in choosing they may give the benefit of the doubt to the innocent.

If one can reasonably affirm either proposition, then one can reasonably conclude that in "Texas," capital punishment is not significantly harsher than necessary and therefore does not violate the Eighth Amendment. So: Can one reasonably affirm either proposition?

I'm inclined to answer in the affirmative but, be that as it may, the important point for our present purposes is this: The question each Supreme Court justice should ask himself or herself is not whether in "Texas" capital punishment (probably) has a deterrent effect, but only whether one can reasonably conclude *either* that it does *or* that the benefit of the doubt may be resolved in favor of protecting the innocent.

Let's assume that there *is* room for a reasonable difference in judgments about whether capital punishment is "cruel and unusual" within the meaning of the Eighth Amendment – and that therefore the Supreme Court should not rule that capital punishment violates the Eighth Amendment. Is there also room for a reasonable difference in judgments about whether inflicting capital punishment *on the mentally retarded,* or *on minors* (that is, those who were not yet eighteen when they committed their crime), is "cruel and unusual"?

- Even if one thinks, contrary to what I have argued earlier, that there may be a retributive justification for *some* capital punishment, it is implausible to think that there is a retributive justification for executing either the mentally retarded or minors, given each group's diminished moral culpability.[32]

- Even if one thinks that *some* capital punishment may have a deterrent effect, it is implausible to think that the deterrent effect that some capital punishment may have would be diminished by the abolition of capital punishment either for the mentally retarded or for minors.[33]

Clearly, then, there is no discernible room for a reasonable difference in judgments about whether executing either the mentally retarded or minors is "cruel" in the relevant sense: *significantly harsher than necessary to serve the legitimate aims of punishment.*

Nor is there room for a reasonable difference in judgments about whether executing either the mentally retarded or minors is "unusual" in the relevant sense: *not commonly used.* As I've already explained, executing *anyone* is exceedingly rare – because systems of capital punishment are exceedingly rare – in liberal-democratic societies.[34]

So even a Supreme Court stacked with justices who are committed Thayerians may conclude – and in my view *should* conclude – that the Eighth Amendment forbids "Texas" to execute either the mentally retarded or minors. As it happens, the Supreme Court, though certainly not stacked with Thayerians, *has* so concluded: in 2002, in *Atkins v. Virginia* (the mentally retarded),[35] and in 2005, in *Roper v. Simmons* (minors).[36] Even from a Thayerian perpective, each ruling is defensible. Defensible, but not inevitable. After all, even Thayerian justices can disagree among themselves:

> Thayer's rule, like all guideposts, is not self-applying. Even limited by the rule of administration, judges, like criminal juries, might differ over what constitutes a reasonable doubt; the possibilities, the stuff of which reasonable doubts are made, do not always strike all men, however reasonable, alike. Even under Thayer's rule of administration, then, the freedom and the burden of decisionmaking remain. But that freedom is narrowed, and that was Thayer's aim. He sought to reduce the scope of judicial freedom without diminishing the judicial duty and burden of judging.[37]

THE SECOND SENTENCE OF SECTION 1 OF THE FOURTEENTH AMENDMENT: WE-THE-PEOPLE'S UNDERSTANDING

This sentence stipulates that

> No State shall make or enforce any law which shall abridge the privileges or immunities of citizens of the United States; nor shall any State deprive any person of life, liberty, or property, without due process of law; nor deny to any person within its jurisdiction the equal protection of the laws.

Does any part of this constitutional provision forbid state government to ban pre-viability abortions? Does any part require state government to extend the benefit of law to same-sex unions? The answer to each question depends partly on the answer to a prior question: In 1866–68, when the Fourteenth Amendment was being ratified, what imperatives did "We the People" understand the three clauses of the second sentence of Section 1 to constitutionalize?[38] I've addressed that question at length in my book *We the People: The Fourteenth Amendment and the Supreme Court*;[39] here it will suffice to recite my principal conclusions. Readers who are skeptical about my conclusions, or who want more detail, may consult *We the People* and weigh my arguments.

In the aftermath of the Civil War, it quickly became clear that a state could, and the former Confederate states did, oppress the ex-slaves, and others, in three basic ways. Each of the three clauses of the second sentence of Section 1 responds to one of the three basic ways – each clause responds to a different way – that some state officials might seek to oppress some human beings. Let's begin with the due process clause.

"No State shall . . . deprive any person of life, liberty, or property, without due process of law . . ." In making this language a part of the Constitution, the People constitutionalized an imperative forbidding state officials to deprive any person of his life, his liberty – that is, his physical freedom – or his property extrajudicially; state officials may execute a person (life), or imprison him (liberty), or fine him or confiscate his property, if at all, only pursuant to "due process of law," which the People understood to refer to the process of law – in the words of the Civil Rights Act of 1866, to the "laws and proceedings for the security of person and property"[40] – that is generally due persons under state law.[41] Whether they understood it to refer to more process – more procedural protections – than that generally due persons under state law is neither clear nor, here, relevant.

"No State shall . . . deny to any person within its jurisdiction the equal protection of the laws." In making this language a part of the Constitution, the People constitutionalized an imperative requiring state officials to give to every person within the state's jurisdiction the same protection ("equal protection") that is generally due persons under state law – the same protection "of the laws." What laws? *Protective* laws: laws – such as those against homicide, kidnapping, or theft – that *protect* a person's life, liberty, or property.[42]

∾

THERE ARE TWO SENTENCES IN SECTION 1 OF THE FOURTEENTH Amendment. The first sentence declares that "[a]ll persons born or naturalized in the United States, and subject to the jurisdiction thereof, are citizens of the United States and of the State wherein they reside." As the Supreme Court emphasized six years after the Fourteenth Amendment was ratified, this sentence was meant to "overturn[] the Dred Scott decision by making *all persons* born within the United States and subject to its jurisdiction citizens of the United States" (and of the state wherein they reside).[43] In *Dred Scott v. Sandford*, 60 U.S. (19 How.) 393 (1857) – surely the single most infamous case in American constitutional law – the Supreme Court ruled, inter alia, that "a man of African descent, whether a slave or not, was not and could not be a citizen of a State or of the United States. . . . That [the] main purpose [of the first sentence of section one of the Fourteenth Amendment] was to establish the citizenship of the negro can admit of no doubt. The phrase, 'subject to its jurisdiction' was intended to exclude from its operation children of ministers, consuls, and citizens or subjects of foreign States born within the United States."[44] But what good would it have been to declare a person to be a citizen of the United States and of the state wherein he resides if a state could treat him as a second-class citizen?

Even if state officials do not deprive persons of their life, liberty, or property except pursuant to the process that is generally due persons under state law, and even if state officials do not fail to perform their legal duty to protect persons from those who would unlawfully deprive them of their life, liberty, or property, there is a third basic way that state officials might seek to oppress, and that some state officials after the Civil War did oppress, some of their citizens: by making and enforcing laws that treat some citizens (for example, ex-slaves) as inferior to other citizens – laws that treat some citizens as second-class citizens (or worse).

"No State shall make or enforce any law which shall abridge the privileges or immunities of citizens of the United States . . ." In making this language a part of the Constitution, the People constitutionalized an imperative forbidding states to make or enforce any law that treats some citizens less well than other citizens[45] *unless the differential treatment serves the public good in a reasonable fashion.*[46] The thought here is that although not every law that treats some citizens less well than others fails to respect the equal citizenship of those the law treats less well, some laws do – namely, laws that do not serve the public good in a reasonable fashion. A law fails to serve the public good in a reasonable fashion if either (1) it fails to serve the public good *at all*, or (2) it serves the public good – it achieves some public benefit or benefits – but fails to do so *in a reasonable fashion*. What sort of laws – what sorts of differential treatment – fit the latter profile?

Differential treatment that serves the public good fails to do so in a reasonable fashion (a) if the differential treatment is based on a demeaning view – a false, deficit-attributing view – about those who are treated less well;[47] or (b) if the cost or costs the differential treatment visits on those who are treated less well are so great relative to the public benefit or benefits the differential treatment achieves that there is no reasonable justification – no reasonable case to be made – for the differential treatment.[48] One may be treated less well than another either because of *who one is* (for example, African-American) or because of *what one does or has done* (for example, had an abortion). I address these two questions (and other, related questions) in the remainder of this chapter: Is a state's refusal to extend the benefit of law to same-sex unions based on a demeaning view about one's being gay or lesbian? Are the costs visited on (some) women by a state ban on pre-viability abortions so great relative to the benefits the ban achieves that there is no reasonable justification for the ban?

In Chapter 8, in discussing the case for Thayerian deference in the exercise of judicial review, I wondered whether it makes sense to generalize across every constitutionally entrenched human right: Perhaps there are reasons for thinking that Thayerian deference is appropriate in cases in which certain human rights are at issue but inappropriate in cases in which certain other human rights are at issue. Thayerian deference seems especially appropriate in cases in which the Supreme Court is enforcing the "regulation for the public good in a reasonable fashion" requirement. Were the Court to ask whether *in its own judgment* the challenged law serves the public good in a reasonable fashion, the Court would be acting like a super-legislature, deliberating *de novo* about an issue that the legislature had already (if implicitly) resolved.[49] Why isn't the proper issue for the Court only whether the legislature's judgment that the law serves the public good in a reasonable fashion is itself a reasonable – plausible – judgment. Unless in the Court's view the legislature's judgment is unreasonable, why should the Court substitute its judgment for the legislature's?[50]

ABORTION AND THE FOURTEENTH AMENDMENT

Does any part of the second sentence of section one of the Fourteenth Amendment forbid the states to ban pre-viability abortions? There is at least one category of pre-viability abortions that no state would choose to ban: pre-viability abortions necessary to save the life of the mother or to prevent grave and irreparable damage to her physical health. So the serious question is whether a state may ban some or all pre-viability abortions *not* necessary to save the life of the mother or to prevent grave and irreparable damage to her physical health. Such a ban doesn't implicate, much less violate, either the due process clause or the equal protection clause: The ban neither deprives any person of her life, liberty (physical freedom), or property – much less deprives her of life, liberty, or property without due process of law – nor denies to any person the equal protection of any law that protects life, liberty, or property.

However, a state ban on pre-viability abortions does implicate the privileges or immunities clause – as does any law that treats some citizens less well than others. (I can't think of a regulatory law that doesn't treat some citizens less well than others.)[51] A state law that bans pre-viability abortions – although it applies to everyone and not just, say, to African-Americans – treats some citizens less well than others: It treats those who have had a pre-viability abortion less well than those who have not, by punishing those who have had a pre-viability abortion. But to implicate is not to violate. Does a law that bans pre-viability abortions violate the privileges or immunities clause? Not if the law – the differential treatment – serves the public good in a reasonable fashion. This, then, is the heart of the matter: Does a law that bans pre-viability abortions serve the public good in a reasonable fashion? The answer is no if either of these propositions is true:

(1) The law fails to serve the public good.
(2) Although the law serves the public good – although it achieves a public benefit or benefits – it fails to do so *in a reasonable fashion*.

We can imagine laws about which one can reasonably wonder whether they serve the *public* good: the good *of the public*, the *common* good, the *commonweal*. (Consider, for example, a law that forbids married couples to use contraceptives.)[52] However, a law that bans the intentional destruction of a human life is not such a law: Such laws – laws against (intentional) homicide – undeniably serve the public good; indeed, if any laws serve the public good, laws against homicide do so.

But is a law that bans pre-viability abortions a law against homicide: Does it ban the intentional destruction of a human life? Although, as H. Tristram Engelhardt has observed, "many describe the status of the embryo imprecisely by asking when human life begins or whether the embryo is a human being . . . no one seriously denies that the human zygote is a human life. The zygote is not dead. It is also not simian, porcine, or canine."[53] Philosopher Peter Singer, who is famously and enthusiastically pro-choice, has acknowledged that "the early embryo is a 'human life.' Embryos formed from the sperm and eggs of human beings are certainly human, no matter how early in their development they may be. They are of the species *Homo sapiens*, and not of any other species. We can tell when they are alive, and when they have died. So long as they are alive, they are human life."[54] Similarly, constitutional scholar Laurence Tribe, a staunch pro-choice advocate, has written that "the fetus is alive. It belongs to the human species. It elicits sympathy and even love, in part because it is so dependent and helpless."[55] So a law that bans pre-viability abortions *is* a law against homicide.

Or is it? One might be tempted to say that a law that bans pre-viability abortions is not a law against homicide *in the relevant sense:* a law that bans the intentional destruction of a human life that has *full moral status*. Even if we accept *arguendo* this characterization of laws against homicide, one can reasonably conclude, as I explained in Chapter 6, that every unborn human life has full moral status from the earliest stage of its development; therefore, one can reasonably conclude that a law that bans pre-viability abortions *is* a law against homicide in the relevant sense – and, as such, serves the public good.

The serious question, then, is not whether a law that bans pre-viability abortions serves the public good. It does. The serious question is whether the law serves the public good *in a reasonable fashion:* Are the costs that such a law visits on those it treats less well so great relative to the public benefits achieved that there is no reasonable justification – no reasonable case to be made – for the law? Or, instead, do the benefits of banning pre-viability abortions justify the costs of doing so? This is a famously controversial – indeed, famously divisive – question.

What are the costs? This is what the Supreme Court said in *Roe v. Wade*, on its way to ruling that laws criminalizing pre-viability abortions violate the Fourteenth Amendment:

> The detriment that the State would impose upon the pregnant woman by denying this choice altogether is apparent. Specific and direct harm medically diagnosable even in early pregnancy may be involved. Maternity, or additional offspring, may force upon the woman a distressful life and future. Psychological harm may be imminent. Mental and physical health may be taxed by child care. There is also the distress, for all concerned, associated with the unwanted child, and there is the problem of bringing a child into a family already unable, psychologically and otherwise, to care for it. In other cases, as in this one, the additional difficulties and continuing stigma of unwed motherhood may be involved.

Did the Court overstate the costs? Richard Posner has suggested that the Court *understated* the costs:

> No effort is made to dramatize the hardships to a woman forced to carry her fetus to term against her will. The opinion does point out that "maternity, or additional offspring, may force upon the woman a distressful life and future," and it elaborates

on the point for a few more sentences. But there is no mention of the woman who is raped, who is poor, or whose fetus is deformed. There is no reference to the death of women from illegal abortions.[56]

Undeniably, a law that criminalizes pre-viability abortions imposes great costs on pregnant women who want to have an abortion. (Although John Ely was a severe critic of the Court's ruling in *Roe*, he cautioned: "Let us not underestimate what is at stake: Having an unwanted child can go a long way toward ruining a woman's life.")[57] A law that forbids a woman to have a pre-viability abortion is very different, in that regard, from, say, a law that requires a motorcyclist to wear a protective helmet, or a dress code that forbids policemen to wear beards. Preventing a woman from having a pre-viability abortion will profoundly affect the shape of her life for years to come, perhaps for the rest of her life.

However, that the costs of criminalizing pre-viability abortions are undeniably great does not mean that the costs are unreasonable in relation to the benefits of doing so; it does not conclude the question of whether the costs are disproportionate to the benefits. But that the costs of criminalizing pre-viability abortions are great *does* mean that the benefits of doing so must be great too, lest the costs be so disproportionate to the benefits that the laws fail to regulate for the public good in a "reasonable" fashion. The Court in *Roe* was therefore right to insist that because the magnitude of the costs is great, the magnitude of the public benefits must be great too. The latter must be proportionate to – commensurate with – the former. As the Court put it in *Roe*, legislation outlawing abortion "may be justified only by a 'compelling state interest,' . . . [and] must be narrowly drawn to express only the legitimate state interests at stake."[58]

Are the costs of criminalizing pre-viability abortions disproportionate to the benefits of doing so? The principal reason for thinking that the principal benefit of criminalizing pre-viability abortions – the many human beings saved from destruction – is not sufficiently great to justify the costs of doing so is this belief: Unborn human beings do not have full moral status – they do not have inherent dignity – from the earliest stage of their development; they acquire full moral status only at some point well after fertilization.[59] Again, however, one can reasonably conclude that unborn human beings *do* have full moral status from the earliest stage of their development. There is in virtually all liberal democratic societies, including the United States, a deep and widespread controversy about the moral status of (unborn) human beings in the earliest stages of development. Moreover, there is little if any reason to doubt that this controversy is enduring. Referring to "philosophy, neurobiology, psychology, [and] medicine," Garry Wills has observed that "[t]he evidence from natural sources of knowledge has been interpreted in various ways, by people of good intentions and good information. If natural law teaching were clear on the matter, a consensus would have been formed by those with natural reason."[60]

If there is room for a reasonable difference in judgments about the moral status of human beings in the earliest stages of development, then there is room for a reasonable difference in judgments about whether the benefits of criminalizing pre-viability abortions justify the costs of doing so – a reasonable difference in judgments, that is, about whether criminal bans on pre-viability abortions serve the public good in a reasonable (proportionate) fashion and thereby comport with the Fourteenth Amendment. Even one who believes that human beings acquire full moral status only at some point well after fertilization should acknowledge that one can reasonably conclude that human beings have full moral status from the earliest stage of development. Again, the case for concluding that human beings from the earliest stage of development have the same moral status that born human beings have – a case that may be, as I explained, solely secular – is entirely reasonable.

Given that there is ample room for a reasonable difference in judgments about the moral status of human beings in the earliest stages of development, how should the Supreme Court respond to the claim that the costs of a law criminalizing (most) pre-viability abortions greatly outweigh the benefits and the law therefore violates the Fourteenth Amendment? *Pace* Thayer, the Court should insist that the question *for the Court* is not whether the (likely) costs of the challenged law outweigh the (likely) benefits, but only whether one can reasonably conclude that the costs do not outweigh the benefits. As I said at the end of the preceding section of this chapter, were the Court to ask whether *in its own judgment* the costs outweigh the benefits, it would be acting like a super-legislature, deliberating *de novo* about an issue that the legislature had already (if implicitly) resolved. If in the Court's view the legislature's judgment that the costs do not outweigh the benefits is reasonable, there is no good reason for the Court to substitute its judgment for the legislature's.[61] Something Justice David Souter wrote in 1997 is highly relevant here (though Souter, following established Court doctrine, referred to "substantive due process review" rather than to "privileges or immunities clause review"):[62]

> [J]udicial review . . . has no warrant to substitute one reasonable resolution of
> the contending positions for another, but authority to supplant the balance
> already struck between the contenders only when it falls outside the realm of the

reasonable.... [It is] essential to the discipline of substantive due process review [to understand] the basic need to account for the two sides in the controversy and to respect legislation within the zone of reasonableness.... It is no justification for judicial intervention merely to identify a reasonable resolution of contending values that differs from the terms of the legislation under review. It is only when the legislation's justifying principle, critically valued, is so far from being commensurate with the individual interest as to be arbitrarily or pointlessly applied that the statute must give way. Only if this standard points against the statute can the individual claimant be said to have a constitutional right.[63]

Can a state legislature reasonably conclude that the costs of banning pre-viability abortions do not outweigh the benefits of doing so? Yes, because, again, one can reasonably conclude that unborn human beings have full moral status from the earliest stage of their development.[64] (This is not to deny that one can reasonably reject that conclusion.)

If, then, one believes, as many do, that laws banning pre-viability abortion do not serve the public good in a proportionate fashion, it does not follow that one should want the Supreme Court to so rule.[65] Neither the premise that such laws serve the public good, nor the premise that they do so in a proportionate fashion, is unreasonable.

SAME-SEX UNIONS AND THE FOURTEENTH AMENDMENT

Again, if a law or policy that treats some persons less well than others is based on a demeaning view about those the law treats less well, the differential treatment fails to serve the public good *in a reasonable fashion*. (In saying that a law/policy is based, even partly, on a view, I mean that government would not have enacted the law or adopted the policy but for the view.) By a "demeaning" view, I mean a view that *falsely* attributes a deficit of some kind – a lack, an inferiority – to a person in virtue of some aspect of (what we may call) the person's particularity: her race, for example, or her sex. An example: Women are, as such (that is, because they are women), not fit for the practice of law.[66]

In refusing to recognize – in refusing to extend the benefit of law to – same-sex unions, as most states do, a state

effectively excludes [same-sex partners] from a broad array of legal benefits and protections incident to the marital relation, including access to a spouse's medical, life, and disability insurance, hospital visitation and other medical decisionmaking privileges, spousal support, intestate succession, homestead protections, and many other stautory protections.[67]

Are state refusals to recognize same-sex unions based on a demeaning view –
a false, deficit-attributing view – about persons (gays and lesbians) in virtue
of their homosexuality? If so, a state's non-recognition policy fails to respect
the equal citizenship of those the policy treats less well; more precisely, the
policy fails to serve the public good *in a reasonable fashion*, thereby violating
the Fourteenth Amendment.

In Chapter 7, I argued that there is no non-demeaning basis for government's refusal to recognize same-sex unions. It does not follow, however,
that the Supreme Court should rule that state refusals to recognize same-sex
unions violate the Fourteenth Amendment. Whether the Court should do so
is a separate question.

A state that wants to defend its refusal to recognize same-sex unions against
a privileges-or-immunities-clause challenge must articulate a plausible and
therefore nondemeaning rationale for its nonrecognition policy. *Pace* Thayer,
the question for each Supreme Court justice, in responding to that defense, is
not whether in his/her judgment the rationale is true; rather, the question is
whether the rationale is plausible: a rationale that state legislators can plausibly
accept (even if they can also plausibly reject the rationale).

Even if, as I suggested in Chapter 7, there is no plausible *secular* rationale for government's refusal to recognize same-sex unions, it is a separate
question as to whether there is a plausible *religious* rationale. For many citizens of the United States, the most persuasive religious rationale for a state's
refusal to recognize same-sex unions is this: "According to the Bible, which
discloses to us the will of God, same-sex unions are contrary to the will
of God. Government should not affirm, by extending the benefit of law to,
relationships that are contrary to the will of God." I explained in my book
Under God? why a religiously grounded moral argument like this is not an
illegitimate basis for political decision making in a liberal democracy – even
a liberal democracy that, like the United States, is constitutionally committed to the non-establishment of religion;[68] I also explained there, however,
why Christians, *as Christians*, have good reason to be wary about relying on
this reading of the Bible as a ground for opposing the legal recognition of
same-sex unions.[69] For our present purposes, suffice it to say that for many
of us – including many of us who identify ourselves as Christian – a biblically
based claim that same-sex unions are contrary to the will of God is simply not
believable.

Nonetheless, many citizens of the United States firmly believe that same-
sex sexual relationships, including same-sex unions, are contrary to the will
of God. Should the Supreme Court reject as implausible a religious rationale
that so many Americans – indeed, probably a majority of them – affirms;

should it do so, that is, if neither any provision of the constitutional text nor well established constitutional law is clearly inconsistent with the rationale?

In 1967, in *Loving v. Virginia*,[70] the Court ruled that no state may ban interracial marriages. *Loving* involved Virginia's antimiscegenation law, and no doubt some Virginia citizens believed that interracial marriages were contrary to the will of God. By 1967, however, most Americans – even, probably, most Virginians – rejected that belief. As the Court noted, in the fifteen years before *Loving* reached the Court, fourteen states had repealed their antimiscegenation laws; only sixteen states retained such laws, which were largely unenforced. Thus, by the time the Court decided *Loving*, forty-four states did not have antimiscegenation laws on their books.

- In ruling as it did, the Court did not reject a religious rationale that a large number of Americans affirmed.
- Moreover, even before 1967 it was constitutional bedrock that no policy based on an ideology of White Supremacy is consistent with the Fourteenth Amendment (even if the ideology is religious).

What if tomorrow the Court were to rule that the states must recognize same-sex unions?

- In so ruling, the Court would be rejecting a religious rationale that a very large number of Americans affirms.
- Moreover, neither any provision of the constitutional text nor well established constitutional law is clearly inconsistent with the rationale.

Why should these differences matter?

After the Court finally got around to striking down antimiscegenation laws in 1967, there was no outcry for a constitutional amendment to overrule the Court's decision. But if tomorrow the Court were to rule that the states must extend the benefit of law to same-sex unions, this would be the predictable result: a constitutional amendment not merely overruling the Court's decision – not merely handing back to the states their discretion not to recognize same-sex unions – but forbidding states to recognize same-sex unions.[71] Thus, in addition to James Bradley Thayer's powerful argument from democracy, there is an important prudential reason for concluding that the Court, if faced anytime soon with a constitutional challenge to a state's non-recognition policy, should exercise its power of judicial ultimacy as deferentially as it conscientiously can.[72] Surely the Court can conscientiously decline to reject as implausible a religious rationale that so many Americans affirm, if neither any provision of the constitutional text nor well-established constitutional law is clearly inconsistent with the rationale. Listen, in that regard, to Richard Posner:

> I think the main basis for the opposition [to gay marriage] is religious and . . . that such opposition is different from opposition based on a scientific error. Religion is not scientific, but there is a difference between a belief that is demonstrably based on error and a belief based on a system of thought that science neither supports nor refutes. . . . In a democratic society, one has to respect religious beliefs; and no reasonable theory of the meaning of the religion clauses of the First Amendment permits one to argue that religious belief cannot be permitted to influence secular law.[73]

CONCLUSION

In this chapter, I've pursued the implications of Thayerian deference for three constitutional controversies at the epicenter of the American culture wars: capital punishment, abortion, and same-sex unions. Let me summarize:

1. Assume you agree with me that, for the reasons I've given in this chapter, capital punishment violates the Eighth Amendment. It does not follow that we should want the Supreme Court to so rule. The Court should not so rule if the Court concludes that the responsible policymakers (state or national) can themselves reasonably conclude that capital punishment is not significantly harsher than necessary to serve the legitimate aims of punishment.

2. Assume you believe that laws banning pre-viability abortion violate the Fourteenth Amendment because (in your view) they do not serve the public good in a reasonable fashion. It does not follow that you should want the Court to so rule. Indeed, the Court should not so rule, because the conclusion that such laws *do* serve the public good in a reasonable fashion is not unreasonable.

3. Assume you agree with me that because there is no non-demeaning basis for state refusals to recognize same-sex unions, such refusals violate the Fourteenth Amendment. As I just explained, it does not follow that we should want the Court, *just yet*, to so rule.[74]

It may appear strange for one who concludes that X (for example, capital punishment) is unconstitutional to oppose the Court's ruling that X is unconstitutional. But, of course, appearances can be deceiving. I explained in Chapter 8 why it doesn't make sense for the supreme court of a country to accept the Thayerian plea for judicial deference if, as in Canada, the court has only the power of judicial penultimacy; indeed, it makes sense for such a court to *reject* the Thayerian plea. But, as I've argued here, it may make sense, all things considered, for the supreme court of a country to accept the Thayerian plea if, as in the United States, the court has the power of judicial ultimacy.

A strong case can be made that the United States Supreme Court should have, not the power of judicial ultimacy, but only the power of judicial penultimacy. For better or worse, however, the Court has the power of judicial ultimacy. *Given* that the Court has this power, what role should the Court play in protecting constitutionally entrenched human rights? In his classic work, *The Least Dangerous Branch*, Alexander Bickel wrote: "The search must be for a function . . . which differs from the legislative and executive functions; . . . which can be so exercised as to be acceptable in a society that generally shares Judge [Learned] Hand's satisfaction in a 'sense of common venture'; which will be effective when needed; and whose discharge by the courts will not lower the quality of the other departments' performance by denuding them of the dignity and burden of their own responsibility."[75] I'm inclined to think that in exercising its power of judicial ultimacy in a Thayerian fashion, the Court would be playing its proper role – it would be serving its proper function – in protecting constitutionally entrenched human rights.

Nonetheless, how appealing Thayerian deference is, *all things considered*, depends partly on what the implications of Thayerian deference turn out to be. Although here I've pursued the implications of Thayerian deference for capital punishment, abortion, and same-sex unions, there are other questions to be answered: Can Thayerian deference accommodate the Supreme Court's most important free speech decisions? Its most important antidiscrimination decisions – including, of course, *Brown v. Board of Education*[76]? Its most important criminal procedure decisions? Indeed, perhaps we should not generalize across every constitutionally entrenched human right; perhaps there are reasons for thinking that Thayerian deference is appropriate in cases in which certain human rights are at issue but inappropriate in cases in which certain other human rights are at issue – the right to freedom of speech, for example, or the right not to be discriminated against on the basis of a demeaning view about an aspect of one's particularity.[77] In any event, the implications – the consequences – of Thayerian deference surely bear on our estimate of the all-things-considered appeal of Thayerian deference.[78]

Summation

At the beginning of the Introduction to this book, I quoted philosopher John Searle's recent observation that "we [do not] have a clear theory of human rights. On the contrary, . . . the necessary work is just beginning."[1] My aim in this book, as the book's title indicates, has been to contribute to "the necessary work [that] is just beginning."

There are (at least) three major issues with which a theory of human rights must deal – and with which I have dealt in this book. The first and most fundamental of the three issues is whether there is a non-religious (secular) ground for the morality of human rights – for the claim that each and every (born) human being has inherent dignity and is inviolable. (That there is a religious ground – indeed, more than one religious ground – is undeniable.) As I noted in the Introduction, the claim that every human being has inherent dignity and is inviolable is deeply problematic for many secular thinkers, because the claim is difficult – perhaps to the point of being impossible – to align with one of their reigning intellectual convictions, what Bernard Williams called "Nietzsche's thought": "[T]here is, not only no God, but no metaphysical order of any kind . . . "[2]

The second major issue concerns the relationship between the morality of human rights and the law of human rights: What laws should we who affirm that every human being has inherent dignity and is inviolable, *because* we affirm it, press our government – our elected representatives – to enact? What policies should we press them to adopt? What laws and policies should we press them to avoid?

As I explained in Chapter 8, many human rights laws and policies are constitutionally entrenched. The third major issue that a comprehensive theory of human rights should address is the proper role of courts, in a liberal democracy, in protecting – and therefore in interpreting – constitutionally entrenched human rights laws and policies.

What I have said in this book about each of these three major issues – and about the other principal issues addressed here: capital punishment, abortion, and same-sex unions – is conspicuously controversial. Is there anything of consequence to say about any of these issues that is *not* conspicuously controversial? The challenge is not to deal with these issues in a non-controversial way; the challenge is to deal with them in a way that advances the conversation and thereby invites and facilitates further productive conversation. If to some degree I have met that challenge here, it is because I have had the help of many fine interlocutors.

Notes

INTRODUCTION

1. John R. Searle, "Social Ontology and Free Speech," The Hedgehog Review, Fall 2004, 55, 66. For a recent contribution to "the necessary work [that] is just beginning," see Amartya Sen, "Elements of a Theory of Human Rights," 32 Philosophy & Public Affairs 315 (2004). For a brief overview of the subject of human rights, see James Nickel, "Human Rights," Stanford Encyclopedia of Philosophy, <http://plato.stanford.edu/entries/rights-human/> (2003).
2. In Chapter 6, in discussing abortion, I inquire as to whether we who affirm that every *born* human being has inherent dignity and is inviolable should also affirm that some or even all *unborn* human beings have inherent dignity.
3. Charles Taylor, A Catholic Modernity? 16 (1999). Taylor writes "that modern culture, in breaking with the structures and beliefs of Christendom, also carried certain facets of Christian life further than they ever were taken or could have been taken within Christendom. In relation to the earlier forms of Christian culture, we have to face the humbling realization that the breakout was a necessary conditon of the development." Id. For Taylor's development of this point, with particular reference to modern liberal political culture's affirmation of universal human rights, see id. at 18–19. Cf. Charles Taylor, "Closed World Structures," in Mark A. Wrathall, ed., Religion after Metaphysics 47, 53–54 & 61 (2003).
4. Bernard Williams, "Republican and Galilean," New York Rev., Nov. 8, 1990, at 45, 48 (reviewing Charles Taylor, Sources of the Self: The Making of Modern Identity (1989)).
5. "Rights" and "duties" are correlative, in this sense: If A has a right against B that B do, or refrain from doing, X to A – if, say, A has a right against B that B not torture A – then B has a duty (obligation) to A not to torture A. Although my comments in this part of the introduction are explicitly about rights-talk, they are also, albeit implicitly, about correlative duties-talk.
6. See James W. Nickel, Making Sense of Human Rights [95] (rev. ed. 2006): "Many people take legal rights as their paradigm of rights. If legal rights provide the model, moral rights may be thought of as phony rights, as lacking key features that real rights have." (Nickel then adds: "Prior to the implementation of human rights in international law, this view would have led to their rejection. Today, however, human

rights exist in international law through widely accepted treaties, and this makes it possible for those who deny the existence of non-legal rights to endorse human rights as legal rights.") Consider, in that regard, these statements by Jeremy Bentham:

> Of a natural right who has any idea? I, for my part, have none: a natural right is a round square, – an incorporeal body. What a legal right is I know. I know how it was made. I know what it means when made. To me a right and a legal right are the same thing . . . Right and law are correlative terms: as much so as son and father. Right is with me the child of law: from different operations of the law result different sorts of rights.

Jeremy Bentham, Supply Without Burthen or Escheat *Vice* Taxation, in Jeremy Waldron, ed., Nonsense Upon Stilts: Bentham, Burke and Marx on the Rights of Man 70, 72–73 (1987).

> *Right*, the substantive *real* laws come *real* rights, but from laws of nature, fancied and invented by poets, rhetoricians, and dealers in moral and intellectual poisons come *imaginary* rights, a bastard brood of monsters, "gorgons and chimeras dire."

Jeremy Bentham, Anarchical Fallacies, in id. at 46, 69.

> *Natural rights* is simple nonsense: natural and imprescriptible rights, rhetorical nonsense – nonsense upon stilts.

Id. at 53. See also Sen, n. 1, at 316:

> Bentham insisted that "natural rights is simple nonsense; natural and imprescriptible rights (an American phrase), rhetorical nonsense, nonsense upon stilts." That suspicion remains very alive today, and despite the persistent use of the idea of human rights in practical affairs, there are many who see the idea of human rights as no more than "bawling upon paper," to use another of Bentham's barbed portrayals of natural rights claims.

More recently, Alasdair MacIntyre has opined that "[b]elief in [moral] rights . . . is on a par with belief in unicorns." Jeffrey Stout, Democracy and Tradition 206 (2004) (discussing MacIntyre's aversion to moral-rights-talk).

For a defense of moral-rights-talk, see Joel Feinberg, Rights, Justice, and the Bounds of Liberty 143–58 (1980). For a critique of Feinberg's position, see Craig. K. Ihara, "Are Individual Rights Necessary? A Confucian Perspective," in Kwong-loi Shun & David B. Wong, eds., Confucian Ethics: A Comparative Study of Self, Autonomy, and Community 11 (2004). See also Alasdair MacIntyre, "Questions for Confucians," in id. at 203, 211 et seq.

PART ONE. THE MORALITY OF HUMAN RIGHTS

1. Regina Ammicht-Quinn, "Whose Dignity Is Inviolable? Human Beings, Machines and the Discourse of Dignity," in Regina Ammicht-Quinn, Maureen Junker-Kerry & Elsa Tamez, eds., Concilium 2003/2: The Discourse of Human Dignity 35, 40. The claim that "the postulate that all human life is holy no longer exists" was made by Peter Singer, quoted in an interview in Der Spiegel, Nov. 25, 2001.
2. Clifford Orwin, "The Unraveling of Christianity in America," The Public Interest, Spring 2004, at 31–32.

CHAPTER 1. THE MORALITY OF HUMAN RIGHTS

1. Jürgen Habermas, Religion and Rationality: Essays on Reason, God, and Modernity 153–54 (Eduardo Mendieta, ed., 2002).

2. See, e.g., Darcy O'Brien, A Dark and Bloody Ground 1 (1993). Whether "Kentucky" does in fact derive from a Native American word for "a dark and bloody ground" is doubtful. See <http://www.continuitypress.com/faqs.html>. The "dark and bloody ground" refers to the area along the Cumberland River in both Kentucky and Tennessee where many Indians versus Indian battles took place before, and for a time after, the European settlers came into the area. See id.

3. Kim A. McDonald, "Anthropologists Debate Whether War Is Inevitable among Humans," Chronicle of Higher Education, Nov. 22, 1999 (quoting Carol Nordstrom, an anthropologist at the University of Notre Dame).

4. Adam Hochschild, King Leopold's Ghost: A Story of Greed, Terror, and Heroism in Colonial Africa 233 (1998). The causes – all of them related to the system of slave labor – were several: murder, starvation, exhaustion, exposure, disease, and a plummeting birth rate. See id. at 225–234. As Hochschild observes, this was "a death toll of Holocaust dimensions." Id. at 4. See also Alan Riding, "Belgium Confronts Its Heart of Darkness," New York Times, Sept. 21, 2002; Alan Riding, "Art Show Forces Belgium to Ask Hard Questions Abouts Its Colonial Past," New York Times, Feb. 9, 2005. The holocaust in the Congo was not an isolated event. See, e.g., Ross A. Slotten, "AIDS in Namibia," 41 Soc. Sci. Med. 277 (1995):

> In 1884, Namibia formally became a German colony and was known as German South West Africa. During the time of annexation, the Herero and Nama peoples were the largest tribes, inhabiting the most desirable land, which the Germans gradually expropriated between 1893 and 1903. This expropriation led to many battles, culminating in the intentional genocide of 60% of the population. To this day, the Hereros and Namas have not recovered their original numerical strength.

See also Giles Foden, "Rehearsal for Genocide," New York Times Book Rev., Apr. 20, 2003 (reviewing Uwe Timm, Morenga (2003)).

5. Israel W. Charney, ed., I Encyclopedia of Genocide 61–105 (1999); Peter Balakian, The Burning Tigris: The Armenian Genocide and America's Response (2003); Belinda Cooper, "Turks Breach Wall of Silence on Armenians," New York Times, Mar. 6, 2004.

6. Id. at 29 (Table 5). "[The Nazi] genocides likely cost the lives of about 16,300,000 people: nearly 5,300,000 Jews, 260,000 Gypsies, 10,500,000 Slavs, and 220,000 homosexuals, as well as another 10,000 handicapped Germans." Id. at 439. "The Nazi genocide against the Jews – the Holocaust, as it has generally come to be known as – is estimated to have resulted in the murder of about five and a half million Jews in Nazi-occupied Europe, around half the number targeted in the notorious Wannsee Conference of January 1942." Ian Kershaw, "Afterthought: Some Reflections on Genocide, Religion, and Modernity," in Omer Bartov & Phyllis Mack, eds., In God's Name: Genocide and Religion in the Twentieth Century 377 (2001).

7. See, e.g., Philip Gourevitch, We Wish to Inform You that Tomorrow We Will Be Killed with Our Families: Stories from Rwanda (1998). For a narrative of the failures by the United States to respond to recent genocides, see Samantha Power, "A Problem from Hell": America and the Age of Genocide (2002).

8. One could go on and on. See, e.g., Iris Chang, The Rape of Nanking: The Forgotten Holocaust of World War II (1997); Mark Danner, The Massacre at El Mozote: A Parable of the Cold War (1994). See also Philip Dray, At the Hands of Persons Unknown: The Lynching of Black America viii (2002): "Through 1944, when lynchings

first began to decline strongly, [the Tuskegee Institute] recorded 3,417 lynchings of blacks . . . Not until 1952 did a year pass without a single recorded lynching."

9. I Encyclopedia of Genocide, n. 5, at 28. "[G]enocide – intentional acts to elimate in whole, or in substantial part, a specific human population – [has] claimed the lives of some 60 million people in the 20th century, 16 million of them since 1945, when the watchword was 'Never again.' Genocide has, in fact, been so frequent, the number of victims so extensive, and serious attempts to prevent it so few, that many scholars have described the 20th century as 'the age of genocide.'" Roger W. Smith, "American Self-Interest and the Response to Genocide," The Chronicle, July 30, 2004. See also Jonathan Glover, Humanity: A Moral History of the Twentieth Century (1999).

It bears emphasizing here that "religion has played an important role in several outbreaks of genocide since World War I." Omer Bartov & Phyllis Mack, "Introduction," in Bartov & Mack, n. 6, at 1. But the role religion has played is not invariably negative, as Bartov and Mack explain:

> Violence and religion have been closely associated in a variety of intricate, often contradictory ways, since the earliest periods of human civilization. Institutionalized religions have practiced violence against both their adherents and their real or imagined opponents. Conversely, religions have also been known to limit social and political violence and to provide spiritual and material comfort to its victims. Religious faith can thus generate contradictory attitudes, either motivating aggression or restraining it. Individual perpetrators and victims of violence can seek in religious institutions and personal faith both a rationale for atrocity, a justification to resist violence, or a means to come to terms with the legacy of destruction by integrating it into a wider historical or theological context.

Id. Cf. Os Guinness, "On Faith," Wilson Quarterly, Spring 2005: "It's a simple fact, for example, that, contrary to the current scapegoating of religion, more people were slaughtered during the 20th century under secularist regimes, led by secularist intellectuals, and in the name of secularist ideologies, than in all the religious persecutions in Western history."

10. See, e.g., Louis B. Sohn, "The New International Law: Protection of the Rights of Individuals Rather Than States," 32 American U. L. Rev. 1 (1982); Robert F. Drinan, Cry of the Oppressed: The History and Hope of the Human Rights Revolution (1987).

11. See Leszek Kolakowski, Modernity on Endless Trial 214 (1990):

> It is often stressed that the idea of human rights is of recent origin, and that this is enough to dismiss its claims to timeless validity. In its contemporary form, the doctrine is certainly new, though it is arguable that it is a modern version of the natural law theory, whose origins we can trace back at least to the Stoic philosophers and, of course, to the Judaic and Christian sources of European culture. There is no substantial difference between proclaiming "the right to life" and stating that natural law forbids killing. Much as the concept may have been elaborated in the philosophy of the Enlightenment in its conflict with Christianity, the notion of the immutable rights of individuals goes back to the Christian belief in the autonomous status and irreplaceable value of the human personality.

12. Tom J. Farer & Felice Gaer, "The UN and Human Rights: At the End of the Beginning," in Adam Roberts & Benedict Kingsbury, eds., United Nations, Divided World 240 (2d ed. 1993).

13. In the final decade of the twentieth century, the Security Council of the United Nations established two international criminal tribunals, one (in 1993) to deal with

atrocities committed in the former Yugoslavia since 1991 and the other (in 1994) to deal with atrocities committed in Rwanda in 1994. In 2001, pursuant to the Rome Statute of the International Criminal Court (1998), the International Criminal Court was established, with jurisdiction over the crime of genocide, crimes against humanity, war crimes, and the crime of aggression. See Henry J. Steiner & Philip Alston, International Human Rights in Context: Law, Politics, Morals 1143–98 (2d ed. 2000).

14. The Universal Declaration was adopted and proclaimed by the General Assembly of the United Nations on Dec. 10, 1948. The International Covenant on Civil and Political Rights (ICCPR) and the International Covenant on Economic, Social, and Cultural Rights (ICESCR), which are treaties and as such are binding on the several state parties thereto, were meant in part to elaborate the various rights specified in the Universal Declaration. The ICCPR and the ICESCR were each adopted and opened for signature, ratification, and accession by the General Assembly of the United Nations on Dec. 16, 1966. The ICESCR entered into force on Jan. 3, 1976, and as of June 2004, had 149 state parties. The ICCPR entered into force on Mar. 23, 1976, and as of June 2004, had 152 state parties. The United States is a party to the ICCPR but not to the ICESCR. In October 1977, President Jimmy Carter signed both the ICCPR and the ICESCR. Although the United States Senate has not ratified the ICESCR, in September 1992, with the support of President George H. W. Bush, the Senate ratified the ICCPR (subject to certain "reservations, understandings and declarations" that are not relevant here; see 138 Cong. Rec. S 4781–84 (daily ed. Apr. 2, 1992)).

15. The relevant wording of the two preambles is as follows:

> *The State Parties to the present Covenant,*
> Considering that . . . recognition of the inherent dignity and of the equal and inalienable rights of all members of the human family is the foundation of freedom, justice, and peace in the world.
> *Recognizing* that these rights derive from the inherent dignity of the human person.
> . . .
> Agree upon the following articles: . . .

16. Homo sapiens sapiens is the name of the subspecies commonly known as modern man, the earliest fossils of which are less than 200,000 years old.

17. For some recent discussions of the idea of human dignity, see Regina Ammicht-Quinn, Maureen Junker-Kerry & Elsa Tamez, eds., Concilium 2003/2: The Discourse of Human Dignity; Robert Kraynak & Glenn Tinder, eds., In Defense of Human Dignity: Essays for Our Times (2003); Vicki C. Jackson, "Constitutional Dialogue and Human Dignity: States and Transnational Constitutional Discourse," 65 Montana L. Rev. 15 (2004).

    The morality of human rights holds not that every human being has inherent dignity, but only that every *born* human being has inherent dignity. See Chapter 6 at 54. Except in Chapter 6, where I discuss abortion, I generally bracket the born/unborn distinction and say simply that according to the morality of human rights, every human being has inherent dignity.

18. The ICCPR, in Article 26, bans "discrimination on any ground such as race, colour, sex, language, religion, political or other opinion, national or social origin, property,

birth or other status." Cf. Charles E. Curran, "Catholic Social Teaching: A Historical and Ethical Analysis 1891 -Present 132 (2002):

> Human dignity comes from God's free gift; it does not depend on human effort, work, or accomplishments. All human beings have a fundamental, equal dignity because all share the generous gift of creation and redemption from God.... Consequently, all human beings have the same fundamental dignity, whether they are brown, black, red, or white; rich or poor, young or old; male or female; healthy or sick.

19. See Jacques Maritain, "Introduction," in UNESCO, Human Rights: Comments and Interpretation 9–17 (1949).

20. For a general definition of what it means to say that one is "inviolable," see 8 Oxford English Dictionary 51 (2d ed. 1989): "not to be violated; not liable or allowed to suffer violence; to be kept sacredly free from profanation, infraction, or assault."

21. See Michael Burleigh & Wolfgang Wipperman, The Racial State: Germany, 1933–1945 (1991); Johannes Morsink, "World War Two iversal Declaration," 15 Human Rights Q. 357, 363 (1993); Claudia Koonz, The Nazi Conscience (2003).

CHAPTER 2. THE MORALITY OF HUMAN RIGHTS: A RELIGIOUS GROUND

1. Raimond Gaita, A Common Humanity: Thinking about Love and Truth and Justice 23–24 (2000). Cf. Jürgen Habermas, Religion and Rationality: Essays on Reason, God, and Modernity 162 (Eduardo Mendieta, ed., 2002): "[T]he basic concepts of philosophical ethics, as they have developed up to this point, also fail to capture all the intuitions that have already found a more nuanced expression in the language of the Bible, and which we have only come to know by means of a halfway religious socialization."

2. Though the claim does seem to be axiomatic for liberal democracy. See n. 29. Cf. Charles Larmore, "The Moral Basis of Political Liberalism," 96 J. Philosophy 599, 624–25 (1999) (arguing that "our commitment to [liberal] democracy... cannot be understood except by appeal to a higher moral authority, which is the obligation to respect one another as persons").

3. A variation on the question "Which human beings are inviolable?" is this question: Who is a human being; that is, who is truly, fully human? Women? Non-whites? Jews? Cast as the claim that only some individuals are truly, fully human, the claim that only some human beings are inviolable has been, and remains, quite common. See generally Alain Finkielkraut, In the Name of Humanity: Reflections on the Twentieth Century (2000). According to Nazi ideology, for example, Jews are not truly, fully human. See Michael Burleigh & Wolfgang Wipperman, The Racial State: Germany, 1933–1945 (1991); Johannes Morsink, "World War Two iversal Declaration," 15 Human Rights Q. 357, 363 (1993). There are countless other examples, past and present. See Richard Rorty, "Human Rights, Rationality, and Sentimentality," in Stephen Shute & Susan Hurley, eds., On Human Rights: The Oxford Amnesty Lectures 1993 111, 112 (1993):

> Serbian murderers and rapists do not think of themselves as violating human rights. Further they are not doing these things to fellow human beings, but to Muslims. They are not being inhuman, but rather are discriminating between the true humans and the pseudohumans. They are making the same sort of distinction as the Crusaders made between the humans and the infidel dogs, and the Black Muslims make between humans and blue-eyed devils. [Thomas Jefferson] was able both to own slaves and to think it

self-evident that all men are endowed by their creator with certain inalienable rights. He had convinced himself that the consciousness of Blacks, like that of animals, "participates more of sensation than reflection." Like the Serbs, Mr. Jefferson did not think of himself as violating *human* rights.

The Serbs take themselves to be acting in the interests of true humanity by purifying the world of pseudohumanity.

This position – that only some individuals are truly, fully human – should be painfully familiar to Americans. See Philip Dray, At the Hands of Persons Unknown: The Lynching of Black America 101 (2002): "[T]he bestselling *The Negro Beast, or 'In the Image of God'* (1900) by Charles Carroll[,] a hodgepodge of dubious biblical interpretations and bogus science, ... made the straightforward assertion that the Negro is not really a human being at all, not part of what Carroll called the 'Adamic family' that originated in the Garden of Eden." See also H. Shelton Smith, In His Image, But ...: Racism in Southern Religion, 1780–1910 (1972).

4. Cf. Jeff McMahan, "When Not to Kill or Be Killed," Times Lit. Supp., Aug. 7, 1998, at 31 (reviewing Frances Myrna Kamm, Morality, Mortality (Vol. II): Rights, Duties, and Status (1997)): "Understanding the basis of our alleged inviolability is crucial both for determining whether it is plausible to regard ourselves as inviolable, and for fixing the boundaries of the class of inviolable beings."

5. See, e.g., Asher Maoz, "Can Judaism Serve as a Source of Human Rights?" 64 Heidelberg J. Int' L. 677 (2004); Michael Lerner, "Jesus the Jew," Tikkun, May/June 2004, at 33:

> Jesus' message of love is ... an intrinsic part of Torah Judaism ... It was the Torah, not Jesus, that first taught "Thou shalt love thy neighbor as thyself" and "Thou shalt love the Lord your God with all your heart, with all your soul, and with all your might." It was this same Judaism that taught a truly revolutionary message: "Thou shalt love the stranger (Hebrew: ger, which might also be translated as "The Other" or "the Powerless one," based on the follow-up point made in Torah, "Remember that you were a Ger in Egypt" when the Jewish people were enslaved).

6. See, e.g., Khaled Abou El Fadl, "Islam and the Challenge of Democratic Commitment," in Elizabeth M. Bukar & Barbara Barnett, eds., Does Human Rights Need God? 58 (2005); John Mikhail, "Islamic Rationalism and the Foundation of Human Rights," Georgetown University Law Center Public Law & Legal Theory Working Paper No. 777026, <http://ssrn.com/abstract=777026>. See generally Robert Traer, Faith in Human Rights: Support in Religious Traditions for a Global Struggle (1991).

7. The translations here and elsewhere in this book are those of *The New Jerusalem Bible* (1985).

8. See John D. Caputo, "The Experience of God and the Axiology of the Impossible," in Mark A. Wrathall, ed., Religion after Metaphysics 123, 138 (2003):

> There is no name more closely associated in the Christian Scriptures with "God" than love. That is what God is, and this comes as close as the New Testament does to a "definition" of God, as opposed to defining God onto-theo-logically in terms of possibility and actuality, essence and existence. Even so, it would be at best a quasi-definition because in saying that God is love one is not de-fining God in the sense of setting forth God's limits and boundaries, but saying that God is unbounded and unlimited and unconditional excess, for love is love only in excess and overflow, not in moderation.
>
> So the experience of God is given in the experience of love. But love is perfect not when love is drawn around a closed circle of friends and intimates, which makes perfect

sense and is perfectly possible, but precisely when love is stretched to the breaking point of loving when love is mad and impossible. The God of love and the God of the impossible seem like a nice fit, a kind of pre-fit.

9. Simone Weil wrote: "God created through love and for love. God did not create anything except love itself, and the means to love." Simone Weil, Waiting for God 123 (Emma Craufurd, tr., 1951).

Sarah doesn't mean to put much weight on the distinction between (a) God's "creating" and (b) God's "sustaining" the universe. See Brian Davies, "Creationism and All That," The Tablet [London], May 11, 2002, at 16:

> In the thirteenth century, St Thomas Aquinas, though himself believing that the world had a beginning, argued that this is seriously irrelevant to the doctrine of creation. He said that to believe that the world is created is chiefly to believe that its being there at all and at any time is God's doing.
>
> And this, too, is what we find biblical authors teaching. . . . In these texts God is intimately involved with the world as its ever-present cause.
>
> . . .
>
> At the end of his *Tractatus Logico-Philosophicus*, Ludwig Wittgenstein wrote: "Not *how* the world is, is mystical, but that it is." For Wittgenstein, *how the world is* is a scientific matter with scientific answers (even if we do not have all the answers yet). But, he insists, even when the scientific answers are in, we are still left with the *thatness* of the world, the fact *that* it is. And it is with this fact that we surely need to grapple if we are reasonably to arrive at the notion of creation apart from the testimony of scripture.

Cf. Thomas Nagel, "Much Ado: There Is No Alternative to the Existence of Something," Times Lit. Supp., May 7, 2004, at 3 (reviewing Bede Rundle, Why There Is Something Rather Than Nothing (2004)).

10. Cf. Kristen Renwick Monroe, The Heart of Altruism: Perceptions of a Common Humanity 216 (1996):

> [I]t is the [altruistic] perspective itself that constitutes the heart of altruism. Without this particular perspective, there are no altruists. . . . [The perspective] consists of a common perception, held by all altruists, that they are strongly linked to others through a shared humanity. This self-perception constitutes such a central core to altruists' identity that it leaves them with no choice in their behavior toward others. They are John Donne's people. All life concerns them. Any death diminishes them. Because they are a part of mankind.

11. Hilary Putnam, The Many Faces of Realism 60–61 (1987). In an essay on "The Spirituality of The Talmud," Ben Zion Bokser and Baruch M. Bokser state: "From this conception of man's place in the universe comes the sense of the supreme sanctity of all human life. 'He who destroys one person has dealt a blow at the entire universe, and he who sustains or saves one person has sustained the whole world.'" Ben Zion Bokser & Baruch M. Bokser, "Introduction: The Spirituality of the Talmud," in The Talmud: Selected Writings 7 (1989). They continue:

> The sanctity of life is not a function of national origin, religious affiliation, or social status. In the sight of God, the humble citizen is the equal of the person who occupies the highest office. As one talmudist put it: "Heaven and earth I call to witness, whether it be an Israelite or pagan, man or woman, slave or maidservant, according to the work of every human being doth the Holy Spirit rest upon him." . . . As the rabbis put it: "We are obligated to feed non-Jews residing among us even as we feed Jews; we are obligated to visit their sick even as we visit the Jewish sick; we are obligated to attend to the burial of their dead even as we attend to the burial of the Jewish dead."

Id. at 30–31.

12. Cf. Daniel C. Dennett, Darwin's Dangerous Idea: Evolution and the Meanings of Life 474 (1995) (quoting Lee Khan Yew, Senior Minister of Singapore, on the outcry over the sentence of flogging given to Michael Fay for vandalism): "To us in Asia, an individual is an ant. To you, he's a child of God. It is an amazing concept."

13. See Richard P. McBrien, ed., The HarperCollins Encyclopedia of Catholicism 43 (1995):

> **analogy,** a comparison in the form of "A is to B as C is to D," e.g., God is to the world as the artist is to her work."
>
> All theological language is analogous since we can compare God only to the created things we know; we cannot speak of God except in human terms. The Fourth Lateran Council (1215) declared that "No similarity can be found so great but that the dissimilarity is even greater" (DS 806). Thus every similarity between God and creatures (God is wise; humans are wise) is understood to include a greater dissimilarity (God's wisdom is unlike human wisdom in that it infinitely surpasses it). Thomas Aquinas (d. 1274) is particularly well known for developing the role of analogy in theological discourse.

(But, not *all* theological language is analogical; *some* is negative: e.g, God is not finite, God is not comprehensible.) Continuing to speak analogically, Sarah says that every human being is created "in the image of God." See id. at 654:

> **imago Dei** (Lat., "image of God"), theological concept that denotes the likeness of the human creature to God. According to Gen 1:26, humanity was created "in [God's] image, according to [God's] likeness." Found sparsely in the Hebrew Scriptures, the word "image" was often used in Pauline writings in the NT to interpret Christ's work and became central to early Christian reflections on the human condition, the meaning of redemption in Christ, and hope for humankind. . . .
>
> Early theologians did not consistently separate "image" from "likeness" in interpreting human existence, and they saw the image of God variously in God's intellect, the capacity for moral decision, and the ability to rule over creation; but these theologians usually agreed that it implied a kinship between God and humankind and a call for the imitation of God.

For a discussion of different understandings and uses of the "image of God" language, see Roger Ruston, Human Rights and the Image of God 269–91 (2004).

14. United Church of Christ, Book of Worship 111 (1983).

15. See Jean Porter, Nature as Reason: A Thomistic Theory of the Natural Law 144–45 (2005):

> In the course of reviewing recent work on the biological roots of morality, Stephen Pope contrasts divine command approaches to ethics to the revised natural law theory currently being developed by some contemporary Catholic moral theologians, including himself, observing that this latter approach "understands the authority of moral claims to be warranted not by divine dictates but by their contribution to human flourishing." The Thomistic theory of natural law to be developed here shares in this fundamental approach, insofar as it takes happiness to be the aim of, and correlatively the ultimate criterion for, moral behavior.

(Quoting Stephen Pope, "The Evolutionary Roots of Morality in Theological Perspective," 33 Zygon 545, 554 (1998).)

16. In e-mail discussion, Steve Smith has characterized Sarah's views this way: "Human fulfillment generally, and my own fulfillment, will be served by learning to love and respect that which is sacred. Human beings are sacred. Therefore, human fulfillment is served by . . . etc." As Smith observes: "In this presentation, the claims that

(a) my fulfillment is served by learning to love Bill, Jane, et al. and (b) Bill, Jane, et al. are sacred are hardly independent claims, or independent reasons to care about others . . . Both the 'fulfillment' and the 'sacredness' parts are necessary to the argument. But at the same time, they are not just different phrasings of the same claim." E-mail from Steven Smith to Michael Perry, Aug. 28, 2002.

17. David M. Gallagher, "Thomas Aquinas on Self-Love as the Basis for Love of Others," 8 Fascicolo 23 (1999) (emphasis in original).
    On the relationship between loving one another and loving God, see n. 20.

18. For Christians, the basic shape of the good life is indicated by the instruction given by Jesus at a Passover seder on the eve of his execution: "I give you a new commandment: love one another; you must love one another just as I have loved you." John 13:34. See also John 15:12, 17.

19. In his book *After Theory* (2003), Terry Eagleton writes that "Aristotle thought that there was a particular way of living which allowed us . . . to be at our best for the kind of creatures we are. This was the life conducted according to the virtues. The Judaeo-Christian tradition considers that it is the life of charity or love. What this means . . . is that we become the occasion of each other's self-realization. It is only through being the means of your fulfillment that I can attain my own." Quoted in David Lodge, "Goodbye to All That," New York Rev., May 27, 2004, at 39, 41.

20. In the Gospel, there are two great commandments, not one. See Matthew 22:34-40: "But when the Pharisees heard that he had silenced the Sadducees they got together and, to put him to the test, one of them put a further question, 'Master, which is the greatest commandment of the Law?' Jesus said to him, 'You must love the Lord your God with all your heart, with all your soul, and with all your mind. This is the greatest and the first commandment. The second resembles it: You must love your neighbor as yourself. On these two commandments hang the whole Law, and the Prophets too." See also Mark 12:28–34; Luke 10:25–28. Cf. J.L. Mackie, Ethics: Inventing Right and Wrong 243 (1977): "D. D. Raphael, in 'The Standard of Morals,' in Proceedings of the Aristotelian Society 75 (1974–75) follows Edward Ullendorff in pointing out that whereas 'Thou shalt love thy neighbor as thyself' represents the Greek of the Septuagint (Leviticus 19:18) and of the New Testament, the Hebrew from which the former is derived means rather 'You shall treat your neighbor lovingly, for he is like yourself.'"

    What is the relation between the two commandments? In the view of great German Catholic theologian Karl Rahner, not only is there no tension between the commandment to love God and the commandment to love one another, there is "a radical identity of the two loves." Karl Rahner, 6 Theological Investigations 231, 236 (1969). In his "Reflections on the Unity of the Love of Neighbor and the Love of God", Rahner wrote: "It is radically true, i.e. by an ontological and not merely 'moral' or psychological necessity, that whoever does not love the brother whom he sees, also cannot love God whom he does not see, and that one can love God whom one does not see only by loving one's visible brother lovingly." Id. at 247. Rahner's reference is to a passage in John's First Letter in which it is written: "Anyone who says 'I love God' and hates his brother, is a liar, since whoever does not love the brother whom he can see cannot love God whom he has not seen." 1 John 4:20. In Rahner's view, it is only by loving one's neighbor that one achieves the ontological/existential state of being/consciousness that constitutes "love of God", even though one may not "believe in God". See Rahner, this n., at 238–39. If Rahner is right, then there is, in the following sense, not two great commandments, but one: Compliance with the first great commandment (to love God) requires compliance with the second (to love one another), and compliance with the second entails compliance with the first. See id. at 232. Consider, in that regard, the Last Judgment passage in Matthew's Gospel:

> When the Son of man comes in his glory, escorted by all the angels, then he will take his seat on his throne of glory. All nations will be assembled before him and he will separate people from one another as the shepherd separates sheep from goats. He will place the sheep on his right hand and the goats on his left. Then the King will say to those on his right hand, "Come, you whom my Father has blessed, take as your heritage the kingdom prepared for you since the foundation of the world. For I was hungry and you gave me food, I was thirsty and you gave me drink, I was a stranger and you made me welcome, lacking clothes and you clothed me, sick and you visited me, in prison and you came to see me." Then the upright will say to him in reply, "Lord, when did we see you hungry and feed you, or thirsty and give you drink? When did we see you a stranger and make you welcome, lacking clothes and clothe you? When did we find you sick or in prison and go to see you?" And the King will answer, "In truth I tell you, in so far as you did this to one of the least of these brothers of mine, you did it to me." Then he will say to those on his left hand, "Go away from me, with your curse upon you, to the eternal fire prepared for the devil and his angels. For I was hungry and you never gave me food, I was thirsty and you never gave me anything to drink, I was a stranger and you never made me welcome, lacking clothes and you never clothed me, sick and in prison and you never visited me." Then it will be their turn to ask, "Lord, when did we see you hungry or thirsty, a stranger or lacking clothes, sick or in prison, and did not come to your help?" Then he will answer, "In truth I tell you, in so far as you neglected to do this to one of the least of these, you neglected to do it to me." And they will go away to eternal punishment, and the upright to eternal life.

Matthew 25:31–46. In Matthew's Gospel, these are Jesus's final words to his disciples before the beginning of the passion narrative. Matthew 26:1–2 states: "Jesus had now finished all he wanted to say, and he told his disciples, 'It will be Passover, as you know, in two days' time, and the Son of Man will be handed over to be crucified.'"

It seem to follow, from Rahner's view, that it is a mistake, a confusion, to say that we should love one another *because* we love, or should love, God and God wants us to – or because we fear, or should fear, God and God wants us to. We should say, instead, that for us to love one another is also for us to love God, and that we should achieve the ontological/existential state of being/consciousness that constitutes "love of one another" (= "love of God") because that state is the highest human good; to have achieved that radically unalienated condition is to have become *truly, fully* human.

21. Cf. Helmut Gollwitzer et al., Dying We Live: The Final Messages and Records of the Resistance (New York: Pantheon Books, Inc. 1956). Dietrich Bonhoeffer wrote that "when Christ calls us, his call leads to death." Dietrich Bonhoeffer, The Cost of Discipleship 41 (R. H. Fuller, tr., 1995; originally published 1937).

22. Cf. Charles Taliaferro, "Why We Need Immortality," 6 Modern Theology 367 (1990).

23. Cf. Graham Greene, Monsignor Quixote 221 (1982): "The Mayor didn't speak again before they reached Orense; an idea quite strange to him had lodged in his brain. Why is it that the hate of a man – even of a man like Franco – dies with his death, and yet love, the love which he had begun to feel for Father Quixote, seemed now to

live and grow in spite of the final separation and the final silence – for how long, he wondered with a kind of fear, was it possible for that love of his to continue? And to what end?"

24. Compare, with Sarah's eschatological vision, the view of Jürgen Habermas:

> [By confronting] the conscientious question about deliverance for the annihilated victims[,] we become aware of the limits of that transcendence from within which is directed to this world. But this does not enable us to ascertain the *countermovement* of a compensating transcendence from beyond. That the universal covenant of fellowship would be able to be effective retroactively, toward the past, only in the weak medium of our memory, of the remembrance of the living generations, and of the anamnestic witnesses handed down falls short of our moral need. But the painful experience of a deficit is still not a sufficient argument for the assumption of an "absolute freedom which saves in death."

Habermas, n. 1, at 80.

25. The literature in Christian ethics on *agape* is voluminous. Some recent titles include: Colin Grant, Altruism and Christian Ethics (2001); Garth L. Hallett, Christian Neighbor-Love: An Assessment of Six Rival Versions (1989); Stephen J. Pope, The Evolution of Altruism and the Ordering of Love (1994); Edmund N. Santurri & William Werpehowski, eds., The Love Commandments: Essays in Christian Ethics and Moral Philosophy (1992); Edward Collins Vacek, SJ, Love, Human and Divine: The Heart of Christian Ethics (1994); Timothy P. Jackson, Love Disconsoled: Meditations on Christian Charity (1999); André Comte-Sponville, A Small Treatise on the Great Virtues 222–90 (Catherine Temerson, tr., 2001); Timothy P. Jackson, The Priority of Love: Christian Charity and Social Justice (2003).

26. For Sarah, to love another, in the sense of *agape*, is not to feel a certain way but to act in a certain way. Cf. Jeffrie G. Murphy, "Law Like Love," 55 Syracuse L. Rev. 15, 21 (2004):

> There are, of course, many fascinating questions that can be asked about the love commandment. Does it command love as an emotion or simply that we act in a certain way? Kant, convinced that we can be morally bound only to that which is in our control, called emotional love pathological love and claimed that it could not be our duty to feel it. What is actually commanded he called practical love – which is simply acting morally as Kant conceived acting morally.

Murphy explained to me in discussion that by "pathological" (which is the English word commonly used to translate the German word Kant used) Kant did not mean diseased or sick but simply something from our passions with respect to which we are passive and thus not in voluntary control.

27. Timothy Chappell, Book Review, 111 Mind 411, 412 (2202) (reviewing Raimond Gaita, A Common Humanity: Thinking about Love and Truth and Justice (2000)). Chappell is here describing "Gaita's view" and says that it is "reminiscent of course of Simone Weil and Iris Murdoch." Id. See Gaita, n. #, at xxxiii:

> Iris Murdoch said that understanding the reality of another person is a work of love, justice and pity. She meant, I believe, that love, justice and pity are *forms* of understanding rather than merely conditions that facilitate understanding – conditions like a clear head, a good night's sleep, an alcohol-free brain. Real love is hard in the sense of hardheaded and unsentimental. In ridding oneself of sentimentality, pathos and similar afflictions, one is allowing justice, love and pity to do their cognitive work, their work of disclosing reality. It is the same love, [Simone] Weil tells us, that sees what is invisible.

Compare Finkielkraut, n. 3, at 5–6 (commenting on Primo Levi's encounter at Auschwitz with the German chemist Doktor Engineer Pannwitz): "To Doktor Pannwitz, the prisoner standing there [Levi], before the desk of his examiner, is not a frightened and miserable man. He is not a dangerous or inferior or loathsome man either, condemned to prison, torture, punishment, or death. He is, quite simply, not a man at all."

28. See also Luke 6:27–35. Recall here the parable of the Good Samaritan (Luke 10:29–37):

> But the man was anxious to justify himself and said to Jesus, "And who is my neighbour?" In answer Jesus said, "A man was once on his way down from Jerusalem to Jericho and fell into the hands of bandits; they stripped him, beat him and then made off, leaving him half dead. Now a priest happened to be travelling down the same road, but when he saw the man, he passed by on the other side. In the same way a Levite who came to the place saw him, and passed by on the other side. But a Samaritan traveller who came on him was moved with compassion when he saw him. He went up to him and bandaged his wounds, pouring oil and wine on them. He then lifted him onto his own mount and took him to an inn and looked after him. Next day, he took out two denarii and handed them to the innkeeper and said, 'Look after him, and on my way back I will make good any extra expense you have.' Which of these three, do you think, proved himself a neighbour to the man who fell into the bandits' hands?" [The man] replied, "The one who showed pity towards him." Jesus said to him, "Go, and do the same yourself."

In *The New Jerusalem Bible*, a note attached to "Samaritan" explains that "[t]he contrast is between the element in Israel most strictly bound to the law of love, and the heretic and stranger, . . . from whom normally only hate could be expected."

29. Norman Geras, The Contract of Mutual Indifference: Political Philosophy after the Holocaust 67 (1998). Cf. Samuel Brittan, "Making Common Cause: How Liberals Differ, and What They Ought To Agree On," Times Lit. Supp., Sept. 20, 1996, at 3, 4:

> [P]erhaps the litmus test of whether the reader is in any sense a liberal or not is Gladstone's foreign-policy speeches. In [one such speech,] taken from the late 1870s, around the time of the Midlothian campaign, [Gladstone] reminded his listeners that "the sanctity of life in the hill villages of Afghanistan among the winter snows, is as inviolable in the eye of almighty God as can be your own . . . that the law of mutual love is not limited by the shores of this island, is not limited by the boundaries of Christian civilization; that it passes over the whole surface of the earth, and embraces the meanest along with the greatest in its unmeasured scope." By all means smile at the oratory. But anyone who sneers at the underlying message is not a liberal in any sense of that word worth preserving.

(There is an echo of Gladstone in something said by Michael Gerson, President Bush's chief speech writer: "To put it simply, it's a fairly radical belief that a child in an African village whose parents are dying of AIDS has the same importance before God as the president of the United States." Quoted in Elisabeth Bumiller, "Evangelicals Sway White House on Human Rights Issues Abroad," New York Times, Oct. 26, 2003.) Listen, too, to Herman Melville: "But this august dignity I treat of, is not the dignity of kings and robes, but that abounding dignity that has no robed investiture. Thou shalt see it shining in the arm that wields a pick or drives a spike; that democratic dignity which, on all hands, radiates without end from God Himself! The great God absolute! The centre and circumference of all democracy! His omnipresence, our divine equality!" Herman Melville, Moby Dick 126 (Penguin Classics ed. 1992). Thanks to George Wright for calling this passage to my attention.

30. Gaita, n. 1, at xviii–xix.

31. Graham Greene, The Power and the Glory 131 (Penguin ed. 1940). For a dissenting view on hate, see Meir Y. Soloveichik, "The Virtue of Hate," First Things, Feb. 2003, at 41. As the Chronicle of Higher Education stated, in an e-mail notice on this article dated Feb. 13, 2003: "Rabbi Soloveichik asks: 'Is an utterly evil man . . . deserving of a theist's love?' and, reflecting on his conversations with Christian clergymen, concludes that there is 'no minimizing the difference between Judaism and Christianity on whether hate can be virtuous.' He examines the 'theological underpinnings' for each faith's approach to hate and notes that 'the crucifixion is a story of a loving God seeking humanity's salvation,' but that 'not a single Jewish source asserts that God deeply desires to save all humanity.'" For vigorous criticism, by religious Jews and others, of Soloveichik's essay, and a response by Soloveichik, see "Correspondence: Jews and Christians, Hate and Forgiveness," First Things, May 2003, at 2–9.

32. It seems to have been an implausible ideal for Ivan Karamazov:

> I have never been able to understand how it was possible to love one's neighbors. And I mean precisely one's neighbors, because I can conceive of the possibility of loving those who are far away. I read somewhere about a saint, John the Merciful, who, when a hungry frozen beggar came to him and asked him to warm him, lay down with him, put his arms around him, and breathed into the man's reaking mouth that was festering with the sores of some horrible disease. I am convinced that he did so in a state of frenzy, that it was a false gesture, that this act of love was dictated by some self-imposed penance. If I must love my fellow man, he had better hide himself, for no sooner do I see his face than there's an end to my love for him.

Fyodor Dostoevsky, The Brothers Karamazov, opening of ch. 5, IV (Constance Garnett, tr., 1933).

33. Distinguishing "reasons" from "motives" in this context is deeply problematic. See Henry B. Veatch, "Modern Ethics, Teleology, and Love of Self," 75 Monist 52, 60 (1992):

> [T]he stock answer given to this question ["Why should I be moral?"] has long been one of trying to distinguish between a *reason* and a *motive* for being moral. For surely, it is argued, if I recognize something to be my duty, then surely I have a reason to perform the required action, even though I have no motive for performing it. In fact, even to ask for a motive for doing something, when one already has a reason for doing it, would seem to be at once gratuitous and unnecessary – at least so it is argued. Unhappily, though, the argument has a dubious air about it at best. For does it amount to anything more than trying to prove a point by first attempting to make a distinction, implying that the distinction is no mere distinction, but a distinction with a difference – viz. the distinction between a reason and a motive. But then, having exploited the distinction, and yet at the same time insinuating that one might conceivably have a reason for doing something, but no motive for doing it, the argument draws to its conclusion by surreptitiously taking advantage of the fact that there possibly is no real distinction between a reason and a motive after all, so that if one has a reason for doing a thing, then one has a motive for doing it as well. In other words, it's as if the argument only succeeds by taking back with its left hand what it had originally given with its right.

34. Thus, Sarah rejects as false Vacek's distinction between "natural-law ethics" and "mutual-love ethics." See Edward Collins Vacek, SJ, "Divine-Command, Natural-Law, and Mutual-Love Ethics," 57 Theological Studies 633 (1996): "In natural-law ethics, something is right because it fulfills human nature, and the task is to discover and realize that nature. In mutual-love ethics, something is finally right because it is appropriate to our love relationship with God, and the fundamental moral task is to

live in accord with this relationship." For Sarah, what fulfills human nature is to live in a relationship of love with God and with other human beings. Vacek's "mutual-love ethics" seems to me better understood not as an alternative to, but as a version of, "natural-law ethics." For an excellent explication of Aquinas's understanding of the relation between self-love and other-love (and also between self-love and love of God), see Gallagher, n. 17; see also Porter, n. 15, at 209–10.

35. Stephen Scott, "Motive and Justification," 85 J. Philosophy 479, 499 (1988). On the term "happiness," see Julia Annas, "Virtue and Eudaimonism," 15 Social Philosophy & Policy 37, 53 n. 35 (1998): "Despite the differences between *eudaimonia* and happiness which I have explored in this essay, and which are striking to philosophers reflecting on virtue and happiness, 'happiness' is clearly the correct translation for *eudaimonia* in ancient literature of all kinds, and it would be a mistake to conclude that we should translate *eudaimonia* by some other term." Compare Richard Taylor, "Ancient Wisdom and Modern Folly," 13 Midwest Studies in Philosophy 54, 57, 58 (1988): "The Greek *eudaimonia* is always translated 'happiness,' which is unfortunate, for the meaning we attach to the word *happiness* is thin indeed compared to what the ancients meant by *eudaimonia*. *Fulfillment* might be a better term, though this, too, fails to capture the richness of the original term. . . . The concept of happiness in modern philosophy, as well as in popular thinking, is superficial indeed in comparison."

   For an insightful, clarifying discussion of how sharply Kant's understanding of happiness differs from Aristotle's, see James Bernard Murphy, "Practical Reason and Moral Psychology in Aristotle and Kant," 18 Social Philosophy & Policy 257, 273–76 (2001).

36. Sarah's eudaimonistic, love-animated morality will not sit well with those whose thinking is under the influence of Kant. (They are many: "Kant's footprints are all over modern moral theory." Richard A. Posner, "The Problematics of Moral and Political Theory," 111 Harvard L. Rev. 1637, 1664 n. 48 (1998).) I concur in what Simon Blackburn says to such thinkers: "We can still do moral philosophy if we recognize that many of our concerns have passion and desire as their ancestors rather than truth and reason." Simon Blackburn, "Am I Right?" New York Times Book Rev., Feb. 28, 1999, at 24 (reviewing T. M. Scanlon, What We Owe to Each Other (1999)). Referring to "the view that reasons that are seen only in the pull of the will and of love are not real reasons at all," Blackburn continues: "[W]hen we reflect what a cold picture of human nature that [view] implies, I think we should find it rather sad." Id. I concur, too, in what Roger Scruton and Richard Rorty say, in the following passages, to such thinkers:

> The weakness of the Kantian position lies in its attribution of a "motivating force" to reason – in its denial of Hume's principle that reason alone cannot be a motive to action. The Aristotelian position involves no commitment to the idea of a "pure practical reason." It recognises that practical reasoning concludes in action only because it begins in desire. The "practical syllogism" has a practical premise, and to the agent with evil desires no reason can be given that will, by its sheer force as a reason, suffice to make him good. . . .

> Aristotle's invocation of happiness, as the final end of human conduct, is essentially correct. Happiness is the single final answer to the question "why do that?", the answer that survives the conflict with every rival interest or desire. In referring to happiness we refer, not to the satisfaction of impulses, but to the fulfillment of the person. . . . But what is happiness? Kant dismissed the idea as empty: happiness, he argued, simply stands for the generality of human desires: it means different things for different people, and provides no coherent

motive of its own. Following Aristotle, however, I shall propose an idea of happiness as a kind of "flourishing."

Roger Scruton, Sexual Desire: A Moral Philosophy of the Erotic 325, 326 (1986).

Would it be a good idea to treat "justice" as the name for loyalty to a certain very large group, the name for our current largest loyalty, rather than the name for something distinct from loyalty? Could we replace the notion of "justice" with that of loyalty to that group – for example, one's fellow-citizens, or the human species, or all living things? Would anything be lost by this replacement?

Moral philosophers who remain loyal to Kant are likely to think that a *lot* would be lost. Kantians typically insist that justice springs from reason, and loyalty from sentiment. Only reason, they say, can impose universal and unconditional moral obligations, and our obligation to be just is of this sort. It is on another level from the sort of affectional relations that create loyalty. Jürgen Habermas is our most prominent contemporary philosopher to insist on this Kantian way of looking at things: the thinker least willing to blur either the line between reason and sentiment, or the line between universal validity and historical consensus. But contemporary philosophers who depart from Kant, either in the direction of Hume (like Annette Baier) or in the direction of Hegel (like Charles Taylor) or in that of Aristotle (like Alasdair MacIntyre), are not so sure. . . .

What Kant would describe as [a conflict] between moral obligation and sentiment, or between reason and sentiment, is, on a non-Kantian account of the matter, a conflict between one set of loyalties and another set of loyalties. The idea of a *universal* moral obligation to respect human dignity gets replaced by the idea of loyalty to a very large group – the human species.

Richard Rorty, "Justice as a Larger Loyalty," in Ron Bontekoe & Marietta Stepaniants, eds., Justice and Democracy: Cross-Cultural Perspectives 9, 11 (1997).

Listen, too, to Charles Taylor, who is speaking about neo-Kantian moral philosophy:

Much contemporary moral philosophy, particularly but not only in the English-speaking world, has given such a narrow focus to morality . . . This moral philosophy has tended to focus on what it is right to do rather than on what it is good to be, on defining the content of obligation rather than the nature of the good life . . . This philosophy has accredited a cramped and truncated view of morality in a narrow sense, as well as of the whole range of issues involved in the attempt to live the best possible life, and this not only among professional philosophers, but with a wider public.

Charles Taylor, Sources of the Self: The Making of the Modern Identity 3 (1989). Taylor continues:

[Such moral theories] leave us with nothing to say to someone who asks why he should be moral. . . . But this could be misleading, if we seemed to be asking how we could convince someone who saw none of the point of our moral beliefs. There is nothing we can do to 'prove' we are right to such a person. But imagine him to be asking another question: he could be asking us to make plain the point of our moral code, in articulating what's uniquely valuable in cleaving to these injunctions. Then the implication of these theories is that we have nothing to say which can impart insight. We can wax rhetorical and propagandize, but we can't say what's good or valuable about [the injunctions], or why they command assent.

Id. See also id. at 4, 14–15, 63–64, 79, 87; Charles Taylor, "A Most Peculiar Institution," in J. E. J. Altham & Ross Harrison, eds., World, Mind, and Ethics: Essays on the Ethical Philosophy of Bernard Williams 132 (1995); Charles Taylor, "Iris Murdoch and Moral

Philosophy," in Maria Antonaccio & William Schweiker, eds., Iris Murdoch and the Search for Human Goodness 3 (1996).

37. Grant, n. 25, at xix. Sarah agrees with Grant. She understands Aquinas to have defended substantially the same position. See note 15. Cf. David O. Brink, "A Puzzle about the Rational Authority of Morality," 6 Philosophical Perspectives 1, 22 (1992): "Unless agent-neutral reasons are necessarily superior reasons, the best solution would be to argue that agent-relative reasons, properly understood, support other-regarding moral requirements as well. So friends of agent-neutrality would do well to cultivate the resources of strategic and metaphysical egoists, even if they reject the rational egoist assumption that all reasons for action are agent-relative." (For Brink's discussion of "metaphysical egoism", see id. at 18–22. See also David O. Brink, "Self-Love and Altruism," 14 Social Philosophy & Policy 122 (1997). I suppose that we could say that Augustine, Aquinas, and Sarah are a species of what Brink calls "metaphysical egoists.")

38. Indeed, for some religious believers, such a "God" is an idol. Cf. Charles Larmore, "Beyond Religion and Enlightenment," 30 San Diego L. Rev. 799, 799–802 (1993).

39. John Dominic Crossan, "Case Against Manifesto," 5 Law Text Culture 129, 144 (2000). For a version of Divine Command Theory – albeit, an unconventional version – that has a strong affinity with Sarah's moral "theory", see Martin Kavka & Randi Rashkover, "A Jewish Modified Divine Command Theory," 32 J. Religious Ethics 387 (2004). In discussion, Recep Senturk said that he doesn't see any conflict between a loving God and a legislating God. The holy scriptures of Judaism, Christianity, and Islam (Senturk said) always portray God as both a loving God and a legislating God. I don't mean to suggest that there is a conflict. For Sarah, nonetheless, "the Law of God is not what God legislates but what God is, just as the Law of Gravity is not what gravity legislates but what gravity is." Cf. id. at 411: "[W]e think that there is no philosophical ground for understanding 'obedience to God' in the sense [of] 'obedience to propositional sentences uttered by God.' "

40. See Peter Geach, God and the Soul 127–28 (1969).

41. Jürgen Habermas has acknowledged "that a philosophy that thinks post-metaphysically cannot answer the question that [David] Tracy . . . calls attention to: why be moral at all?" Habermas, n. 1, at 81. What Habermas then goes on to say is really quite remarkable:

> At the same time, however, this philosophy can show why this question does not arise meaningfully for communicatively socialized individuals. We acquire our moral intuitions in our parents' home, not in school. And moral insights tell us that we do not have any good reasons for behaving otherwise: for this, no self-surpassing of morality is necessary. It is true that we often behave otherwise, but we do so with a bad conscience. The first half of the sentence attests to the weakness of the motivational power of good reasons; the second half attests that rational motivation by reasons is more than nothing [auch nicht nichts ist] – moral convictions do not allow themselves to be overridden without resistance.

Id. Let's put aside the fact that "we" acquire our moral "intuitions" in many places besides (or in addition to) our parents' home – in the streets, for example. The more important point, for our present purposes, is that we don't all acquire the same moral intuitions. Some of us acquire moral intuitions that enable us to ignore, and perhaps even to brutalize, the Other without any pangs of "conscience." It is incredible that in the waning days of this unbearably brutal century, Habermas – writing in Germany of all places – could suggest otherwise. We need not even look at the oppressors themselves; we need look only at those whose passivity makes them complicitors. The real world is full of what Primo Levi called "us-ism": "Those on the Rosenstrasse who risked their lives for Jews did not express opposition to anti-semitic policies per se. They displayed primarily what the late Primo Levi, a survivor of Auschwitz, called 'selfishness extended to the person closest to you . . . us-ism.' In most of the stories that I have heard of Aryans who risked their lives for Jews to whom they were married, they withdrew to safety, one by one, the moment their loved ones were released. Their protests bring home to us the iron limits, the tragically narrow borders, of us-ism." Nathan Stoltzfus, "Dissent in Nazi Germany," Atlantic monthly, September 1992, at 87, 94.

42. "In an old rabbinic text three other questions are suggested: '*Whence* did you come?' '*Whither* are you going?' 'Before *whom* are you destined to give account?'" Abraham J. Heschel, Who Is Man? 28 (1965). "All people by nature desire to know the mystery from which they come and to which they go." Denise Lardner Carmody & John Tully Carmody, Western Ways to the Center: An Introduction to Religions of the West 198–99 (1983). "The questions Tolstoy asked, and Gauguin in, say, his great Tahiti triptych, completed just before he died ('Where Do We Come From? What Are We? Where Are We Going?'), are the eternal questions children ask more intensely, unremittingly, and subtly than we sometimes imagine." Robert Coles, The Spiritual Life of Children 37 (1990).

43. Communities, especially historically extended communities – "traditions" – are the principal matrices of religious answers to such questions: "Not the individual man nor a single generation by its own power, can erect the bridge that leads to God. Faith is the achievement of many generations, an effort accumulated over centuries. Many of its ideas are as the light of the star that left its source a long time ago. Many enigmatic songs, unfathomable today, are the resonance of voices of bygone times. There is a collective memory of God in the human spirit, and it is this memory which is the main source of our faith." From Abraham Heschel's two-part essay "Faith," first published in volume 10 of *The Reconstructionist*, Nov. 3 & 17, 1944. For a later statement on faith, incorporating some of the original essay, see Abraham J. Heschel, Man is Not Alone 159–76 (1951).

44. David Tracy, Plurality and Ambiguity: Religion, Hermeneutics, Hope 86 (1987).

45. In Milan Kundera's *The Unbearable Lightness of Being*, the narrator, referring to "the questions that had been going through Tereza's head since she was a child," says that "the only truly serious questions are ones that even a child can formulate. Only the most naive of questions are truly serious. They are the questions with no answers. A question with no answer is a barrier than cannot be breached. In other words, it is questions with no answers that set the limits of human possibilities, describe the boundaries of human existence." Milan Kundera, The Unbearable Lightness of Being 139 (1984).

46. David Tracy, The Analogical Imagination 4 (1981). Tracy adds: "To formulate such questions honestly and well, to respond to them with passion and rigor, is the work of all theology. . . . Religions ask and respond to such fundamental questions . . . Theologians, by definition, risk an intellectual life on the wager that religious traditions can be studied as authentic responses to just such questions." Id.

47. John Paul II, On the Relation Between Faith and Reason: Fides et Ratio, issued on Sept. 14, 1998. In the introduction to Fides et Ratio, John Paul II wrote:

Moreover, a cursory glance at ancient history shows clearly how in different parts of the world, with their different cultures, there arise at the same time the fundamental questions which pervade human life: Who am I? Where have I come from and where am I going? Why is there evil? What is there after this life? These are the questions which we find in the sacred writings of Israel and also in the Veda and the Avesta; we find them in the writings of Confucius and Lao-Tze, and in the preaching of Tirthankara and Buddha; they appear in the poetry of Homer and in the tragedies of Euripides and Sophocles as they do in the philosophical writings of Plato and Aristotle. They are questions which have their common source in the quest for meaning which has always compelled the human heart. In fact, the answer given to these questions decides the direction which people seek to give to their lives.

Id. at Introduction, pt. 1. See also id. at chapter 3, pt. 26. (*Fides et Ratio* would more accurately be named *Fides et Philosophia.*) We find a similar statement in the Second Vatican Council's Declaration on the Relation of the Church to Non-Christian Religions (*Nostra Aetate*, 1):

People look to their different religions for an answer to the unsolved riddles of human existence. The problems that weigh heavily on people's hearts are the same today as in ages past. What is humanity? What is the meaning and purpose of life? Where does suffering originate, and what end does it serve? How can genuine happiness be found? What happens at death? What is judgement? What reward follows death? And finally, what is the ultimate mystery, beyond human explanation, which embraces our entire existence, from which we take our origin and toward which we tend?

CHAPTER 3. THE MORALITY OF HUMAN RIGHTS: A NON-RELIGIOUS GROUND?

1. Leo Tolstoy, A Confession and Other Religious Writings 150 (Jane Kentish, tr., 1987). Cf. John M. Rist, Real Ethics: Rethinking the Foundations of Morality 2 (2002): "[Plato] came to believe that if morality, as more than 'enlightened' self-interest, is to be rationally justifiable, it must be established on metaphysical foundations. . . . "

2. This passage – quoted in George Parkin Grant, English Speaking Justice 77 (1985) – appears in Nietzsche's *Thus Spoke Zarathustra*, Part IV ("On the Higher Man"), near the end of section 1.

     John Mackie asked: "[W]hat [can we] make of morality without recourse to God, . . . what [can we] say about morality if, in the end, we dispense with religious belief?" J.L. Mackie, Ethics: Inventing Right and Wrong 48 (1977). Richard Joyce, from a secular perspective, offers one response to Mackie's inquiry: Morality is a myth. See Richard Joyce, The Myth of Morality (2001). J. Budziszewski, from a religious perspective, offers substantially the same response. See J. Budziszewski, "The Second Tablet Project," First Things, June/July 2002, at 23. By contrast, Michael Moore argues that morality has no need for God. See Michael S. Moore, "Good Without God," in Robert P. George, ed., Natural Law, Liberalism, and Morality 201 (1996). For a critique of Moore's position, see Steven D. Smith, "Natural Law and Contemporary Moral Thought: A Guide from the Perplexed," 42 American J. Jurisprudence 299 (1997).

3. The question of whether any ground for claiming that every human being has inherent dignity is, *qua* religious, plausible is substantially a question about the plausibility of religious faith – a question well beyond the scope of this book. On the plausibility of religious faith, see, for example, Jürgen Habermas, Religion and Rationality: Essays on Reason, God, and Modernity 162 (Eduardo Mendieta, ed., 2002); Hilary Putnam, "The Depths and Shallows of Experience," May 9, 2002, University of California

at Santa Barbara, <http://www.srhe.ucsb.edu/lectures/text/putnamText.html>. See also Stephen M. Barr, Modern Physics and Ancient Faith (2003).

4. See, for example, Abdullahi A. An-Na'im et al., eds., Human Rights and Religious Values: An Uneasy Relationship? (1995); William Theodore de Bary & Tu Weiming, eds., Confucianism and Human Rights (1998); Dan Cohn-Sherbok, ed., World Religions and Human Rights (1992); Carrie Gustafson & Peter Juviler, eds., Religion and Human Rights: Competing Claims? (1999); John Kelsay & Sumner B. Twiss, eds., Religion and Human Rights (1994); LeRoy S. Rouner, ed., Human Rights and the World's Religions (1988); Max L. Stackhouse, Creeds, Society and Human Rights (1986); Arlene Swidler, ed., Human Rights in Religious Traditions (1982); Robert Traer, Faith in Human Rights: Support in Religious Traditions for a Global Struggle (1991).

5. See Chapter 2, n. 1 and accompanying text.

6. See John Haldane, "The Greatest of These Is Love, As an Atheist Reminds Us," The Tablet [London], Dec. 9, 2000, at 1678 (reviewing Gaita's book).

7. Leszek Kolakowski, Religion, If There Is No God: On God, the Devil, Sin, and Other Worries of the So-Called Philosophy of Religion 191 (1982) (emphasis added).

8. Cf. Rist, n. 1, at 267 ("Although a 'moral saint' may exist without realist (and therefore religious) beliefs, yet his stance as a moral saint cannot be *justified* without recourse to realism."); Charles Taylor, "Closed World Structures," in Mark A. Wrathall, ed., Religion after Metaphysics 47, 61 (2003):

> The logic of the subtraction story is something like this: Once we slough off our concern with serving God, or attending to any other trascendent reality, what we're left with is human good, and that is what modern societies are concerned with. But this radically under-describes what I'm calling modern humanism. That I am left with only human concerns doesn't tell me to take universal human welfare as my goal; nor does it tell me that freedom is important, or fulfillment, or equality. Just being confined to human goods could just as well find expression in my concerning myself exclusively with my own material welfare, or that of my family or immediate milieu. The, in fact, very exigent demands of universal justice and benevolence which characterize modern humanism can't be explained just by the subtraction of earlier goals and allegiances.

9. Habermas, n. 3, at 81–82.

10. Glenn Tinder, "Can We Be Good without God: The Political Meaning of Christianity," Atlantic monthly, December 1989, at 69, 80 (passages rearranged and emphasis added). For Tinder's book-length treatment of the relevant issues, see Glenn Tinder, The Political Meaning of Christianity: An Interpretation (1989).

11. Kristen Monroe's study of altruists and altruism is relevant here. See Kristen Renwick Monroe, The Heart of Altruism: Perceptions of a Common Humanity 216 (1996).

12. See Desmond Tutu, quoted in Jim Wurst, "Archbishop Tutu Examines Link Between Religion and Politics," U.N. Wire, March 18, 2004 (reporting on Tutu's speech "God's Word and World Politics"):

> Religion . . . is neither automatically good or bad, it can be either depending on what it inspires its adherents to do. Religion has the capacity to produce saints, but it also has the capacity to produce rogues. . . . Christians need to be among the most modest because of the many ghastly things that Christians have perpetrated [e.g., slavery, apartheid, Nazi Germany and the Holocaust, fascism in Italy and Spain, the dropping of the atomic bombs on Hiroshima and Nagasaki, the Ku Klux Klan and the Rwanda genocide]. We who are Christians have much that should make us hang our heads in shame.

13. Bruce Ackerman has announced: "There is no moral meaning hidden in the bowels of the universe." Bruce A. Ackerman, Social Justice in the Liberal State 368 (1980). See also Bertrand Russell, Mysticism and Logic 47–48 (1917):

> That man is the product of causes which had no prevision of the end they were achieving; that his origin, his growth, his hopes and fears, his loves and his beliefs, are but the outcome of accidental collocations of atoms; that no fire, no heroism, no intensity of thought and feeling, can preserve an individual life beyond the grave; that all the labor of the ages, all the devotion, all the inspiration, all the noonday brightness of human genius, are destined to extinction in the vast death of the solar system, and that the whole temple of man's achievement must inevitably be buried beneath the debris of a universe in ruins – all these things, if not quite beyond dispute, are yet so certain that no philosophy which rejects them can hope to stand. Only within the scaffolding of these truths, only on the firm foundation of unyielding despair, can the soul's habitation henceforth be safely built.

Ackerman's declaration, like Russell's before him, brings to mind one of Nietzsche's sayings:

> Man a little, eccentric species of animal, which – fortunately – has its day; all on earth a mere moment, an incident, an exception without consequences, something of no importance to the general character of the earth; the earth itself, like every star, a hiatus between two nothingnesses, an event without plan, reason, will, self-consciousness, the worst kind of necessity, *stupid* necessity – Something in us rebels against this view; the serpent vanity says to us: "all that *must* be false, *for* it arouses indignation – Could all that not be merely appearance? And man, in spite of all, as Kant says – "

Friedrich Nietzsche, The Will to Power 169 (Walter Kaufmann & R. J. Hollingdale, trs., & Walter Kaufmann, ed., 1967).

14. For the person deep in the grip of, the person claimed by, the problem of meaning, "[t]he cry for meaning is a cry for ultimate relationship, for ultimate belonging," wrote Heschel. "It is a cry in which all pretensions are abandoned. Are we alone in the wilderness of time, alone in the dreadfully marvelous universe, of which we are a part and where we feel forever like strangers? Is there a Presence to live by? A Presence worth living for, worth dying for? Is there a way of living in the Presence? Is there a way of living compatible with the Presence?" Abraham J. Heschel, Who Is Man? 75 (1965). See also Fyodor Dostoevsky, The Brothers Karamazov 235 (Norton ed. 1976): "For the secret of man's being is not only to live but to have something to live for. Without a stable conception of the object of life, man would not consent to go on living, and would rather destroy himself than remain on earth, though he had bread in abundance." (This is one of the Grand Inquisitor's statements in chapter 5 of Book Five.) Cf. W. D. Joske, "Philosophy and the Meaning of Life," in E. D. Klemke, ed., The Meaning of Life 248, 250 (1981) ("If, as Kurt Vonnegut speculates in *The Sirens of Titan*, the ultimate end of human activity is the delivery of a small piece of steel to a wrecked space ship wanting to continue a journey of no importance whatsoever, the end would be too trivial to justify the means."); Robert Nozick, Philosophical Explanations 586 (1981) ("If the cosmic role of human beings was to provide a negative lesson to some others ('don't act like them') or to provide needed food to passing intergalactic travelers who *were* important, this would not suit our aspirations – not even if afterwards the intergalactic travelers smacked their lips and said that we tasted good.")

15. Paul Edwards, "Life, Meaning and Value of," 4 Encyclopedia of Philosophy 467, 470 (Paul Edwards, ed., 1967). Whether Clarence Darrow was in fact "one of the most compassionate men who ever lived" is open to question. For a revisionist view of Darrow, see Gary Wills, Under God: Religion and American Politics, chs. 8–9 (1990).

16. John Leslie, "Is It All Quite Simple? The Physicist's Search for a Theory of Everything," Times Lit. Supp., Jan. 29, 1993, at 3 (reviewing, inter alia, Steven Weinberg, Dreams of a Final Theory (1992)). Cf. Paul Davies, "The Holy Grail of Physics," New York Times Book Rev., Mar. 7, 1993, at 11 (reviewing, inter alia, Weinberg's book): "Reductionism [in physics] may be a fruitful research method, but it is a bleak philosophy. . . . If the world is but a collection of inert atoms interacting through blind and purposeless forces, what happens to . . . the meaning of life?"

17. Richard A. Posner, "The Problematics of Moral and Political Theory," 111 Harvard L. Rev. 1637, 1687 (1998) (citing Thomas Nagel, The Last Word 130 (1997)). Cf. James Boyd White, "Talking about Religion in the Language of Law: Impossible but Necessary," 81 Marquette L. Rev. 177, 197–99 (1998) (explaining why he has difficulty understanding what one who is not a religious believer might be saying in affirming the Declaration of Independence's insistence on the "equality" of all human beings).

18. J. M. Winter & D. M. Joslin, eds., R. H. Tawney's Commonplace Book 67 (1972). On Aug. 13, 1913, Tawney wrote in his diary the passage accompanying this note. Three days earlier, on Aug. 10, he quoted in his diary T. W. Price, Midland secretary of the Workers' Educational Association and lecturer at Birmingham University: "Unless a man believes in spiritual things – in God – altruism is absurd. What is the sense of it? Why shld [sic] a man recognize any obligation to his neighbor, unless he believes that he has been put in the world for a special purpose and has a special work to perform in it? A man's relations to his neighbors become meaningless unless there is some higher power above them both." Id. Cf. Dennis Prager, "Can We Be Good Without God?," 9 Ultimate Issues 3, 4 (1993): "If there is no God, you and I are purely the culmination of chance, pure random chance. And whether I kick your face in, or support you charitably, the universe is as indifferent to that as whether a star in another galaxy blows up tonight."

19. Jeffrie Murphy, "Afterword: Constitutionalism, Moral Skepticism, and Religious Belief," in Alan S. Rosenbaum, ed., Constitutionalism: The Philosophical Dimension 239, 248 (1988) (emphasis added).

20. Raimond Gaita, A Common Humanity: Thinking about Love and Truth and Justice 5 (2000). I have trouble squaring what Gaita says in the passage accompanying this note, and in other passages I've quoted in this chapter, with what he says in this passage:

> Although I fully acknowledge that it is our religious tradition that has spoken most simply (and perhaps most deeply) about this when it declared that all human beings are sacred, I think that the conception of individuality I have been articulating, even as transformed by a language of love nourished by the love of saints, can stand independently of explicit religious commitment and independently of speculation about supernatural entities. What grew and was nourished in one place, I say, might take root and flourish elsewhere.

> Id. at xx.

21. Nietzsche, The Will to Power, n. 13, at 157.

22. Arthur Allen Leff, "Unspeakable Ethics, Unnatural Law," 1979 Duke L. J. 1229, 1249. See also John T. Noonan, Jr., "Posner's Problematics," 111 Harvard L. Rev. 1768 (1998): "These three propositions [if no lawgiver, no law; if no law, no judge; if no judge, no judgment], which have the strength of self-evidence, sum up the predicament of most of the academic moralists who are Judge Posner's targets. These moralists acknowledge no lawgiver and no judge. Their vulnerability is patent. The attempts to pronounce moral judgments are doomed to failure."

23. See, John Finnis, Natural Law and Natural Rights (1980); John Finnis, Aquinas: Moral, Political, and Legal Theory (1998). Alan Wolfe has remarked that "[a]mong Catholic intellectuals, as well as some who are not Catholic, the most important Catholic inheritance is the natural-law tradition . . . " Alan Wolfe, "The Intellectual Advantages of a Roman Catholic Education," Chronicle of Higher Education, May 31, 2002.

24. Thomas W. Smith, "Finnis' Questions and Answers: An Ethics of Hope or Fear?" 40 American J. Jurisprudence 27, 29 (1995).

25. Finnis, Natural Law and Natural Rights, n. 23, at 107.

26. Recall from the preceding chapter that Sarah "understands the authority of moral claims to be warranted . . . by their contribution to human flourishing." See Chapter 2, n. 15.

27. Finnis, Natural Law and Natural Rights, n. 23, at 107.

28. To say that X is of value (or that X has value) is to say that X is of value *to* (or that X has value *for*) someone(s) (e.g., John Finnis) or something(s) (e.g., a cat or a plant). That X is of value, whether instrumental or intrinsic, to A does not entail that X is also of value to B. Similarly, that Y is a reason for A – a *practical* reason, a reason for choosing to do *this* rather than *that* – does not entail that Y is a also reason for B.

29. See Joyce, The Myth of Morality, n. 2, at 126: "[E]ven if we allow that in valuing his own humanity, Al, on pain of irrationality, must accept that others value their own humanity as he does, this falls dramatically short of his being rationally required to value their humanity." For Joyce's response – his persuasive response, in my judgment – to the claim that reasons are agent-neutral rather than agent-relative, see id. at 126–33. See also David O. Brink, "A Puzzle about the Rational Authority of Morality," 6 Philosophical Perspectives 1, 18–22 (1992); David O. Brink, "Self-Love and Altruism," 14 Social Philosophy & Policy 122 (1997). Cf. Richard Rorty, "Justice as a Larger Loyalty," in Ron Bontekoe & Marietta Stepaniants, eds., Justice and Democracy: Cross-Cultural Perspectives 9, 19 (1997): "I see no point in saying that it is more rational to prefer one's neighbors to one's family in the event of a nuclear holocaust, or more rational to prefer leveling off incomes around the world to preserving the institutions of liberal Western societies. To use the word 'rational' to commend one's chosen solution to such dilemmas, or to use the term 'yielding to the force of the better argument' to characterize one's way of making up one's mind, is to pay oneself an empty compliment."

   Terence Cuneo has observed, in correspondence, that my critique of Finnis presupposes an "internalist" (or "agent-relative") rather than an "externalist" (or "agent-neutral") account of reasons – in particular, of reasons for action. He then suggests that I "conditionalize" my critique: If Internalism is true and Externalism is false, then Finnis's and similar arguments fail. E-mail from Terence Cuneo to Michael

Perry, Nov. 13, 2002. In my judgment, internalism *is* true and externalism *is* false. See Peter Geach, God and the Soul xix, 121–22 (1969).

30. J. D. Goldsworthy, "God or Mackie? The Dilemma of Secular Moral Philosophy," 1985 American J. Jurisprudence 43, 73–77. See also Mark R. Discher, "Does Finnis Get Natural Rights for Everyone?" 80 New Blackfriars 19 (1999). Cf. Jeffrey Goldsworthy, "Fact and Value in the New Natural Law Theory," 1996 American J. Jurisprudence 21.

31. Id. at 75.

32. A prominent secular argument for human rights is Alan Gewirth's. See Alan Gewirth, Reason and Morality, chs. 1–2 (1978); Alan Gewirth, The Community of Rights, ch. 1 (1996). Examining Gewirth's argument here would take us too far afield. Suffice it to say that Gewirth's argument has been extremely controversial. For a careful restatement and defense of Gewirth's argument, see Deryck Beyleveld, The Dialectical Necessity of Morality: An Analysis and Defense of Alan Gewirth's Argument to the Principle of Generic Consistency (1991). For a skeptical response to Beyleveld, see Marcus G. Singer, "Gewirth, Beyleveld, and Dialectical Necessity," 13 Ratio Juris 177 (2000); for Beyleveld's reply, see Deryck Beyleveld, "A Reply to Marcus G. Singer on Gewirth, Beyleveld and Dialectical Necessity," 15 Ratio Juris 458 (2002). For a powerful – and, in my judgment, sound – explanation of why Gewith's argument fails, see Timothy S. Bishop, "Gewirth on the Justification of Moral Rights" (undated; on file with author).

33. Finnis gestures in this direction in the final chapter of *Natural Law and Natural Rights*. See Finnis, Natural Law and Natural Rights, n. 23, at 371–410 ("Nature, Reason, God"). See also John Finnis, Moral Absolutes: Tradition, Revision, and Truth (1991).

34. Rist, n. 1, at 259–60.

35. Finnis teaches in two English-speaking law schools: Oxford University and the University of Notre Dame.

36. Like Finnis, Dworkin, and Nussbaum, I teach in a university law school. This explains the fact that my focus in this chapter is on moral philosophers who teach in university law schools.

37. Ronald Dworkin, "Life Is Sacred. That's the Easy Part," New York Times Magazine, May 16, 1993, at 36.

38. Id.

39. Ronald Dworkin, Life's Dominion: An Argument About Abortion, Euthanasia, and Individual Freedom 195 (1993).

40. Id. at 25.

41. Id. at 78.

42. Id. at 82. See id. at 81–84.

43. Id. at 82.

44. Id. at 83.

45. Id. at 84.

46. Id. at 82.

47. Id. at 83.

48. Id. at 78.

49. Id. at 71.

50. Martha C. Nussbaum, "Skepticism about Practical Reason in Literature and the Law," 107 Harvard L. Rev. 714, 718 (1994).

51. Id. at 744. Michael Ignatieff seems to follow much the same approach as Nussbaum. See Michael Ignatieff, Human Rights as Politics and as Idolatry 88–89 (2001).

52. See also Martha C. Nussbaum, "Compassion: The Basic Social Emotion," 1996 Social Philosophy & Policy 27 (1996); Martha C. Nussbaum, "Compassion and Terror," Daedalus, Winter 2003, at 10.

53. Not everyone is an altruist – indeed, few are – and those who are strike us as remarkable and exemplary, even saintly, human beings. See Kristen Renwick Monroe, The Heart of Altruism: Perceptions of a Common Humanity 216 (1996).

54. Claude Lévi-Strauss, Structural Anthropology, vol. 2, 329 (Monique Layton, tr., 1983). See also Alain Finkielkraut, In the Name of Humanity: Reflections on the Twentieth Century 5–14 (2000).

> To accept the idea that all people in the world form a single humanity is not . . . the same thing as recognizing that they all belong to the human species. What distinguishes mankind from most other animals is precisely the fact *that he does not identify with others of his kind.* A cat for a cat has always been another cat. A man, on the other hand, must fulfill a set of Draconian conditions or be crossed off the list, without any recourse, of those counted as members of human society. From the very beginning, man jealously reserved the title of man for only those identified with his own community.

Id. at 5.

55. Richard Rorty, "Human Rights, Rationality, and Sentimentality," in Stephen Shute & Susan Hurley, eds., On Human Rights: The Oxford Amnesty Lectures 1993 111, 123–24 (1993).

56. Id. Rorty's "much more common case" is also much more common than the person at the other extreme from the psychopath: someone actively concerned about the well-being of every human being. We sometimes mark just how *uncommon* such an exemplary person is, in the real world, by calling her a "saint."

57. See Richard Joyce, "The Fugitive Thought," 34 J. Value Inquiry 463, 470 (2000):

> [A] thesis of natural sympathy is only sensible when this sentiment is presented as a natural disposition or propensity. To present the-good-of-fellows as the object of a desire which all people have, a desire from which no one could escape, is to divest the thesis of much of its attraction. We are all too familiar with counter-examples. Besides, we may credit the wielder of the ring of Gyges with all sorts of non-selfish desires. Perhaps his caring for the interests of his friends, family and community is not motivated by self-interest at all. But none of this will be sufficient for grounding imperatives proscribing his inflicting harm upon the inhabitants of the neighboring valley.

58. Nietzsche, The Will to Power, n. 13, at 147. Commenting on "anthropocentrism, [which] by abolishing all horizons of significance, threatens us with a loss of meaning and hence a trivialization of our predicament," Charles Taylor has written: "At one moment, we understand our situation as one of high tragedy, alone in a silent universe, without intrinsic meaning, condemned to create value. But at a later moment, the same doctrine, by its own inherent bent, yields a flattened world, in which there aren't very meaningful choices because there aren't any crucial issues." Charles Taylor, The Ethics of Authenticity 68 (1991).

59. Philippa Foot, Natural Goodness 103 (2001). Cf. Alan Levine, "Introduction: The Prehistory of Toleration and Varieties of Skepticism," in Alan Levine, ed., Early Modern Skepticism and the Origins of Toleration 1, 4 (1999): "Far from attempting to justify liberalism to outsiders or on first principles, Rorty and Rawls prefer not to

take up the challenge. Content to harmonize our preexisting opinions, they do not and cannot address the fundamental challenges that Nietzsche, for example, poses."

Finnis, Dworkin, and Nussbaum are not Kantian or neo-Kantian moral philosophers. Frances Kamm, however, is one of the most important contemporary neo-Kantian philosophers. See F.M. Kamm, Morality, Mortality: Death, and Whom to Save from It (1993); Frances Myrna Kamm, Morality, Mortality (Vol. II): Rights, Duties, and Status (1997). Unfortunately, Kamm fails even to address the question why every human being is inviolable. In an otherwise laudatory review of a book by Kamm, philosopher Jeff McMahan writes:

> The burden of the third and final part of the volume is to explain why it is generally not permissible for one to engage in killing even when, by doing so, one could prevent a greater number of killings from occurring. Here, Kamm's central contention is that people must be regarded as inviolable, as ends-in-themselves.... [Kamm's] arguments often raise difficult questions that the book fails to address. A conspicuous instance of this is Kamm's failure to identify the basis of our moral inviolability. Understanding the basis of our alleged inviolability is crucial both for determining whether it is plausible to regard ourselves as inviolable, and for fixing the boundaries of the class of inviolable beings.

Jeff McMahan, "When Not to Kill or Be Killed," Times Lit. Supp., Aug. 7, 1998, at 31 (reviewing Kamm, Morality, Mortality (Vol. II) (1997)).

Christine Korsgaard is another of the most important contemporary neo-Kantian moral philosophers. See Christine M. Korsgaard, Creating the Kingdom of Ends (1996); Christine M. Korsgaard with G.A. Cohen, Raymond Geus, Thomas Nagel, and Bernard Williams, The Sources of Normativity (Onora O'Neill, ed., 1996). Unlike Kamm, Korsgaard does address the question of "the basis of our alleged inviolability". For a critique of Korsgaard's argument, which she presents in *The Sources of Normativity*, see Joyce, The Myth of Morality, n. 2, at 123–33. Joyce's critique is, in my judgment, persuasive.

60. I am grateful to Chris Eberle and Steve Smith for suggesting this position to me.
61. See n. 15 and accompanying text.
62. See Chapter 2, n. 13.
63. In e-mail discussion, Steve Smith has observed that "[w]ithout some suitable meta-story, it just seems incredible that everyone would find happiness/fulfillment in becoming the kind of person who cares about [all] others.... [I]f 'evolution' is the substitute story, then it seems more plausible to imagine that we would be constructed for struggle, and would find fulfillment in squashing our competitors. I realize that a degree of altruism can be accounted for in terms of promoting the survival of a group with similar genes, but any broader inclination to serve others seems incompatible with the evolution story. And if no story at all is offered, so that the line is 'I don't know how, but that's just the way we're made – basically we're all cut out to be nice guys,' the contrary evidence seems overwhelming." E-mail from Steven Smith to Michael Perry, Sept. 16, 2002. See also Michael Ruse, "Evolutionary Ethics: A Defence," in Holmes Rolston III, ed., Biology, Ethics, and the Origins of Life 93, 104–05 (1995); H. Allen Orr, "Darwinian Storytelling," New York Rev., Feb. 27, 2003, at 17, 20 (reviewing Steven Pinker, The Blank Slate: The Modern Denial of Human Nature (2002)):

> [T]he moral circle expands, [Pinker] says, by the principle of reciprocal altruism, a socio-biological theory that shows how kindness can spread even among unrelated individ-

uals. To Pinker, then, the moral circle is primarily "pushed outward by the expanding networks of reciprocity that make other human beings more valuable alive than dead." This network is facilitated by "trade, cultural exchanges, and people-to-people activities."

But this is silly. The notion that our moral circle expanded by reciprocity is in many instances ahistorical nonsense. Men had plenty of "people-to-people" interaction with women while condemning them to second-class citizenship. And slave-holding Southerners had more "cultural exchanges" and "people-to-people activities" with African-Americans than did abolitionist Northerners. At what point in history did our "networks of reciprocity" with women and slaves become sufficiently dense that the calculus of reciprocity demanded that we grant them the vote and freedom? The question is absurd. The fact is that for every case in which morality plausibly expanded by reciprocity there is another in which it expanded by selfless moral reasoning, political or religious struggle, or even court rulings that forced a rule of conduct on those who initially opposed it. And it should be evident that a morality that bids us care for the severely handicapped cannot be explained by an expectation of reciprocity.

64. Cf. Rorty, "Human Rights, Rationality, and Sentimentality," n. 55, at 123–24 (contrasting "the rather rare figure of the psychopath, the person who has no concern for any human being other than himself[,]" to "the much more common case: the person whose treatment of a rather narrow range of featherless bipeds is morally impeccable, but who remains indifferent to the suffering of those outside this range, the ones he or she thinks of as pseudohumans").

If, like Sarah, one believes that every human being is truly sacred – truly a beloved child of God and a sister/brother to oneself – and that our created nature is truly fulfilled by becoming persons who "love another just as I have loved you," then one also believes that to act contrary to God's creation is to violate no less a reality than God. (If I violate your beloved children, do I not violate you as well as your children?) By contrast, if one believes neither in God nor, therefore, in the metaphysical sacredness of every human being, but does believe that our evolved nature is fulfilled by becoming persons who love one another, then one believes that to act contrary to one's nature is violate . . . what? Evolution? To speak of "violating" evolution is surely to speak metaphorically: How does one "violate" evolution? Sarah says: "In violating the Jews, the Nazis violated God's creation and, therefore, God." What does Sarah's interlocutor say? That in violating the Jews, the Nazis acted contrary to blind evolution?

65. Warren Christopher, "Democracy and Human Rights: Where America Stands," 4 U.S. Department of State Dispatch 441, 442 (1993). See also William F. Schultz, In Our Own Best Interests: How Defending Human Rights Benefits Us All xix (2002) ("Respect for human rights both in the United States and abroad has implications for our welfare far beyond the maintenance of our ethical integrity. Ignoring the fates of human rights victims almost anywhere invariably makes the world – *our* world – a more dangerous place. If we learned nothing else from the horrific events of September 11, perhaps we learned that."); William W. Burke-White, "Human Rights and National Security: The Strategic Connection," 17 Harvard Human Rights J. 249 (2004). Cf. Jerome J. Shestack, "An Unsteady Focus: The Vulnerabilities of the Reagan Administration's Human Rights Policy," 2 Harvard Human Rights Yearbook 25, 49–50 (1989) (listing several reasons that should "motivate an administration to

afford human rights a central role in United States foreign policy as a matter of national interest").

66. Richard B. Bilder, "Human Rights and U.S. Foreign Policy: Short-Term Prospects," 14 Virginia J. International L. 597, 608 (1974).

67. Richard Rorty, Contingency, Irony, and Solidarity xiii (1989).

68. Id.

69. Rorty, "Human Rights, Rationality, and Sentimentality," n. 55, at 126.

70. Bernard Williams, "Auto-da-Fé," New York Rev., Apr. 28, 1983, at 33.

71. Rorty, "Human Rights, Rationality, and Sentimentality," n. 55, at 116.

72. See, e.g., id. at 124–25: "Kant's account of the respect due to rational agents tells you that you should extend the respect you feel for people like yourself to all featherless bipeds. That is an excellent suggestion, a good formula for secularizing the Christian doctrine of the brotherhood of man. But it has never been backed up by an argument based on neutral premises, and it never will be."

73. Id. at 116.

74. Id. at 117. See id. at 117–18. See also Rorty, Contingency, Irony, and Solidarity, n. 67, ch. 9 ("Solidarity"). In this regard, Rorty stands in stark contrast to John Paul II, who was a religious defender of the morality of human rights, and to Noam Chomsky, who is a secular defender.

> The great concern of our contemporaries for historicity and for culture has led some to call into question . . . the existence of "objective norms of morality" valid for all peoples of the present and the future, as for those of the past. . . . It must certainly be admitted that man always exists in a particular culture, but it must also be admitted that man is not exhaustively defined by the same culture. . . . [T]he very progress of cultures demonstrates that there is something in man which transcends those cultures. This "something" is precisely human nature: This nature is itself the measure of culture and the condition ensuring that man does not become the prisoner of any of his cultures, but asserts his personal dignity by living in accordance with the profound truth of his being.

John Paul II, Veritatis Splendor, 23 Origins 297, 314 (1993).

> A vision of future social order is . . . based on a concept of human nature. If in fact man is an indefinitely malleable, completely plastic being, with no innate structures of mind and no intrinsic needs of a cultural or social character, then he is a fit subject for the "shaping behavior" by the state authority, the corporate manager, the technocrat, or the central committee. Those with some confidence in the human species . . . will try to determine the intrinsic human characteristics that provide the framework for intellectual development, the growth of moral consciousness, cultural achievement, and participation in a free community.

Noam Chomsky, For Reasons of State 404 (1973).

75. Rorty, "Human Rights, Rationality, and Sentimentality," n. 55, at 122.

76. Id. at 119.

77. Rorty, "Justice as a Larger Loyalty," n. 29, at 19–20.

78. Jean E. Hampton, The Authority of Reason 120 (Richard Healey, ed., 1998). Thanks to George Wright for calling this passage to my attention.

79. Richard Rorty, Consequences of Pragmatism xlii (1982).

80. We would be left with a morality based on rational self-interest, but such a morality is too slender a reed to bear the cause of human rights. David Gauthier's Morals By

Agreement (1987), which is an example of such a morality, is illustrative. (Cf. Robert Sugden, "The Contractarian Enterprise," in David Gauthier & Robert Sugden, eds., Rationality, Justice and the Social Contract: Themes from *Moral By Agreement* 1, 8 (1993): "At the core of [Gauthier's project] is the thought that traditional moral theory relies on the supposed existence of entities, such as God or goodness, which are external to human life yet somehow matter. A defensible morality should dispense with such mysterious entities, and accept that life has no meaning outside itelf.") Gauthier argues "that rational persons will recognize a role for constraints, both unilateral and mutual, in their choices and decisions, that rational persons would agree ex ante on certain mutual constraints were they able to do so, and that rational persons will frequently comply with those mutual constraints in their interactions." David Gauthier, "Rational Constraint: Some Last Words," in Peter Vallentyne, ed., Contractarianism and Rational Choice: Essays on David Gauthier's *Morals By Agreement* 323, 330 (1991). As Peter Vallentyne observes, "[Gauthier's] main interest is to give an account of rational and impartial constraints on conduct. If this does not capture the traditional conception of morality, so much the worse for the traditional conception. Rationality – not morality – is the important notion for him." Peter Vallentyne, "Gauthier's Three Projects," in id. at 1, 2. Vallentyne's next comment helps us see the chasm between a morality like Gauthier's and a morality that can support human-rights-claims:

> [Gauthier's contractarian] view of the relationship between the individual and society has some implications about which even the most committed contractarians are uneasy. If justice is wholly a matter of reciprocity, do we have any obligation to support people who are so severely handicapped that they can offer us nothing in return? . . . Gauthier has to concede that the handicapped lie 'beyond the pale of morality tied to mutuality'; if we have moral duties in these cases, [Gauthier's] theory cannot account for them. Each of us may feel *sympathy* for the handicapped, and if so, the welfare of the handicapped will be among the ends we pursue; but this is a matter of preference, not moral obligation.

Id. It is not only the handicapped that lie beyond the pale of a morality of rational self-interest; it is also all those other persons around the world – the weakest of the weak, the most marginalized of the marginalized – whom we in rich, powerful nations need not fear and whose cooperation to achieve our goals we need not secure.

Gauthier has written that *Morals By Agreement* "is an attempt to challenge Nietzsche's prescient remark, 'As the will to truth . . . gains self-consciousness . . . morality will gradually perish'. It is an attempt to write moral theory for adults, for persons who live consciously in a post-anthropomorphic, post-theocentric, post-technocratic world. It is an attempt to allay the fear, or suspicion, or hope, that without a foundation in objective value or objective reason, in sympathy or in sociality, the moral enterprise must fail." David Gauthier, "Moral Artifice," 18 Canadian J. Philosophy 385, 385 (1988). In the end, however, Gauthier does not challenge Nietzsche so much as he embraces a Nietzschean conception of justice. Nietzsche wrote: "Justice (fairness) originates among those who are approximately *equally powerful*, as Thucydides . . . comprehended correctly. . . . [J]ustice is repayment and exchange on the assumption of an approximately equal power position. . . . Justice naturally derives from prudent concern with self-preservation; that means, from the egoism of the consideration: 'Why should I harm myself uselessly and perhaps not attain my goal anyway?'" Friedrich Nietzsche, "All Too Human," in Basic Writings of Nietzsche 148 (Walter Kaufmann, tr., 1973). I suspect that if we abandon the claim that every human being is inviolable, all we will be left with is a Nietzschean morality that not only cannot support, but that is deeply hostile to, many of the most basic human-rights-claims that we who embrace the cause of human rights want to make.

81. Czeslaw Milosz, "The Religious Imagination at 2000," New Perspectives Quarterly, Fall 1997, at 32. See also Gaita, n. 20, at xviii-xix:

> [T]he language of love . . . compels us to affirm that even those who suffer affliction so severe that they have irrevocably lost everything that gives sense to our lives, and the most radical evil-doers, are fully our fellow human beings. On credit, so [to] speak, from this language of love, we have built a more tractable structure of rights and obligations. If the language of love goes dead on us, however, if there are no examples to nourish it, either because they do not exist or because they are no longer visible to us, then talk of inalienable natural rights or of the unconditional respect owed to rational beings will seem lame and improbable to us. Indeed, exactly that is happening.

In e-mail discussion, Steve Smith has written:

> Insofar as humans have the quality of "dignity" or (as I prefer) "sacredness," perceptive sincere persons may well be able to perceive that quality without even knowing or giving much thought to the "ground" of the quality. So they don't need to believe in God in order to accord this respect to human beings. Their understanding would be seriously incomplete, of course, but their moral commitment might still be perfectly sincere.
>
> The problems arise when (a) they try to give a secular account of this quality – because the account will be deficient – and/or (b) they affirmatively embrace a naturalist cosmology of the sort you associate with Darrow and Weinberg, because that cosmology will tend to subvert their initial more innocent perception of the sacredness of life. In other words, "sacredness" won't be intelligible in the naturalist ontological worldview, and so the worldview and the moral commitment will be inconsistent.
>
> But even so, insofar as people are able to maintain inconsistencies (and many of us are prodigiously talented at that), they can hold both to a naturalist worldview and to genuine moral commitments, including commitments to human rights.

E-mail from Steven Smith to Michael Perry, Mar. 18, 2005. This seems right to me – though the accommodation that Smith describes seems to me ultimately unstable.

82. Ludwig Wittgenstein, Philosophical Investigations, sec. 217 (1953), quoted in Hilary Putnam, The Many Faces of Realism 85 (1987).

83. See Amartya Sen, "Elements of a Theory of Human Rights," 32 Philosophy & Public Affairs 315, 317 (2004):

> Human rights activists are often quite impatient with such critiques. The invoking of human rights tends to come mostly from those who are concerned with changing the world rather than interpreting it (to use a classic distinction made famous, oddly enough, by that overarching theorist, Karl Marx). It is not hard to understand their unwillingness to spend time trying to provide conceptual justification, given the great urgency to respond to terrible deprivations around the world. This proactive stance has its practical rewards, since it has allowed immediate use of the colossal appeal of the idea of human rights to confront intense oppression or great misery, without having to wait for the theoretical air to clear.

Sen then adds:

> However, the conceptual doubts must also be satisfactorily addressed, if the idea of human rights is to command reasoned loyalty and to establish a secure intellectual standing. It is

critically important to see the relationship between the force and appeal of human rights, on the one hand, and their reasoned justification and scrutinized use, on the other.

84. Bernard Williams, "Republican and Galilean," New York Rev., Nov. 8, 1990, at 45, 48 (reviewing Charles Taylor, Sources of the Self: The Making of Modern Identity (1989)).

85. See n. 80.

86. Cf. Timothy P. Jackson, "The Theory and Practice of Discomfort: Richard Rorty and Pragmatism," 51 Thomist 270, 284–85 (1987):

> [T]he loss of realism . . . means the loss of any and all realities independent of or transcendent to inquiry. In this respect, God must suffer the same fate as any other transcendent subject or object. Because faith makes sense only when accompanied by the possibility of doubt, Rorty's distancing of scepticism means a concomitant distancing of belief in "things unseen." He, unlike Kant, denies both knowledge and faith; but for what, if anything, is this supposed to make room? Faith may perhaps be given a purely dispositional reading, being seen as a tendency to act in a certain way, but any propositional content will be completely lost. The pull toward religious faith is at best a residue of metaphysical realism and of the craving for metaphysical comfort. The taste for the transcendent usually associated with a religious personality will find little place in a Rortian world. Similarly, hope and love, if thought to have a supernatural object or source, lose their point. The deconstruction of God must leave the pious individual feeling like F. Scott Fitzgerald after his crackup: "a feeling that I was standing at twilight on a deserted range, with an empty rifle in my hand and the targets down." The deconstructed heart is ever restless, yet the theological virtues stand only as perpetual temptations to rest in inauthenticity. We live in a world without inherent *telos*; so there simply is no rest as Christianity has traditionally conceived it.

CHAPTER 4. FROM MORALITY TO LAW

1. Dietrich Bonhoeffer, "After Ten Years: A Letter to the Family and Conspirators," in Dietrich Bonhoeffer, A Testament to Freedom 482, 486 (Geoffrey B. Kelly & F. Burton Nelson, eds.; rev. ed., HarperSanFrancisco 1995). "After Ten Years" bears the date "Christmas 1942."

2. See Amartya Sen, "Elements of a Theory of Human Rights," 32 Philosophy & Public Affairs 315, 321–22 (2004).

3. Id. at 322.

4. Id. at 341. See id. at 340–42.

5. Id. at 322–23.

6. I have not been able to locate the source for this statement.

7. Quoted in Nicholas D. Kristof, "The American Witness," New York Times, March 2, 2005.

8. Charles L. Black, Jr., A New Birth of Freedom: Human Rights, Named and Unnamed 133 (1999).

CHAPTER 5. CAPITAL PUNISHMENT

1. According to Amnesty International, 84 countries have abolished the death penalty for all crimes (40 of which have have done so since 1990); 12 countries have abolished it for all but exceptional crimes, such as wartime crimes; 24 countries can be considered abolitionist in practice: they retain the death penalty in law but have not carried

out any executions for the past 10 years or more and are believed to have a policy or established practice of not carrying out executions. Thus, 120 countries have abolished the death penalty in law or practice. The number of countries that retain and use the death penalty is 76, though the number that actually execute prisoners in any one year is much smaller. Amnesty International, Facts and Figures on the Death Penalty, <http:www.amnesty.org./pages/deathpenalty-facts-eng> (visited on Apr. 21, 2005). See also Kathryn F. King, "The Death Penalty, Extradition, and the War against Terrorism: U.S. Responses to European Opinion about Capital Punishment," 9 Buffalo Human Rights L. Rev. 161, 171 (2003):

> Today, all members of the European Union have banned the death penalty. Abolition has been made a prerequisite for EU membership, giving Eastern and Central European nations who desire to join the EU strong incentives to prohibit the practice. In principle and in practice, Western European governments are unequivocally opposed to capital punishment.

According to Amnesty International, supra:

> During 2004, at least 3,797 prisoners were executed in 25 countries and at least 7,395 people were sentenced to death in 64 countries. . . . In 2004, 97 per cent of all known executions took place in China, Iran, Viet Nam and the USA. In China, limited and incomplete records available to Amnesty International at the end of the year indicated that at least 3,400 people were executed, but the true figure was believed to be much higher. In March 2003 a delegate at the National People's Congress said that "nearly 10,000" people are executed per year in China. Iran executed at least 159 people, and Viet Nam at least 64. There were 59 executions in the USA, down from 65 in 2003.

2. In the United States, we may ask: If we live in a state that has not already done so, should we press our state government to abandon reliance on capital punishment?

3. See generally William A. Schabas, The Abolition of the Death Penalty in International Law (3d ed. 2002).

4. As of June 2004, there were fifty state parties to the Second Optional Protocol, including Australia, Austria, Belgium, Denmark, Germany, Greece, Hungary, Ireland, Italy, Netherlands, New Zealand, Norway, Portugal, Slovakia, South Africa, Spain, Sweden, Switzerland, and the United Kingdom of Great Britain and Northern Ireland. (Of the listed states, only Greece and Spain entered a reservation under Article 2; Spain subsequently withdrew its reservation.) See <http://web.amnesty.org/pages/deathpenalty-treaties-eng>.

5. As of April 2004, 44 states have ratified Protocol No. 6. See http://web.amnesty.org/pages/deathpenalty-treaties-eng.

6. As of April 2004, twenty-four states have ratified, and eighteen other states have signed but not yet ratified, Protocol No. 13. Id.

7. The Protocol to the American Convention on Human Rights to Abolish the Death Penalty, adopted by the General Assembly of the Organization of American States in 1990, provides for the total abolition of the death penalty but allows a state "to reserve the right to apply the death penalty in wartime in accordance with international law, for extremely serious crimes of a military nature," if the state makes a reservation to that effect at the time it ratifies the Protocol. The Protocol "shall enter into force among the States that ratify or accede to it when they deposit their respective instruments of ratification or accession with the General Secretariat of the Organization of American States." As of April 2005, there were eight state parties to the Protocol: Brazil (which entered a reservation under Article 2), Costa Rica,

Ecuador, Nicaragua, Panama, Paraguay, Uruguay, and Venezuela. Chile has signed but not yet ratified the Protocol.

8. See Collins v. Collins, 510 U.S. 1143, 1145 (Blackmun, J., dissenting from the denial of certiorari) (1994): "From this day forward, I no longer shall tinker with the machinery of death."

9. See Lawrence C. Marshall, "The Innocence Revolution and the Death Penalty," 1 Ohio State J. Criminal Law 573 (2004); "Wrongful Convictions Symposium," 52 Drake L. Rev. 587–738 (2004). Cf. Adam Liptak, "Study Suspects Thousands of False Convictions," New York Times, April 19, 2004.

10. See, e.g., Hilary Mantel, "The Right to Life," New York Rev., May 12, 2005; Hugo Adam Bedau & Paul G. Cassell, eds., Debating the Death Penalty: Should America Have Capital Punishment? The Experts on Both Sides Make Their Best Case (2004); Symposium, "Race to Execution," 53 DePaul L. Rev. 1403–1737 (2004); Symposium, "Rethinking the Death Penalty: Can We Define Who Deserves Death?" 24 Pace L. Rev. 107–86 (2003).

11. Cf. Pam Belluck, "State Panel Suggests Death Penalty Safeguards," New York Times, May 3, 2004: "A commission appointed by [Massachusetts] Gov. Mitt Romney has come up with what it considers the first virtually foolproof formula for [insuring that no innocent person is executed], and Mr. Romney is expected to use the plan to try to bring back capital punishment to the state, where it was abolished two decades ago."

12. To say that this is one of the most fundamental questions about capital punishment for those of us who affirm the morality of human rights is not to say that it is the most important question. In the real world, where systems of capital punishment are, and probably always will be, far from perfectly functioning, the most important question may be whether these imperfect systems (as distinct from imaginary perfect systems) are morally tolerable. See n. 64.

13. Jeffrie Murphy writes:

> In a letter to Marcellinus, the special delegate of the Emperor Honorius to settle the dispute between Catholics and Donatists, Augustine is concerned with the punishment to be administered for what must have, to him, seemed the most vicious of crimes: the murder of one Catholic priest and the mutilation of another by members of a radical Donatist faction.

Jeffrie G. Murphy, Getting Even: Forgiveness and Its Limits 109 (2003). Murphy then quotes from Augustine's letter:

> I have been a prey to the deepest anxiety for fear your Highness might perhaps decree that they be sentenced to the utmost penalty of the law, by suffering a punishment in proportion to their deeds. Therefore, in this letter, I beg you by the faith which you have in Christ and by the mercy of the same Lord Christ, not to do this, not to let it be done under any circumstances. For although we [bishops] can refuse to be held responsible for the death of men who were not manifestly presented for trial on charge of ours, but on the indictment of officers whose duty it is to safeguard the public peace, we yet do not wish that the martyrdom of the servants of God should be avenged by similar suffering, as if by way of retaliation. . . . We do not object to wicked men being deprived of their freedom to do wrong, but we wish it to go just that far, so that, without losing their life or being maimed in any part of their body, they may be restrained by the law from their mad frenzy, guided into the way of peace and sanity, and assigned to some useful work to replace their criminal activities. It is true, this is called a penalty, but who can fail to see that it should be called a benefit rather than a chastisement when violence and cruelty are held in check, but the remedy of repentance is not withheld?

Id. at 110.

14. E. Christian Brugger, Capital Punishment and Roman Catholic Moral Tradition 26 (2003). Brugger quotes this passage from Aquinas:

> By sinning man departs from the order of reason, and therefore falls away from *human dignity*, insofar as man is naturally free and exists for his own sake, and falls somehow into the slavery of the beasts, so that he may be disposed of according to what is useful to others.... Therefore, although it is evil in itself to kill a man who preserves his *human dignity*, nevertheless to kill a man who is a sinner can be good, just as it can be good to kill a beast...

Id. at 173 (emphasis in original). For a magisterial history of Western – in particular, Christian – thinking about capital punishment, see James J. Megivern, The Death Penalty: An Historical and Theological Survey (1997).

15. Brugger, Capital Punishment and Roman Catholic Moral Tradition, n. 14, at 26–27 (emphasis in original).

16. A Culture of Life and the Penalty of Death: A Statement of the United States Conference of Catholic Bishops Calling for an End to the Use of the Death Penalty 6 (2005). The Administrative Committee of the U.S. Conference of Catholic Bishops recently declared that "each person's life and dignity must be respected, whether that person is an innocent unborn child in a mother's womb... or even whether that person is a convicted criminal on death row." USCCB Administrative Committee, "Faithful Citizenship: A Catholic Call to Political Responsibility," 33 Origins 321, 325 (2003).

17. Raimond Gaita, A Common Humanity: Thinking about Love and Truth and Justice xviii-xix (2000).

18. According to U.S. Supreme Court Justice William Brennan, "the fundamental premise of the [Cruel and Unusual Punishments] Clause [of the Eighth Amendment to the U.S. Constitution is] that even the vilest criminal remains a human being possessed of common human dignity." Furman v. Georgia, 408 U.S. 238, 273 (1972) (concurring opinion).

19. In 1992, three of seven judges on the Canadian Supreme Court apparently thought so: "[The death penalty] is the supreme indignity to the individual, the ultimate corporal punishment, the final and complete lobotomy and the absolute and irrevocable castration. [It is] the ultimate desecration of human dignity." Kindler v. Canada, (1992) 6 CRR (2d) SC 4.

20. See Brugger, Capital Punishment and Roman Catholic Moral Tradition, n. 14, at 191–92n. 5:

> For example, in his "*Urbi et Orbi*" address in December 1998, Pope John Paul II said: "May Christmas help to strengthen and renew, throughout the world, the consensus concerning the need for urgent and adequate measures... to end the death penalty." *Origins* 28, no. 29 (7 January 1999): 506. In January 1999, during a trip to St. Louis, he appealed to Governor Mel Carnahan of Missouri to commute the death sentence of Darrell Mease to life without parole; on January 28 the governor announced he had done what the pope had asked; in the pope's homily at the St. Louis World Dome several days later he said: "I renew the appeal I made most recently at Christmas for a consensus to end the death penalty which is both cruel and unnecessary." *Origins* 28, no. 34 (11 February 1999): 601. At an international congress on the death penalty in June 2001, the Holy See stated that it "has consistently sought the abolition of the death penalty and His Holiness John Paul II has personally and indiscriminately appealed on numerous occasions in order that such sentences should be commuted to a lesser punishment." It added, "It is surely more necessary than ever that the inalienable dignity of human life be universally respected and recognized for its immeasurable value." Zenit, *Weekly News Analysis*, 19 January 2002.

See also New York Times, Jan. 28, 1999, at A14:

> Preaching consistency in moral values, Pope John Paul II today urged America's Roman Catholics to extend the crusade to protect human life to include murderers on death row. "The new evangelization calls for followers of Christ who are unconditionally pro-life," the Pope preached to 100,000 people [in St. Louis]. "Modern society has the means of protecting itself, without definitively denying criminals the chance to reform." He called the death penalty "cruel and unnecessary," and said it was so "even in the case of someone who has done great evil."

21. See n. 14.
22. See Brugger, Capital Punishment and Roman Catholic Moral Tradition, n. 14, at 184–85:

> What is the morally relevant basis for distinguishing between what one intends and what one merely foresees? . . . Intention is an act of the will whereby some good or apparent good is chosen in response to reason moving it to act. Since the will is a rational appetite, what one intends is what one desires, or what one endeavors to have, be, or bring about; we might say it is what one sets one's heart upon, what one seeks to possess, or rest in. A foreseen effect that lies outside one's intention is not absent from one's deliberations, but it is not what one directly commits oneself to when acting; it is not for the effect's sake that one chooses to act. The two effects stand in a different relationship to the will of the actor. To be sure, in foreseeing such a state of affairs resulting from one's freely chosen action, one is willing to do an act which brings about those states of affairs. In intending action x with consequence y, I consent to bring about y (i.e., I choose a y-bringing-about action). But I have no commitment to y, no morally relevant interest in bringing about y, and no morally relevant desire to see y happen.

23. Id. at 185.
24. See n. 22.
25. Brugger, Capital Punishment and Roman Catholic Moral Tradition, n. 14, at 173. For a development of the point, see E. Christian Brugger, "Aquinas and Capital Punishment: The Plausibility of the Traditional Argument," 18 Notre Dame J. L., Ethics & Social Policy 357, 358 et seq. (2004).
26. See n. 22.
27. J. L. Mackie, Ethics: Inventing Right and Wrong 243 (1977).
28. In November 2000, in a statement titled "Responsibility, Rehabilitation and Restoration: A Catholic Perspective on Crime and Criminal Justice," the U.S. Catholic bishops wrote: "We are guided by the paradoxical Catholic teaching on crime and punishment: We will not tolerate the crime and violence that threaten the lives and dignity of our sisters and brothers, *and we will not give up on those who have lost their way.* We seek both justice and mercy." (Emphasis added.) During Lent of 2004, 45 U.S. Catholic bishops from twelve southern states issued a statement of their own, in which they declared that "[a] Catholic approach never gives up on those who violate laws. We believe that both victims and offenders are children of God. Despite their very different claims on society, their lives and dignity should be protected and respected. We seek justice, not vengeance. We believe punishment must have clear purposes: protecting society and rehabilitating those who violate the law." Southern U.S. Bishops, "Toward Restorative, Not Retributive, Criminal Justice," 34 Origins 63 (2004). See also Helen Prejean, "Above All Else, Life," New York Times, April 4, 2005.

29. See Nathan Thornburgh, "When a Killer Wants to Die," Time, Apr. 25, 2005, at 43. Cf. Richard W. Garnett, "Sectarian Reflections on Lawyers' Ethics and Death-Row Volunteers," 77 Notre Dame L. Rev. 795 (2002).

30. David Boonin, A Defense of Abortion 223 (2003) (emphasis added). Hypothetical No. 2 was inspired by a hypothetical in Boonin's book. See id. at 222–27.

31. See Gene Outka, "The Ethics of Human Stem Cell Research," in Brent Waters & Ronald Cole-Turner, eds., God and the Embryo: Religious Voices on Stem Cell and Cloning 29, 46 (2003): "While [the great Christian ethicist Paul Ramsey] was committed to an absolute prohibition against murder as the intentional killing of innocent life, he was prepared to attach two *exempting conditions* to it. One *may* directly kill when (1) the innocent will die in any case and (2) other innocent life will be saved." See Paul Ramsey, War and the Christian Conscience 171–91 (1961).

32. See H. David Baer, "Proportionalism Defended," First Things, May 1994, at 3–4.

33. See n. 25 and accompanying text.

34. Harvard legal philosopher Charles Friend has written that "[w]e can imagine extreme cases where killing an innocent person may save a whole nation. In such cases it seems fanatical to maintain the absoluteness of the judgment, to do right even if the heavens will in fact fall." Charles Fried, Right and Wrong 10 (1977). By contrast, Catholic natural lawyer John Finnis has written:

> There are hard cases, as everybody knows. The prospect . . . of damage apparently avertable by violating the moral absolutes, can seem indubitable and be felt as overwhelming. But these are cases in which we do not see the relevant parts of the scheme of providence – a scheme of which we never, in this life, see the whole or even much. . . . To deny the truth of moral absolutes . . . is incoherent with faith in divine providence. . . . [T]o respect the moral absolutes which are made known to us by God through reason and faith is to cooperate with God, who has practical knowledge of everything without limit.

John Finnis, Moral Absolutes: Tradition, Revision, and Truth 12, 20 (1991). Those of us who find ourselves unable to accept Finnis's theology of providence will likely side with Fried in this dispute.

35. See E. Christian Brugger, Capital Punishment and Roman Catholic Moral Tradition 38–56 (2003). Cf. John E. Witte, Jr. & Thomas C. Arthur, "The Three Uses of the Law: A Protestant Source of the Purposes of Criminal Punishment," 10 J. L. & Religion 433, 452–65 (1993–1994).

36. Larry Alexander, "The Philosophy of Criminal Law," in Jules Coleman & Scott Shapiro, eds., The Oxford Handbook of Jurisprudence & Philosophy of Law 815, 816 (2002). For a useful discussion of different kinds of retributive theories of punishment, see Brugger, Capital Punishment and Roman Catholic Moral Tradition, n. 14, at 38–56.

37. Andrew Oldenquist, "Retribution and the Death Penalty," 20 U. Dayton L. Rev. 335, 340 (2004).

38. See Robert A. Pugsley, "A Retributivist Argument Against Capital Punishment," 9 Hofstra L. Rev. 1501 (1981); John P. Conrad, "The Retributivist's Case against Capital Punishment," in Ernest van den Haag, ed., The Death Penalty: A Debate 19 (1983); David McCord. "Imagining a Retributivist Alternative to Capital Punishment," 50 Florida L. Rev. 1 (1998); Dan Markel, "State, Be Not Proud: A Retributivist Defense of the Commutation of Death Row and the Abolition of the Death Penalty," 40 Harvard Civil Rights-Civil Liberties L. Rev. 407 (2005).

39. Albert Camus, "Reflections on the Guillotine," in Albert Camus, Resistance, Rebellion, and Death 230 (Justin O'Brien, tr., 1974).
40. See n. 13 and accompanying text.
41. See n. 14. See also Brugger, "Aquinas and Capital Punishment," n. 25.
42. See Brugger, Capital Punishment and Roman Catholic Moral Tradition, n. 14, at 9–37.
43. It bears mentioning that incarceration can present serious human rights problems of its own. See, e.g., Human Rights Watch, "Out of Sight: Super-Maximum Security Confinement in the United States (2000), <http://www.hrw.org/reports/2000/supermax/>; Adam Liptak, "Inmate Was Considered 'Property' of Gang, Witness Tells Jury in Prison Rape Lawsuit," New York Times, Sept. 25, 2005.
44. In this chapter, by deterrence I mean marginal deterrence. See Robert Weisberg, "The Death Penalty Meets Social Science: Deterrence and Jury Behavior Under New Scrutiny," 1 Annual Rev. L. & Social Science 151, 152 (2005):

    [O]ther things being equal, the presence or enforcement of the death penalty obviously will produce fewer homicides than not punishing homicides at all. Thus, the question is one of *marginal* deterrence – i.e., whether the death penalty deters more homicides than the next most severe penalty, which in all jurisdictions [in the United States] is some form of life imprisonment, and in most of the relatively new sentence of life without the possibility of parole. So it is solely for convenience that throughout this review deterrence stands for marginal deterrence.

45. In one study, for example, the three co-authors – one of whom is my Emory colleague, economist Joanna Shepherd – conclude "that capital punishment has a strong deterrent effect; each execution results, on average, in 18 fewer murders – with a margin of error of plus or minus 10. Tests show that results are not driven by tougher sentencing laws, and are also robust to many alternative specifications." The quoted language is from the abstract of the article: Hashem Dezhbakhsh, Paul H. Rubin & Joanna M. Shepherd, "Does Capital Punishment Have a Deterrent Effect? New Evidence from Post-Moratorium Panel Data," 5 American Law & Economics Rev. 344 (2003).
46. See John Donohue & Justin Wolfers, "Uses and Abuses of Empirical Evidence in the Death Penalty Debate," 58 Stanford L. Rev. 791, 794 (2005) (reviewing that the Dezhbakhsh/Rubin/Shepherd study cited in the preceding note and concluding that "the existing evidence for deterrence is surprisingly fragile . . . "). See also Richard Berk, "New Claims About Executions and General Deterrence: Déjà Vu All Over Again?" 2 J. Empirical Legal Studies 303 (2005); Jeffrey Fagan, Deterrence and the Death Penalty: A Critical Review of the New Evidence, Testimony to the New York State Assembly Standing Committee (Jan. 21, 2005), <http://www.deathpenaltyinfo.org/FaganTestimony.pdf>; Jeffrey Fagan, "Death and Deterrence Redux: Science, Alchemy and Causal Reasoning on Capital Punishment," Ohio St. J. Criminal L. (forthcoming 2006); Rudolph J. Gerber, "Economic and Historical Implications for Capital Punishment Deterrence," 18 Notre Dame J. L., Ethics & Public Policy 437 (2004); Lawrence Katz, Steven D. levitt & Ellen Shustorovich, "Prison Conditions, Capital Punishmenty, and Deterrence," 5 American Law & Economics Rev 318 (2003); Weisberg, n. 44.
47. In a more recent paper than that cited earlier (n. 45), Joanna Shepherd reaches a more nuanced conclusion: that in the United States, "executions deter murders in six states and have no effect on murders in eight states. In thirteen states, executions *increase*

murders – what I call the 'brutalization effect.'" Joanna M. Shepherd, "Deterrence versus Brutalization: Capital Punishment's Differing Impacts Among States" (draft, February 2005), forthcoming in the *Michigan Law Review*.

> In general, the states that have executed more than nine people in the last twenty years experience deterrence. In states that have not reached this threshold, executions generally increase murders or have no significant impact. On average across the U.S., executions deter crime because the states with deterrence execute many more people than do the states without it. . . . My results have three important policy implications. First, if deterrence is the objective, then capital punishment succeeds in the few states with many executions. Second, the many states with numbers of executions below the threshold may be executing people needlessly. Indeed, instead of deterring crime, the executions may be inducing additional murders: a rough total estimate is that, in the many states where executions induce murders rather than deter them, executions cause an additional 250 murders a year. Third, to achieve deterrence, states must generally execute many people. If a state is unwilling to establish such a large execution program, it should consider abandoning capital punishment.

48. I suppose that *if* incarceration for life were much more expensive than execution, and *if* the money saved by executing rather than incarcerating for life were going to be spent to save many human lives . . . But in the United States, incarceration for life is not more expensive than execution. See, e.g., ACLU Capital Punishment Project, The High Costs of the Death Penalty (n.d.), <http://www.deathpenaltyinfo.org/FactSheet.pdf>. Nor is there any reason to think that if incarceration for life were more exspensive, the money saved would be spent, for example, on medical research.

In commenting on a draft of this chapter, Rick Garnett asked: "Why isn't [an adequate] justification [for capital punishment] supplied by the need to communicate adequately the magnitude of [the convict's] wrong and to redress the disorder caused by his offense?" E-mail from Richard W. Garnett to Michael J. Perry, Nov. 16, 2005. I suspect that few of us would argue that of the available punishments for even the most depraved crimes, *only* capital punishment can "communicate adequately the magnitude of the wrong and redress the disorder caused by the offense." Have all the jurisdictions that have forsaken reliance on capital punishment – Michigan, for example, or England – thereby forsaken their *only* means of communicating adequately the magnitude of the wrong and of redressing the disorder caused by the offense? Is that a plausible position? Is it plausible to believe that the only way to restore the disorder caused by some heinous murders is by killing – executing – the murderers? Isn't it at least as plausible to believe that killing the murderers *obscures* the magnitude of the wrong they did rather than communicates it, by obscuring the value of human life – of *every* human life? That seems to be the position of the United States Conference of Catholic Bishops in their recent statement of opposition to the death penalty. See A Culture of Life and the Penalty of Death: A Statement of the United States Conference of Catholic Bishops Calling for an End to the Use of the Death Penalty 2, 7, 8, 10 (2005):

> We have other ways to punish criminals and protect society. The sanction of death when it is not necessary to protect society undermines respect for human life and dignity.
>
> . . .
>
> Some ask whether those who commit the most heinous crimes or who are found guilty of repeated violence constitute the "rare" occasions when the death penalty is

appropriate. . . . [T]he existence of a "rare" occasion when the death penalty may be used is determined not by the gravity of the crime but by whether "it would not be possible otherwise to defend society." No matter how heinous the crime, if society can protect itself without ending a human life, it should do so.

. . .

The pursuit of the common good is linked directly to the defense of human life. At a time when the sanctity of life is threatened in many ways, taking life is not really a solution but may instead effectively undermine respect for life. In many ways the death penalty is about us: the actions taken in our name, the values which guide our lives, and the dignity that we accord human life. Public policies that treat some lives as unworthy of protection, or that are perceived as vengeful, fracture the moral conviction that human life is sacred.

. . .

[W]e are convinced that working together to defend the use of the death penalty is an integral and important part of resisting a culture of death and building a true culture of life.

49. I chose the number eighteen because of the Dezhbakhsh/Rubin/Shepherd study cited in n. 45.

50. If a system of torture-plus-capital-punishment would deter about thirty-six murders per execution, would that warrant establishing a system of torture-plus-capital-punishment? See Henry Schwarzschild, "Reflections on Capital Punishment," 25 Israel L. Rev. 505, 508 (1991).

51. Quoted in Brugger, Capital Punishment and Roman Catholic Moral Tradition, n. 14, at 191–92n. 5.

52. Carol S. Steiker, "No, Capital Punishment Is Not Morally Required: Deterrence, Deontology, and the Death Penalty," 58 Stanford L. Rev. 751, 785 (2005).

53. CF. id.:

If the dollars spent on an execution that would prevent eighteen murders could be spent to prevent an equal number of people from dying in workplace accidents or from AIDS *without* violating any categorical moral prohibition, why should a threshold deontologist agree that any catastrophic threshold permitting violation of such a moral prohibition has been met? Given the costliness of the administration of capital punishment, it seems unlikely that a deontologist would ever properly conclude that the marginal deterrence afforded by executions so far outweighed other possible savings of lives with the same dollars so as to cross some catastrophic threshold.

54. See Sanjay Gupta, "A Montana Ordinance Has a Surprising Effect – and Triggers a CDC Warning," Time, May 10, 2004, at 82 (reporting that the Centers for Disease Control estimate that in the United States, "secondhand smoke causes 35,000 deaths a year from heart disease – a figure some experts believe will have to be revised upward"). Cf. Steiker, n. 52, at 786:

Capital punishment is morally required, under a consequentialist view, not merely if the government saves more lives by punishing than it sacrifices; rather, capital punishment is morally required only if the government can save more lives through capital punishment than it could save by deploying those resources in some other way. If it turns out that the government could save *more* AIDS patients, avert *more* fatal accidents, or cure *more* childhood diseases with the resources that executions would require, why should a consequentialist feel morally compelled to insist on capital punishment? Indeed, shouldn't a "life-life tradeoff" perspective *require* that capital punishment be abandoned to fund such other initiatives? Of course, the comparative savings of lives might not work out in this particular way, but the point remains: Our collective moral duties cannot be considered in artificial isolation, but rather must be determined in the broader context of all government action.

55. Cf. Graham Greene, The Power and the Glory [page] (1940): "When you visualized a man or a woman carefully, you could always begin to feel pity.... When you saw the corners of the eyes, the shape of the mouth, how the hair grew, it was impossible to hate. Hate was just a failure of imagination."

56. See n. 46.

57. Donohue & Wolfers, n. 46, at 795. See also id. at 841–45.

58. Editorial, "No Airtight Case for Death," Birmingham [Alabama] News, Nov. 10, 2005, at 8A. This editorial is one in a recent six-part series in which the editorial page of the Birmingham News came out in opposition to use of the death penalty in Alabama.

> The truth is, there is no proof that the death penalty deters – or that it doesn't. Deterrence supporters can argue that the murder rate would be even higher in states with the death penalty if they didn't use it, just as detractors can point to high murder rates seemingly corresponding to high use of the death penalty. There's no way to show cause and effect. But most data do suggest that there's plenty of reason to doubt the death penalty's ability to deter other murders.

Id.

59. Id (citing study by University of Florida sociologists Michael L. Radelet and Ronald L. Akers).

60. See Chapter 9 at 125.

61. State v. Makwanyane and Another, 1995 (6) BCLR 665, 693 (Constitutional Court). For some recent confirmation of this view, see Associated Press, "Race, Pleas Affect Ohio Death Penalty," New York Times, May 7, 2005.

62. On systems of capital punishment in the United States, see David R. Dow, Executed on a Technicality: Lethal Injustice on America's Death Row (2005).

63. See n. 1.

64. Cf. Marshall, n. 9, at 576:

> A new group of abolitionists is emerging. These new abolitionists are not particularly interested in the philosophical, theoretical, or theological debate about the propriety of capital punishment. Rather, they have concluded that regardless of whether one believes that the government has the right to take life as an abstract matter, one cannot support the death penalty given the practical issues surrounding the unfairness and inaccuracy of its implementation.

Compare Mantel, n. 10:

> As Sister Helen [Prejean] sees it, attempts to make the death penalty more consistent have failed. Yet where defects are only procedural, they could be remedied; given political will and a bottomless public purse, possibly they could be fixed. If the bureaucrats were wise and the system fair – if the process met tightly defined legal criteria of objectivity – would it be alright to have a death penalty? Many would say yes. Sister Helen is clear in her view: "I don't believe that the government should be put in charge of killing anybody, even those proven guilty of terrible crimes.... Every human being is worth more than the worst act of his or her life."
> The death penalty is not wrong because it is inconsistently administered. If it were fairly administered, it would still be wrong. Finally, the issue is moral; a nation so God-besotted should be able to grasp that. When the government touches a corpse, it contaminates the private citizen. A modern nation that deals in state-sponsored death becomes, in part, dead itself; dead, certainly, to the enlightened ideals from which America derives its existence as a nation.

CHAPTER 6. ABORTION

1. Adam Smith, The Theory of Moral Sentiments (rev. ed. 1790; V.2.15; republished, Oxford: Clarendon Press, 1976), p. 210, quoted in Amartya Sen, "Elements of a Theory of Human Rights," 32 Philosophy & Public Affairs 315, 354–55 (2004).

2. It is a separate question as to whether we should want the law to punish the woman who has a banned abortion or just those, or some of those, who help her to have the abortion. Cf. M. Cathleen Kaveny, "Toward a Thomistic Perspective on Abortion and the Law in Contemporary America," 55 The Thomist 343, 393 (1991): "[C]riminal sanctions . . . should be directed primarily at physicians rather than women, who are likely to be obtaining even the most morally dubious abortions under conditions of duress."

3. H. Tristram Engelhardt, Jr., "Moral Knowledge: Some Reflections on Moral Controversies, Incompatible Moral Epistemologies, and the Culture Wars," 10 Christian Bioethics 79, 84 (2004).

4. Peter Singer, The President of Good and Evil: The Ethics of George W. Bush 37 (2004).

5. Laurence H. Tribe, "Will the Abortion Fight Ever End: A Nation Held Hostage," New York Times, July 2, 1990, at A13.

6. As of June 2004, there were 192 state parties to the Convention on the Rights of the Child. The United States, which has signed but not ratified the Convention, was not one of them.

7. See Cynthia Price Cohen, "United Nations Convention on the Rights of the Child: Introductory Note," 44 International Commission of Jurists Rev. 36, 39 (1990); Dominic McGoldrick, "The United Nations Convention on the Rights of the Child," 5 International J. L. & Family 132, 133–34 (1991).

8. See Chapter 5 at 37–39.

9. Cf. Case of Vo v. France, European Court of Human Rights, Application No. 53924/00, July 8, 2004 (Article 2 of the European Convention on Human Rights and Fundamental Freedoms, which states that "[e]veryone's right to life shall be protected by law," does not apply to "unborn child").

    Note, however, that the American Convention on Human Rights states, in Article 1(2), that "[f]or the purposes of this Convention, 'person' means *every* human being"; it then states, in Article 4(1), that "[e]very person has the right to have his life respected" and that "[t]his right shall be protected by law *and, in general, from the moment of conception.*" (Emphasis added.) As of April 2005, the American Convention on Human Rights, which entered into force in 1978, had 25 state parties. The United States was not one of them.

    It is worth noting that the international law of human rights does not remain silent on the issue of reproductive health. See Rebecca J. Cook & Bernard M. Dickens, "Human Rights Dynamics of Abortion Law Reform," 25 Human Rights Quarterly 1 (2003).

10. Sheryl Gay Stolberg, "Shifting Certainties in the Abortion War," New York Times, Jan. 11, 1998, §4, at 3.

11. See Mary B. Mahowald, "Conception vs. Fertilization," Commonweal, Sept. 9, 2005, at 40:

    > Although these terms ["conception" and "fertilization"] are often used interchangeably, even in papal documents, "conception" refers to the beginning of a pregnancy within

a woman's body, when the embryo is implanted within her uterus several days after an egg is fertilized. In contrast, "fertilization" refers to the process by which any embryo is formed either in vivo or in vitro through union of egg and sperm. (Cloned embryos are not formed through union of egg and sperm.) Infertility practitioners and some people who are publicly opposed to abortion (for example, [Utah Senator] Orrin Hatch) support stem-cell retrieval from in vitro embryos on grounds of this distinction, arguing that new life begins at conception or the onset of pregnancy. The Catholic position should be clearly stated as one that opposes termination of the life of any fertilized egg or embryo (even if the latter has been cloned) regardless of whether conception has yet occurred.

12. See Chapter 2, n. 13.
13. See id. at 8–9.
14. See id, n. 13.
15. Garry Wills, "The Bishops vs. the Bible," New York Times, June 27, 2004. For the views of some Roman Catholics on the issue, see Joseph F. Donceel, SJ, "Immediate Animation and Delayed Homonization," 31 Theological Studies 76 (1970); Joseph F. Donceel, SJ, "A Liberal Catholic's View," in Robert Hall, ed., Abortion in a Changing World 39 (1970); Thomas A. Shannon, "Human Embryonic Stem Cell Therapy," 62 Theological Studies 811, 814–21 (2001); Jean Porter, "Is the Embryo a Person? Arguing with the Catholic Traditions," Commonweal, Feb. 8, 2002, at 8; John Haldane & Patrick Lee, "Aquinas on Ensoulment, Abortion and the Value of Life," 78 Philosophy 255 (2003); Robert Pasnau, "Souls and the Beginning of Life (A Reply to Haldane & Lee)," 78 Philosophy 521 (2003); John Haldane & Patrick Lee, "Rational Souls and the Beginning of Life," 78 Philosophy 532 (2003). Cf. Anthony Kenny, "The Soul Issue," Times Lit. Supp., March 7, 2003, at 12. Consider these passages from an essay that Peter Steinfels, at the time the editor of the Catholic weekly *Commonweal*, published in *Commonweal* in 1981:

> [T]he right-to-life movement is naively overconfident in its belief that the existence of a unique "genetic package" from conception onwards settles the abortion issue. Yes, it does prove that what is involved is a human individual and not "part of the mother's body." It does not prove that, say, a twenty-eight-day-old embryo, approximately the size of this parenthesis (–), is *then and there* a creature with the same claims to preservation and protection as a newborn or an adult. . . . Although it is not *logically* impossible, for example, to consider the great number of fertilized eggs that fail to implant themselves in the uterus as lost "human beings", a great many people find this idea totally incredible. Similarly, very early miscarriage usually does not trigger the sense of loss and grief that miscarriage does. Can we take these instinctive responses as morally helpful? . . . It is simply *not* the case that a refusal to recognize Albert Einstein or Anne Frank as human beings deserving of full legal rights is equivalent to the refusal to see the same status in a disc the size of a period or an embryo one-sixth of an inch long and with barely rudimentary features.

Peter Steinfels, "The Search for an Alternative," Commonweal, Nov. 20, 1981, reprinted in Patrick Jordan & Paul Baumann, eds., Commonweal Confronts the Century: Liberal Convictions, Catholic Tradition 204, 209–11 (1999). Cf. Porter, supra this note, at 8:

> What can we [Catholics] say to convince men and women of good will who do not share our theological convictions or our allegiance to church teaching that early-stage embryos have exactly the same moral status as we and they do? It will not serve us to fall back at this point on blanket denunciations such as "the culture of death." Naturally, these tend to be conversation stoppers. What is worse, they keep us from considering the possibility

that others may not be convinced by what we are saying because what we are saying is – not convincing.

16. Garry Wills, Papal Sin 229 (2000).

17. See David Boonin, A Defense of Abortion 91–115 & 129–32 (2003).

18. See id. at 115–29.

19. Id. at 115.

20. One should read Boonin's impressive book for his careful presentation of the argument.

21. See David DeGrazia, "Identity, Killing, and the Boundaries of Our Existence," 31 Philosophy & Public Affairs 414, 428–30. (2003).

22. Assume that for a human being that, like a post-OCBA fetus, has desires, respecting her ideal, dispositional desires and respecting her well-being amount to the same thing as a practical matter, because her fundamental ideal, dispositional desire is to achieve, to the greatest extent possible, well-being. Nonetheless, for a pre-OCBA fetus, respecting her ideal, dispositional desires and respecting her well-being cannot amount to the same thing: The former is an impossible feat; the latter is not. One cannot respect a pre-OCBA fetus's desires; a pre-OCBA fetus has no desires. But one *can* respect a pre-OCBA fetus's well-being – by not acting to impair or destroy, or by acting to protect or improve, the fetus's well-being.

23. One of the reviewers of this book in manuscript for the Cambridge University Press suggested consideration of "a possible position regarding the time at which individual human life begins: the early embryo possesses the possibility of twinning (one fertilized egg splits into two) and recombination (two fertilized eggs combine into one). So, eminent pro-life thinkers such as Paul Ramsey seriously considered the possibility that the end of this phase (14 days or so) should mark the beginning of the life of an individual human being, since individual human beings, unlike individual human cells, don't possess this possibility – individual human beings don't asexually reproduce or combine with one another." The reviewer then noted that "[t]his is the alternative that is most at issue in the stem cell debate." For a defense of this position, see Mary Warnock, An Intelligent Person's Guide to Ethics 43–49 (1998) (giving reasons for drawing the line at "fourteen days from fertilisation").

24. "We can distinguish between being dependent on a particular person and being dependent on some person or other. The viability criterion maintains that the former property[, not the latter,] is morally relevant . . . " Boonin, n. 17, at 130. "The proponent of the viability criterion is best understood as claiming that a fetus is viable if the technological means of keeping it alive outside of the womb are in principle available somewhere, even if not to this particular fetus." Id. at 131–32.

25. See John Langan, "Observations on Abortion and Politics," America, Oct. 25, 2004: "[O]ur increased knowledge of embryology and human genetics . . . [make] clear the continuity and identity of human life from conception forward . . . "

26. Consider what Chris Eberle has said in written comments on a draft of this chapter:

> [T]he viability threshold makes the inherent dignity of human beings depend[] on temporal and perhaps spatial facts that are every bit as arbitrary as the spatial facts that scuttled the birth criterion. Why?
>
> There doesn't seem to be any reason to believe that we can't develop technology that enables us to keep unborn human beings alive and developing long enough for them to [survive] outside the mother's womb *at any point from conception to birth*. We might not now be able to do so, but what of moral relevance is that? In fact, to claim that it's relevant

is to claim that whether one has inherent dignity depends on when one happens to be lucky enough to be born. If we do not now have the requisite technology, but we develop that technology in ten years, then it will turn out that unborn human [beings] will be viable, and thus have inherent dignity, from conception on in ten years, but that those conceived now are just flat out of luck. Their clock doesn't start ticking till they're 24 weeks old. It's not clear that this kind of temporal arbitrariness is any less objectionable than the spatial arbitrariness that scuttled the birth criterion.

Moreover, the viability criterion might be arbitrary in much the same way as the birth criterion. Consider a human being who would be able to live outside the mother's womb if that human being were conceived in the USA, but who happens to live in Darfur, which utterly lacks the technology that keeps American unborns alive. Is that child viable? It's not clear: must life-sustaining technology actually be available or must it be available only in principle?

Suppose you take the former route – well, that seems arbitrary in the extreme. Whether one has inherent dignity seems to depend on chance facts about where one happens to be born.

Suppose that you take the latter route – the in-principle available route. Someone, some-where has the technology necessary to [enable survival] outside the mother's womb. But this seems crazy: what if there are Aliens on another planet with the right technology, but who are not able to get that technology to us any more effectively than Americans can get their technology to the folks in Darfur? Are all unborn human beings viable from conception on if there are Aliens who live on Alpha Centauri who have the technology to keep babies alive from conception on until they [survive] outside the mother's womb?

Maybe not – the technology has to be located here on earth – or at least in our solar system. Well, this is not going to work: do unborn human beings acquire human dignity if an Alien spaceship happens to pass through our solar system (or atmosphere) with the requisite technology? Even if we don't know they are passing through? So unborn [human beings] lose their inherent dignity when the Aliens leave the solar system?

One could spin such silly stories for a long while longer . . .

You get the picture: making the inherent dignity of a human being depend on viability, which is in turn cashed out in terms of the existence and distribution of technology, is objectionably arbitrary.

27. Richard A. McCormick, SJ, Corrective Vision: Explorations in Moral Theology 183 (1994).

28. See Michael J. Wreen, "The Standing Is Slippery," 79 Philosophy 553, 571–72 (2004):

The Abortion Argument offers an indirect argument for its conclusion, one that simply piggybacks on the claim that a given being, a two-year-old, is a human being/person/etc. The fundamental grounds for, say, possession of a right to life are not mentioned, much less explored, in the argument. What this means is that it's a secondary, indirect argument, one that attempts to carry the day without itself tackling any of the weightier issues, both metaphysical and moral, that surround humanity, personhood, moral status, and the right to life. It could be that such an argument is the best that can be done as far as the issue of foetal status and the morality of abortion is concerned . . .

29. Id. at 572. Wreen then adds: " . . . but even so, we can hope for more, and try to find more. I, at least, would feel more confident if there were other, independent, and more fundamental arguments that also lead to the same conclusion." Id.

30. See McCormick, n. 27, at 192: "If the death of the fetus is not the ineluctable result, we should speak of premature delivery."

31. Kaveny, "Toward a Thomistic Perspective on Abortion and the Law in Contemporary America," n. 2, at 393.

32. But cf. Leslie C. Griffin, "*Evangelium Vitae*: Abortion," in Kevin William Wildes, SJ & Alan C. Mitchell, eds., Choosing Life: A Dialogue on *Evangelium Vitae* 159, 171 (1997):

> [Pope John Paul II's 1995 encyclical] *Evangelium Vitae* ["The Gospel of Life"] imposes on [Catholic legislators a] difficult dilemma of conscience. *Evangelium Vitae* . . . asks [them] to enact a theological teaching into law. . . . [It asks them] to impose the Church's teaching on non-Catholics. For pragmatic reasons, Catholics may vote for less restrictive abortion laws when their absolute ban on abortion cannot be passed. Catholics may vote only to restrict abortion rights or to ban abortions altogether. Their goal must be for Catholicism's teaching on abortion to become law for all citizens of the United States, so that no [immoral] abortion is permitted. Moral error has no rights.

33. See Michael J. Perry, Under God? Religious Faith and Liberal Democracy (2003).

34. Cf. Griffin, n. 32, at 159:

> The direct/indirect distinction has faced extensive criticism [within the Catholic Church] as an inadequate formulation of the Church's theological tradition. "No direct killing of the innocent" has been described as a rule, not a principle, and so subject to exceptions. On the subject of abortion, the direct/indirect distinction has been criticized for its excess physicalism. The principle allows, for example, the excision of the cancerous uterus and the ectopic pregnancy, but not other measures calculated to save the life of the mother. Moreover, in these two situations it requires that the mother's fertility not be spared.

35. See n. 30.

36. John Schwartz, "When Torment is Baby's Destiny, Euthanasia Is Defended," New York Times, March 10, 2005. Cf. Associated Press, "Study: Newborn Euthanasia Often Unreported," New York Times, March 10, 2005.

37. With respect to pregnancies like Carla's, it probably makes sense to permit a woman to terminate her pregnancy even after the fetus is viable. (Though, again, when the law permits a woman to terminate her pregnancy in the post-viability period, the law should require that she do it in a way that spares the life of her viable fetus. See n. 31 and accompanying text. Of course, in such cases, the baby, whether full term or prematurely delivered, is destined to die soon after it departs Carla's body.) It is difficult to discern why, in cases like Carla's, a woman who is in the post-viability period of pregnancy should be required to carry her fetus to term.

38. Langan, n. 25. See also Kaveny, "Toward a Thomistic Perspective on Abortion and the Law in Contemporary America," n. 2, at 393–94.

> Mid-term abortions in response to tests revealing serious genetic abnormalities in the fetus are a wrenchingly difficult situation in which to forge an adequate legal response. On the one hand, the quality-of-life judgments implicit in many of these abortion decisions are [morally problematic]. Moreover, these abortions are performed relatively late in pregnancy, at a fairly advanced stage in fetal development. On the other hand, in our culture, this situation is a paradigmatic example of how doing the right thing can sometimes require an extraordinary amount of virtue. The resources to aid parents with handicapped children are scant, and the burden could easily seem intolerable to many persons. The first response of pro-lifers, therefore, should be to increase substantially aid to families with mentally or physically damaged offspring. Yet the fact that the limits of the criminal law are the limits of ordinary virtue weighs against the institution of penal sanctions. In the grim meantime, the law should certainly make clear that its refusal to implement criminal penalties in such cases is a matter of excuse, not justification.

For an illustration of "the limits of ordinary virtue," see Claudette Kane, Letter to the Editor, Commonweal, Sept. 10, 2004, at 38:

> I want to explain why I and many sincere Catholics disagree with the editors' views on abortion and mental retardation. I am the mother of a mentally deficient child who committed suicide. The experience of living with my son's anguish has convinced me that Christ's command that we love one another absolutely forbids deliberately inflicting suffering on our children. I don't believe that the many women who refused to choose retardation for their child acted from selfish motives.

> We all know what being mentally deficient really means: it means we will always be dependent on other people. It means we will be a child in our parents' home forever. It means we will never hold a job which pays enough for us to marry the person we love and have children of our own. Many women have decided that aborting a severely retarded child was the right thing to do; I don't think they were morally blind.

Cf. Amy Harmon, "In New Tests for Fetal Defects, Agonizing Choices for Parents," New York Times, June 20, 2004.

39. Cf. Steinfels, n. 15, at 211–12, recommending

> the protection of unborn life not from conception but from that point when not one but a whole series of arguments and indicators have converged to support the "humanness" of the unborn.

> The goal, in sum, should be the prohibition of abortion after eights weeks of development. At this point, when the embryo is now termed a fetus, all organs are present that will later be developed fully, the heart has been pumping for a month; the unborn individual has a distinctively human appearance, responds to stimulation of its nose or mouth, and is over an inch in size. Electrical activity in its brain is now discernible. . . . [A]t this point "with a good magnifier the fingerprints could be detected. Every document is available for a national identity card."

> The argument is not that this is the "magic moment" when "human life" begins. The argument is rather that this is one moment when an accumulation of evidence should compel a majority, even in a pluralist society and despite whatever obscurities about early life continue to be debated, to agree that the unborn individual now deserves legal protection. After this point, abortion should be permitted only for the most serious reasons: endangerment of the mother's life or risk of her incapacitation. . . .

40. The following Western countries all permit categories of pre-viability abortion, though not all permit exactly the same categories: Australia, Austria, Belgium, Canada, Denmark, Finland, France, Germany, Great Britain, Greece, Italy, Luxembourg, Malta, The Netherlands, New Zealand, Portugal, Spain, Sweden, and Switzerland. (Restrictions on abortion vary by state and territory in Australia; I am referring not to each and every state and territory in Australia, but to the general state of affairs in Australia.) See Republic of Ireland, Green Paper on Abortion, Appendix 3 ("The Law Relating to Abortion in Selected Other Jurisdictions") (1999); Reuters, "Switzerland Votes to Relax Strict Abortion Laws," New York Times, June 2, 2002. The Republic of Ireland is a prominent exception. See James Kingston, Anthony Whelan, and Ivana Bacik, Abortion and the Law (1997); Gerard Hogan & G. F. Whyte, J. M. Kelly's The Irish Constitution 790–810 (3d ed. 1994). But even in Ireland, attitudes toward abortion and preferences concerning its legal regulation are in transition. According to a recent estimate, "about 9 percent of Irish pregnancies end in abortion." Sarah Lyall, "Increasingly, Irish Turn to Britain for Abortions," New

York Times, Dec. 24, 2001. For a sketch by the Irish government of various options for legal reform, see Republic of Ireland, Green Paper on Abortion, supra.

Polling data suggests that in the United States, a majority of citizens opposes the criminalization of early abortions, and a significant minority opposes the criminalization of any pre-viability abortions. In the New York Times/CBS News Poll conducted on Nov. 18–21, 2004, and released on Nov. 23, 2004, the question was asked: "Which of these comes closest to your view? 1. Abortion should be generally available to those who want it; OR 2. Abortion should be available but under stricter limits than it is now; OR 3. Abortion should not be permitted?" The results: 34% said "available," 44% said "available but stricter"; 21 % said "not available"; and 1 % fell into the "DK/NA" category.

41. Garry Wills, "The Bishops vs. the Bible," New York Times, June 27, 2004. On the enduring absence of a consensus to which Wills refers, compare Robert P. George & Patrick Lee, "Acorns and Embryos," The New Atlantis, Fall 2004/Winter 2004, <http://www,thenewatlantis.com/archive/7/georgeleeprint.htm>, with Michael S. Gazzaniga, "The Thoughtful Distinction Between Embryo and Human," The Chronicle Review, Apr. 8, 2005. See also Anthony Kenny, "Life Stories: When an Individual Life Begins – and the Ethics of Ending It," Times Lit. Supp., Mar. 25, 2005, at 3. Jesuit moral theologian Richard McCormick foresaw that because of this dissensus about the moral status of the fetus – in particular, about the fetus's moral status during early pregnancy – "public policy [would] remain sharply contentious and the task of legislators correspondingly complex." Richard A, McCormick, SJ, "The Gospel of Life," America, Apr. 29, 1995, at 12, 13. MaCormick added: "Indeed, a strong case can be made that the attempt to solve the . . . problem [of competing beliefs about the status of the fetus] by legislation bypasses our duty to persuade, to change hearts and minds." Id.

Professor M. Cathleen Kaveny has written that "the pro-life conviction of the immorality of abortion too often translates into a call for stringent criminal penalties, [but this] ignores the proper differences between moral and legal sanctions. . . . " Kaveny, "Toward a Thomistic Perspective on Abortion and the Law in Contemporary America," n. 2, at 345, 374. For further, later argument by Kaveny in support of her suggestion "that stringent criminal penalties for abortion" may not be "the best way for [the law] to express its concern," see M. Cathleen Kaveny, "The Limits of Ordinary Virtue: The Limits of the Criminal Law in Implementing Evangelium Vitae," in Wildes & Mitchell, n. 32, at 132. See also M. Cathleen Kaveny, "Law, Morality and Common Ground," America, Dec. 9, 2000, at 7. Referring in particular to "early abortions," as distinct from "mid-term abortions," Kaveny writes: "[T]he inherent limits of the criminal law make penal sanctions inappropriate . . . The extreme lack of consensus regarding this class of abortions means that laws which do institute such sanctions are likely to be unstable." Kaveny, "Toward a Thomistic Perspective on Abortion and the Law in Contemporary America," n. 2, at . See also Editorial, "Communion Politics," Comonweal, May 21, 2004, at 5, 6.

42. Langan, n. 2. Cf. Clifford Longley, " 'The Church Hasn't Yet Made a Mature Appraisal of What Democracy Demands'," The Tablet [London], May 7, 2005, at 11: "The criminal justice system . . . only works when there is at least a minimal degree of assent by the public to the moral framework in which it operates. . . . [W]hat you

have to persuade the majority of is not just that your moral principle is correct but that it is right to insist that the minority which does not agree with it must nevertheless comply with it too."

43. Langan, n. 25. The American historical experience suggests that imposition of the criminal sanction is best used to support and protect a consensus that already exists, not to coerce behavior when there is deep and widespread dissensus about the morality of the behavior. Think about Prohibition.

44. Id. What William Galston says about embryonic stem-cell research applies to abortion too:

> If embryonic stem-cell research is the moral equivalent of slavery, as many of its foes contend, aren't the moral costs of tolerating it unacceptable? Perhaps so. The difficulty is that many morally and religiously serious people whose views are not tainted by the self-interest of slaveowners reject the analogy altogether. Whatever our stance, we must ask ourselves whether, in the name of inscribing our particular views into public law, we are willing to risk the moral equivalent of civil war.

William A. Galston, "Catholics, Jews, & Stem Cells: When Believers Beg to Differ," Commonweal, May 20, 2005, at 13, 17.

In the passage accompanying this note, Langan refers to the possibility of "further threats to public order." With respect to that possibility, see Janice Nadler, "Flouting the Law," 83 Texas L. Rev. 1399 (2005):

> Does the perception of one particular law as unjust make an individual less likely to comply with related laws? This Article advances the Flouting Thesis – the idea that the perceived legitimacy of one law or legal doctrine can influence one's willingness to comply with unrelated laws – and provides original experimental evidence to support this thesis. The results suggest that willingness to disobey law can extend far beyond the particular unjust law in question [i.e., the particular law perceived as unjust], to willingness to flout unrelated laws commonly encountered in everyday life . . .

45. Cynthia Gorney, "Imagine a Nation Without Roe v. Wade," New York Times, Feb. 27, 2005.

46. Cook & Dickens, n. 9, at 17.

47. Kaveny, "Toward a Thomistic Perspective on Abortion and the Law in Contemporary America," n. 2, at 394.

48. See id. at 374: "To say that the law cannot be *indifferent* to the well-being of the unborn . . . does not mean that stringent criminal penalties for abortion are the best way for [the law] to express its concern." For further, later argument by Kaveny in support of her suggestion "that stringent criminal penalties for abortion" may not be "the best way for [the law] to express its concern," see M. Cathleen Kaveny, "The Limits of Ordinary Virtue: The Limits of the Criminal Law in Implementing *Evangelium Vitae*," in Wildes & Mitchell, n. 32, at 132. See also Kaveny, "Law, Morality and Common Ground," n. 41.

49. Kaveny, "Toward a Thomistic Perspective on Abortion and the Law in Contemporary America," n. 2, at 361.

50. Id. at 392–96.

51. Cf. David Smith, MSC, "What Is Christian Teaching on Abortion?" 42 Doctrine & Life 305, 316 (1992) (focusing on Britain and Ireland):

> As can be observed from this brief survey of certain Christian Churches, all agree that the human embryo has "value" and must be respected. The disagreement concerns what precisely is the "value" of the human embryo. One view, represented explicitly by the

Roman Catholic Church, states that it has exactly the same value as any other human being. Another view, represented by a strong body of opinion in the Church of England, asserts that its value, prior to individuation (consciousness), is less than that of a human being in the proper sense of the word. A third view, represented by the Methodist Conference, would argue that its value depends on its stage of development: thus a progressively increasing value. The Baptist Union seems to favour a similar position, as does the Church in Wales and the Free Churches.

See also Daniel Callahan, Abortion, Law, Choice and Morality 497–98 (1970) (arguing that although abortion "is not the destruction of a human person[, it is] the destruction of an important and valuable form of human life"); Boonin, n. 17, at 300–10 (discussing "pro-life feminism"). Cf. Margaret O'Brien Steinfels, "On Catholics and Democrats," Dissent, Winter 2000, at 86, 88:

> My own church can be described as virtually absolutist on this question, believing as it does that an individual human life is present and to be protected from the moment of conception. That many Catholics do not share that exact understanding does not mean that we do not think that there are better and worse reasons in the decision to seek an abortion, and that some of those decisions will fail the test of moral seriousness. And they often fail, in the minds of many people, Catholics and others, precisely because they seem to be wholly dismissive of the value of the human fetus. How is it at a time that we are becoming more sensitive, and rightly so, to the protection of animal life and endangered species, we can treat the life that comes from our own bodies so indifferently?

52. Cf. Archbishop John Myers, "A Time for Honesty," Origins, May 20, 2004, at 1, 4–5:

> That some Catholics, who claim to believe what the church believes, are willing to allow others to continue directly to kill the innocent is a grave scandal.... [W]ith abortion (and, for example, slavery, racism, euthanasia and trafficking in human persons), there can be no legitimate diversity of opinion. The direct killing of the innocent is always a grave injustice. One should not permit unjust killing anymore than one should permit slave-holding, racist actions or other grave injustices.... Obviously, recognizing the grave injustice of slavery requires one to ensure that no one suffers such degradation. Similarly, recognizing that abortion is unjust killing requires one – in love and justice – to work to overcome the injustice.

The question, however, is whether "recognizing that abortion is unjust killing" requires one to press one's elected representatives to do what one believes they simply will not do: criminalize early abortions. See Langan, n. 25: "The function of bishops, and more generally of the churches, is to bear witness to the moral truth that is at stake, not to determine what is the best legal and political resolution of the problem.... [I]t would be a brave bishop who would claim to know on theological grounds just when such compromises are acceptable or justifiable, and it would be a naive voter who would follow his opinion on such a question." At another point in his essay, with an eye on the 2004 presidential election, Professor Langan wrote:

> [S]ingle issue voting may well be an admirable expression of conscientious conviction about an important matter, but it should not be imposed on voters as a requirement of conscience. Both voters and politicians have to make up their own minds about what issues are opportune, what fights can be won, what results can be achieved.... If a person, whether a political candidate or a citizen, judges that an objective such as the prohibition of abortion is simply not attainable in the present state of American public and legal opinion, then he or she cannot be required to make the prohibition of abortion the decisive consideration in voting or to demand it as an essential plank in the political platform. If I vote for a candidate who professes to be strongly pro-life but is either unable

or unwilling to reduce or eliminate abortions, then I have not succeeded in achieving my pro-life objective.... Politics is not merely the expression of values; it is social action shaped by many discordant forces over time. Moral principles are profoundly important in political life, but they are developed within a larger and, regrettably, less well ordered and unprincipled reality.

Id. See also James L. Heft, SM, "US Catholics and the Presidential Election: Abortion and Proportionate Reasons," 86 New Blackfriars 259 (2005).

53. See n. 40.
54. See BBC News, UK Edition, "Lord Steel's Re-think on Abortion," July 5, 2004; BBC News, UK Edition, "Blair Hints at Abortion Rethink," July 7, 2004. See also Mian Ridge, "Steel Calls for Reduction on Abortion Limit," The Tablet [London], July 10, 2004, at 33.
55. In the United States, are state legislatures constitutionally free to ban some mid-term abortions? On January 22, 1973, in *Roe v. Wade*, the Supreme Court of the United States famously decreed that under the Fourteenth Amendment, no state may ban abortion in the period of pregnancy prior to the time at which the fetus becomes "viable": "[capable] of meaningful life outside the mother's womb." 410 U.S. 113, 163 (1973). Although, according to the Court's decree, a state may ban abortion in the post-viability period of pregnancy, it must provide an exception for any abortion "necessary to preserve the life or health of the mother." Id. at 164. No constitutional decision by the Supreme Court in the period since the end of World War II has been more controversial – certainly none has been more *persistently* controversial – than the Court's ruling in *Roe*. Even after almost a third of a century, the legitimacy of the Court's decision is widely and furiously contested. See Editorial, "*Roe*: Twenty-Five Years Later," First Things, January 1998, at 9; Editorial, "Dead Reckoning," National Review, Jan. 26, 1998. Cf. Carey Goldberg with Janet Elder, "Public Still Backs Abortion, But Wants Limits, Poll Says," New York Times, Jan. 16, 1998, at A1: "[T]he country remains irreconcilably riven over what many consider to be the most divisive American issue since slavery, with half the population considering abortion murder, the poll found. Despite a quarter-century of lobbying, debating and protesting by the camps that call themselves 'pro-choice' and 'pro-life,' that schism has remained virtually unaltered."

In any event, unless/until *Roe v. Wade* is overruled, no state legislature may ban any pre-viability abortions. However, state legislatures are constitutionally free to ban – and most do ban – most *post-viability* abortions. Connecticut's law, for example, provides that no abortion can be performed after viability unless necessary to preserve the women's life or health. Connecticut General Statutes, §19a–602(b). Only ten states are *without* such laws: Alaska, Colorado, Hawaii, Mississippi, New Hampshire, New Jersey, New Mexico, Oregon, Vermont, and West Virginia.
56. See, e.g., William P. Clark, "For Reagan, All Life Was Sacred," New York Times, June 11, 2004 (quoting Reagan): "[T]here is no cause more important... than affirming the transcendent right to life of all human beings, the right without which no other rights have any meaning."). See also Bishop Vincent Galeone, "A Pro-Choice Catholic Politician?," 34 Origins 199, 200 (2004): "[T]he right to life is the foundation of all our other rights. Just as a building without a foundation will ultimately collapse, so too every other right we enjoy will crumble unless buttressed by this most basic right of all."

57. Kaveny, "Toward a Thomistic Perspective on Abortion and the Law in Contemporary America," n. 2, at 395–96. See Steven Ertelt, "Pro-Life Democrats Unveil Legislative Package to Reduce Abortions," <http://www.lifenews.com/nat1294.html>; Nina Kohl, "Pro-Life Democrats: We're Here, We're Sincere. Get Used to It," Tikkun, May/June 2005, at 14.

The controversy over human stem cell research is closely linked to the controversy over abortion. Should one who affirms that every human being, unborn as well as born, has inherent dignity want governmment to ban all embryonic stem cell research? Not necessarily. Consider the position of Gene Outka, Dwight Professor of Philosophy and Christian Ethics at Yale University. Outka "take[s] conception and all that it alone makes possible as *the* point at which one should ascribe a judgment of irreducible value" and opposes the creation of embryos for use in stem cell research. But Outka would permit the use of "excess" embryos, i.e., embryos left over after infertility treatments have been completed. See Gene Outka, "The Ethics of Human Stem Cell Research," in Brent Waters & Ronald Cole-Turner, eds., God and the Embryo: Religious Voices on Stem Cell and Cloning 29 (2003). (The quoted language is on p. 55.)

CHAPTER 7. SAME-SEX UNIONS

1. John Paul II, quoted in Henri de Lubac, At the Service of the Church 172 (Anne Elizabeth Englund trans., 1993); also quoted in David Brooks, "Bigger Than The Nobel," New York Times, Oct. 11, 2003.
2. On the basis of subsection 9(3) of the South African Constitution, the Supreme Court of Appeal of South Africa has developed the common law of marriage to include same-sex "life partnerships." See Fourie & Another v. Minister of Home Affairs & Others, Case No. 232/2003 (2004).
3. "Falsely" according to whose standards of truth/falsity? If the right is being enforced by a court: according to the court's standards. This is not to say, however, that the judiciary necessarily gets the last word. In Chapters 8 and 9, I discuss the proper role of courts in protecting human rights.
4. In Appendix A to this chapter, I inquire about the extent to which existing human rights laws – international, transnational (regional), and national – conforms to this non-discrimination ideal.
5. See Robert Wright, "Two Years Later, a Thousand Years Ago," New York Times, Sept. 11, 2003, at A27:

> [P]rehistoric life seems to have featured frequent hostility among groups, with violence justified by the moral devaluation, even dehumanization, of the victims. And recorded history is replete with such bigotry. The modern idea that people of all races and religions are morally equal is often taken for granted, but viewed against the human past, it is almost bizarre.

6. See Michael Burleigh & Wolfgang Wipperman, The Racial State: Germany, 1933–1945 (1991); Johannes Morsink, "World War Two and the Universal Declaration," 15 Human Rights Q. 357, 363 (1993); Claudia Koonz, The Nazi Conscience (2003). Cf. Christopher Hitchens, "Obit: Edward Said," Slate, Sept. 29, 2003: "[F]or Edward, injustice was to be rectified, not rationalized. I think that it was, for him, surpassingly a matter of dignity. People may lose a war or a struggle or be badly led or poorly advised, but they must not be humiliated or treated as alien or less than human."

7. Philip Dray, At the Hands of Persons Unknown: The Lynching of Black America 101 (2002) (referring to "the bestselling *The Negro Beast, or 'In the Image of God'* (1900) by Charles Carroll[,] a hodgepodge of dubious biblical interpretations and bogus science"). See also H. Shelton Smith, In His Image, But . . . : Racism in Southern Religion, 1780–1910 (1972).

8. Koonz, n. 6, at 1–2. During the period of "ethnic cleansing" in Bosnia, Richard Rorty observed:

> Serbian murderers and rapists do not think of themselves as violating human rights. Further they are not doing these things to fellow human beings, but to *Muslims*. They are not being inhuman, but rather are discriminating between the true humans and the pseudohumans. They are making the same sort of distinction as the Crusaders made between the humans and the infidel dogs, and the Black Muslims make between humans and blue-eyed devils. [Thomas Jefferson] was able both to own slaves and to think it self-evident that all men are endowed by their creator with certain inalienable rights. He had convinced himself that the consciousness of Blacks, like that of animals, "participates more of sensation than reflection." Like the Serbs, Mr. Jefferson did not think of himself as violating *human* rights. The Serbs take themselves to be acting in the interests of true humanity by purifying the world of pseudohumanity.

Richard Rorty, "Human Rights, Rationality, and Sentimentality," in Stephen Shute & Susan Hurley, eds., On Human Rights: The Oxford Amnesty Lectures 1993 111, 112 (1993). "The past provides many instances where the law refused to see a human being when it should have." Baker v. State [of Vermont], 744 A.2d 864, 889 (Vt. 1999).

9. For the interesting details, see Eugene D. Genovese, A Consuming Fire: The Fall of the Confederacy in the Mind of the White Christian South 81 et seq. (1998).

10. This is not to deny that some discrimination against women has been based on the view that women are not truly, fully human. David Richards has rehearsed the classical and medieval antecedents of that view:

> Aristotle . . . place[d] women below men but above slaves, so that considerations of equal justice (with men) do not apply to women . . . The Aristotelian view, absorbed into Christian theoretical thought by St. Thomas, was confirmed for Christian and Jewish thought by scripture as well. . . .
> Such an ancient and powerful tradition of thought has understandably led to a common conception of women as not being moral persons in the full sense. . . . [W]omen are supposed incapable of full public life in the world of work and politics; accordingly, on paternalistic grounds women are by law or convention denied the right to participate in that world, or are given that right in special areas on terms of special protections not afforded men.

David A. J. Richards, The Moral Criticism of Law 174 (1977). On Aquinas's view of women, see Paul J. Weithman, "Complementarity and Equality in the Political Thought of Thomas Aquinas," 59 Theological Studies 277 (1998).

Even today, an ideology implicit in much of American culture – and sometimes explicit – is "that the man is the 'norm' for being human while the woman is an 'auxiliary,' someone defined exclusively by her relationships to men." United States Catholic Bishops, "Fourth Draft/Response to the Concerns of Women for Church and Society," 22 Origins 221, 224 (1992). According to this ideology, "the one sex . . . is superior to the other in the very order of creation or by the very nature of things. . . . This error and the sinful attitudes it generates represent, in fact, a radical distortion of the very order of creation. Unjust discrimination of this sort, whether subtle or overt, distorts interpersonal relations and adversely affects the social patterns and the modes of communication that influence day-to-day life in our world." Id.

11. 83 U.S. (16 Wall.) 130, 141 (1873) (Justice Bradley, joined by Justices Swayne and Field, concurring in the judgment). For a contemporary expression of a similar view, see Neil MacFarquhar, "In Najaf, [Iraq,], Justice Can Be Blind but Not Female," New York Times, July 31, 2003.

12. United States v. Virginia, 518 U.S. 515, 000 n. 9 (1996).

   In 1975, in *Stanton v. Stanton*, the U.S. Supreme Court referred to "the role-typing society has long imposed" on women and to the normative view that "the female [is] destined solely for the home and the rearing of the family, and only the male for the marketplace and the world of ideas." 421 U.S. 7, 14–15 (1975). Michael Levin's statement is a conspicuous example of such a view: "In the human species Man is the aggressor and Woman the accepter." Michael Levin, "Vs. Ms.," in J. English, ed., Sex Equality 216, 217–18 (1977), quoted by Kenneth L. Karst, "Foreword: Equal Citizenship Under the Fourteenth Amendment," 91 Harvard L. Rev. 1, 4 (1977) (categorizing Levin's statement as "Neanderthal").

13. Cf. Edward Collins Vacek, SJ, "Feminism and the Vatican," 66 Theological Studies 159, 162 (2005) (quoting Elizabeth Johnson, CSJ, "Feminism and Sharing the Faith: A Catholic Dilemma, in Thomas J. Massaro & Thomas A. Shannon, eds., American Catholic Social Teaching 107, 108 (Collegeville, MN: Liturgical Press, 2002):

   > What is feminism? Elizabeth Johnson offers the following definition: "Feminism, in a generic sense, is a worldview or stance that affirms the dignity of women as fully human persons in their own right, critiques systems of patriarchy for their violation of this dignity, and advocates social and intellectual changes to bring about freeing relationships among human beings."

14. See n. 1 and accompanying text. Not that there aren't many other exemplifications of that evil.

15. See, generally, Frederick Schauer, Profiles, Probabilities, and Stereotypes (2003). Schauer's book is discussed in Felicia R. Lee, "Discriminating? Yes. Discriminatory? No," New York Times, Dec. 13, 2003.

16. Cost considerations aside, it is not always possible for government to proceed on the basis of individualized determinations rather than on the basis of a generalization, even a generalization about race or ethnicity. See Deborah Hellman, "Classifications and Fair Treatment: An Essay on the Moral and Legal Permissibility of Profiling," University of Maryland School of Law, Public Law and Legal Theory Research Paper Series (2003), <http://ssrn.com/abstract=456460>. Cf. Joshua Engelhart, "Why Prisons Can't Intregrate: Abolishing Segregation Will Incite Violence," Los Angeles Times, March 11, 2005.

17. In *United States v. Virginia*, the Supreme Court emphasized that

   > time and time again . . . we have cautioned reviewing courts to take a "hard look" at generalizations or "tendencies" of the kind pressed by Virginia, and relied upon by the District Court. . . . State actors controlling gates to opportunity, we have instructed, may not exclude qualified individuals based on "fixed notions concering the roles and abilities of males and females." . . . [E]qual protection principles, as applied to gender classifications, means state actors may not rely on "overbroad" generalizations to make "judgments about people that are likely to . . . perpetuate historical patterns of discrimination[.]"

   United State v. Virginia, 518 U.S. 515, 541–42 (1996).

18. Cf. David Boonin, A Defense of Abortion 262 (2003) (referring to "the claim that it is prima facie wrong to impose burdens on the members of an oppressed group when those burdens are likely to perpetuate their oppression").

19. I don't address here the question of whether the law should recognize same-sex unions as "marriages" or, instead, as something else (for example, "civil unions"). See David S. Buckel, "Government Affixes a Label of Inferiority on Same-Sex Couples When It Imposes Civil Unions & Denies Access to Marriage," 16 Stanford L. & Pol'y Rev. 73 (2005). Compare Andrew Koppelman, "Civil Conflict and Same-Sex Civil Unions," Responsive Community, Spring/Summer 2004, at 20. Cf. Adam Liptak, "Caution in Court for Gay Rights Groups," New York Times, Nov. 12, 2004. For a debate about whether states should abolish *civil* marriage, see <http://www.legalaffairs.org/webexclusive/debateclub·mo505.msp>.

20. Baker v. State [of Vermont], 744 A.2d 864, 870 (Vt. 1999). For a fuller specification of the benefits in question, see id. at 883–84. See also Goodridge v. [Massachusetts] Department of Public Health, ... (2003).

21. See Richard Posner, Sex and Reason 346 (1992) (emphasis added):

> [S]tatutes which criminalize homosexual behavior express *an irrational fear and loathing of a group that has been subjected to discrimination, much like that directed against the Jews, with whom indeed homosexuals – who, like Jews, are despised more for who they are than for what they do – were frequently bracketed in medieval persecutions.* The statutes thus have a quality of invidiousness missing from statutes prohibiting abortion or contraception. The position of the homosexual is difficult at best, even in a tolerant society, which our society is not quite; and it is made worse, though probably not much worse, by statutes that condemn the homosexual's characteristic methods of sexual expression as vile crimes ... There is a gratuitousness, an egregiousness, a cruelty, and a meanness about [such statutes].

Cf. Louis Crompton, Homosexuality and Civilization (2003). Crompton's book is discussed in Edward Rothstein, "Annals of Homosexuality: From Greek to Grim to Gay," New York Times, Dec. 13, 2003.

As history teaches, "an irrational fear and loathing" of *any* group "more for who they are than for what they do" has tragic consequences. The irrational fear and loathing of homosexuals – that is, the fear and loathing of them *more for who they are than for what they do* – is no exception. There is, for example, the horrible phenomenon of "gay bashing." "The coordinator of one hospital's victim assistance program reported that 'attacks against gay men were the most heinous and brutal I encountered.' A physician reported that injuries suffered by the victims of homophobic violence he had treated were so 'vicious' as to make clear that 'the intent is to kill and maim' ... " Andrew Koppelman, Antidiscrimination Law & Social Equality 165 (1996). As "[a] federal task force on youth suicide noted[,] because 'gay youth face a hostile and condemning environment, verbal and phyical abuse, and rejection and isolation from family and peers,' young gays are two to three times more likely than other young people to attempt and to commit suicide." Id. at 149.

22. Andrew Koppelman, "Are the Boy Scouts Being as Bad as Racists? Judging the Scouts' Antigay Policy," 18 Public Affairs Quarterly 363, 372 (2004).

23. It is sometimes observed that for Roman Catholics, it is not the Bible that is supremely authoritative but the "magisterium" of the Church. The magisterium is the "teaching office and authority of the Catholic Church; also the hierarchy as holding this office." The HarperCollins Encyclopedia of Catholicism 805 (Richard P. McBrien et al. eds.

1995). "The whole episcopal college is the bearer of supreme magisterium, which it exercises both when dispersed throughout the world and when gathered in an ecumenical council. The pope, as head of the episcopal college, can exercise the supreme teaching authority that resides in this college." Id. "At the present time the term 'magisterium' refers, for all practical purposes, to the hierarchical magisterium alone, especially that of the pope." Id. at 807. For a fuller discussion, see id. at 805–808. See also Francis A. Sullivan, "The Magisterium in the New Millennium," *America*, Aug. 27, 2001, at 12; Bernard Hoose, Authority in Roman Catholicism (2002).

24. USCCB Administrative Committee, "Statement on Marriage and Homosexual Unions," 33 Origins 257, 259 (2003). Cf. Robert F. Nagel, "Playing Defense in Colorado," First Things, May 1998, at 34, 35: "There is the obvious but important possibility that one can 'hate' an individual's behavior without hating the individual."

25. Such conduct obviously includes extramarital sex: sexual conduct between two persons who are not married to one another, at least one of whom is married.

26. Cf. Loving v. Virginia, 388 U.S. 1 (1967).

27. Commonwealth [of Kentucky] v. Wasson, 842 S.W.2d 487, 501 (Ky. 1992).

28. Id.

29. Id.

30. Id. at 501.

31. Consider, too, a decision handed down by the Supreme Court of Canada in 1998: Vriend v. Alberta, 1 S.C.R. 493. The province of Alberta had a law on its books called the Human Rights, Citizenship and Multiculturalism Act, which banned discrimination in certain domains (public accommodations, employment practices, and so on) on any of several listed bases, including race or color, ancestry, place of origin, religious beliefs, sex, physical disability, mental disability, age, or marital status. Sexual orientation was not on the list. As the Court explained, the omission was not inadvertent: "Despite repeated calls for its inclusion sexual orientation has never been included in the list of those groups protected from discrimination." The Court concluded – indeed, *unanimously* concluded – that the refusal to include sexual orientation as a prohibited basis of discrimination violated section 15(1) of Charter of Rights and Freedoms (which, in Canada, has constitutional status). Section 15(1) states, in relevant part: "Every individual is equal before and under the law and has the right to the equal protection and equal benefit of the law without discrimination . . . " The Court reasoned that an "implicit message was conveyed by the exclusion" – namely,

> that gays and lesbians, unlike other individuals, are not worthy of protection. This is clearly an example of a distinction which demeans the individual and strengthens and perpetrates the view that gays and lesbians are less worthy of protection as individuals in Canada's society. The potential harm to the dignity and perceived worth of gay and lesbian individuals constitutes a particularly cruel form of discrimination.
>
> . . .
>
> In excluding sexual orientation from the [Act's] protection, the Government has, in effect, stated that "all persons are equal in dignity and rights", except gay men and lesbians. Such a message, even if it is only implicit, must offend s. 15(1), the "section of the *Charter*, more than any other, which recognizes and cherishes the innate human dignity of every

individual". This effect, together with the denial to individuals of any effective legal recourse if they are discriminated against on the ground of sexual orientation, amount to a sufficient basis on which to conclude that the distinction created by the exclusion from the [Act] constitutes discrimination [in violation of s. 15(1)].

In the Court's judgment, Alberta failed to explain its exclusion of sexual orientation in terms that rebutted the strong suspicion that the exclusion was based on an demeaning view about homosexuals (that is, about homosexuals as such). The plaintiff in *Vriend* had been dismissed from his position by the president of a college pursuant to the college's policy on homosexual practice. Bear in mind that in ruling that Alberta was obligated by the Charter to prohibit a college or other employer from discriminating against employees on the basis of sexual orientation, the Court was not saying that Alberta was obligated to prohibit an employer from dismissing employees for engaging in non-marital sexual activity – only that Alberta was obligated to prohibit an employer from discriminating against homosexuals in implementing such a policy. As the Supreme Court of Kentucky understood, a policy against all non-marital sexual activity, heterosexual as well as homosexual, is one thing; a policy against just homosexual sexual activity is something else.

32. Rosemary Ruether, "The Personalization of Sexuality," in Eugene Bianchi & Rosemary Ruether, eds., From Machismo to Mutuality: Essays on Sexism and Woman-Man Liberation 70, 83 (1976) (emphasis added). Cf. Edward Collins Vacek, SJ, "The Meaning of Marriage: Of Two Minds," Commonweal, Oct. 24, 2003, at 17, 18–19: "When, after Vatican II, Catholics began to connect sexual activity more strongly with expressing love than with making babies, it became harder to see how homosexual acts are completely different from heterosexual acts." For a critical comment on one desperate, tortured effort to justify tolerating heterosexual non-marital sex while criminalizing homosexual nonmarital sex, see Andrew Sullivan, "Unnatural Law," New Republic, March 24, 2003, at 18.

None of this means that with respect to non-marital sex, including non-marital sex between two persons of the same sex, anything goes. Consider what Margaret Farley, a Catholic sister and Stark Professor of Christian Ethics at Yale University, has written:

> My answer [to the question of what norms should govern same-sex relations and activities] has been: the norms of justice – the norms which govern all human relationships and those which are particular to the intimacy of sexual relations. Most generally, the norms are respect for persons through respect for autonomy and rationality; respect for relationality through requirements of mutuality, equality, commitment, and fruitfulness. More specifically one might say things like: sex between two persons of the same sex (just as two persons of the opposite sex) should not be used in a way that exploits, objectifies, or dominates; homosexual (like heterosexual) rape, violence, or any harmful use of power against unwilling victims (or those incapacitated by reason of age, etc.) is never justified; freedom, integrity, privacy are values to be affirmed in every homosexual (as heterosexual) relationship; all in all, individuals are not to be harmed, and the common good is to be promoted.

Margaret A. Farley, "An Ethic for Same-Sex Relations," in Robert Nugent, ed., A Challenge to Love: Gay and Lesbian Catholics in the Church 93, 105 (1983). Farley then adds that "[t]he Christian community will want and need to add those norms of faithfulness, forgiveness, of patience and hope, which are essential to any relationships between persons in the Church." Id.

33. See, generally, "Developments – The Law of Marriage and the Family," 116 Harvard L. Rev. 1996, 2004–27 (2003).
34. See id. at 2007–12.
35. "Voters in eighteen states have already passed [constitutional] bans [on same-sex marriage] . . . " Benjamin Wittes, "Marital Differences," Atlantic Monthly, May 2006. The eighteen states are Alaska, Arkansas, Georgia, Kansas, Kentucky, Louisiana, Michigan, Mississippi, Missouri, Montana, Nebraska, Nevada, North Dakota, Ohio, Oklahoma, Oregon, Texas, and Utah. Because "the ballot initiatives have proven to be a major base-mobilizer for conservatives[, and] this year [2006], there will be more. At least six states–Alabama, South Carolina, South Dakota, Tennessee, Virginia, and Wisconsin–will certainly hold referenda, and Arizona and Colorado are likely to do so as well. And given the success such measures have enjoyd at the ballot box, they will probably pass with strong majorities." Id.
36. See Michael J. Perry, Under God? Religious Faith and Liberal Democracy 20–52 (2003).
37. See id. at 55–80. Cf. Nicholas D. Kristof, "Lovers Under the Skin," New York Times, Dec. 3, 2003: "A 1958 poll found that 96 percent of whites disapproved of marriages between blacks and whites. . . . In 1959 a judge justified Virginia's ban on interracial marriage by declaring that 'Almighty God . . . did not intend for the races to mix.' "
38. See, e.g., David G. Meyers & Letha Dawson Scanzoni, What God Has Joined Together? A Christian Case for Gay Marriage (2005).
39. USCCB Administrative Conference, "Statement on Marriage and Homosexual Unions," 33 Origins 257, 259 (2003) (emphasis added).
40. Roderick M. Hills, Jr., "You Say You Want a Revolution? The Case Against the Transformation of Culture Through Nondiscrimination Laws," 95 Michigan L. Rev. 1588, 1610–11 (1997) (citing Roger Scruton, Sexual Desire: A Moral Philosophy of the Erotic 305–11 (1986)).
41. But see Martha C. Nussbaum, "Platonic Love and Colorado Law: The Relevance of Ancient Greek Norms to Modern Sexual Controversies," 80 Virginia L. Rev. 1515, 1601 (1994):

> Scruton's argument was always a peculiar one: for why should one believe that all individuals of one sex are more like each other in quality than any of them is like any member of the opposite sex? And would Scruton really wish to generalize his argument, as consistency seems to demand, preferring relationships between partners different in age, and race, and nationality, and religion? Even if he were to do so, Plato's dialogues offer good argument against him. Along with Aristotle's ethical thought, they argue that people who are alike in the goals they share and the aspirations they cherish may be more likely to promote genuine social goods than people who are unlike in character and who do not share any aspirations. In addition, the dialogues show that the kind of "otherness" that is valuable in love relationships – that one's partner is another separate and, to some extent, hidden world; that the body shows only traces of the soul within; and that lovers never can be completely welded together into a single person – is quite different from the "qualitative" otherness of physiology and character. Indeed, the "otherness" of mystery and separateness is actually defended in Scruton's argument, as it is in Plato's, as an erotic good.

42. Andrew Koppelman has argued that "even in the present regime in which they are not permitted to marry, same-sex couples do not seem to be much less stable than

heterosexual couples. [The] data suggests that same-sex couples are not all that different in terms of their capacity to function or to remain stable from heterosexual couples." Koppelman, "Three Arguments for Gay Rights," 95 Michigan L. Rev. 1636, 1666. See id. at 1664–66.

43. See Andrew Sullivan, "Three's a Crowd," New Republic, June 17, 1996, at 10, 12:

> [M]arriage acts both as an incentive for virtuous behavior – and as a social blessing for the effort. In the past, we have wisely not made nitpicking assessments as to who deserves the right to marry and who does not. We have provided it to anyone prepared to embrace it and hoped for the best. . . . For some, it comes easily. For others, its responsibilities and commitments are crippling. But we do not premise the right to marry upon the ability to perform its demands flawlessly. We accept that human beings are variably virtuous, but that, as citizens, they should be given the same rights and responsibilities – period.

> See also David Brooks, "The Power of Marriage," New York Times, Nov. 22, 2003.

44. See USCCB Administrative Committee, n. 39, at 259. The argument that *even in the short run* legalizing same-sex unions would have subversive consequences for traditional marriage is difficult to take seriously. See Stephen J. Pope, "The Magisterium's Arguments against 'Same-Sex Marriage': An Ethical Analysis and Critique," 65 Theological Studies 530, 555 (2004):

> The magisterium argues that support for marriage, and especially for children, requires opposition to the legal recognition of same-sex marriage. There is, however, no convincing evidence showing that currently functioning gay households are causally related to the deterioration of marriage in the wider society. The biggest threat to marriage comes from the high incidence of divorce that has followed the development of the "no fault" divorce laws of the 1970s.

> See also Stephen J. Pope, "Same-Sex Marriage: Threat or Aspiration?" America, Dec. 6, 2004, at 11.

45. Id. at 559 (citing Judith S. Wallerstein & Sandra Blakeless, The Good Marriage: How and Why Love Lasts (1995)). Cf. Geoffrey Nunberg, "We the People? (In Order to Form a More Perfect Gay Union)," New York Times, Feb. 22, 2004: "For opponents [of recognizing same-sex unions as marriages], broadening the definition of marriage is like opening an exclusive hotel to package tours, with the result that the traditional clientele will no longer feel like checking in."

46. See Jonathan Rauch, "Family's Value: Gay Marriage is Good for Kids," New Republic, May 30, 2005, at 15; Rosemary Radford Ruether, "Marriage Between Homosexuals Is Good for Marriage," National Catholic Rptr., Nov. 18, 2005, at 20.

47. Though evidently skeptical of the argument, Catholic theologian Stephen Pope has suggested that "[i]t is possible for people of good faith to differ on this issue. At the very least, further discussion, investigation, and deliberation are in order." Pope, n. 44, at 562.

48. Berkeley Electronic Press, Issues in Legal Scholarship, Symposium: Single-Sex Marriage (2004), Article 4, <http://www.bepress.com/ils/iss5/art4>.

> In the 1990s, the opponents of same-sex marriage created a new line of argument critique . . . The new line, which has been embraced within the White House and the most anti-gay circles of Capitol Hill, is this: "We love gays and lesbians – but as a society we cannot give them things that would undermine traditional marriage, which is the foundation of America's values and culture. Same-sex marriage would do precisely that – undermine marriage and the nuclear family. For that reason, neutral people should be skeptical of complete equality for these people. . . . We traditionalists love just about

everyone – and look what we've done for homosexuals, we don't put them in jail anymore. But a positive and loving approach requires that we consider the public welfare, especially the welfare of children, our most vulnerable charges. So we cannot go along with the entire 'homosexual agenda,' for it sacrifices a great institution and the public welfare."

Id. at 4.

49. See Editorial, "Bishop Brings Reason to Issue of Gay Benefits," National Catholic Rptr., Nov. 7, 2003, at 24:

[Daniel P.] Reilly[, Roman Catholic bishop of Worcester, Massachusetts,] told legislators that the Massachusetts Catholic Conference, made up of the dioceses of Boston, Worcester, Springfield and Fall River, was unequivocally opposed to legislation that would recognize gay "marriage" or "civil unions." But the church is open, he said, to discussing what public benefits should accrue to those in non-traditional relationships. . . . "If the goal is to look at individual benefits and determine who should be eligible beyond spouses, then we will join the discussion," said Reilly. . . . [Reilly] engaged the issue on the church's terms, saying such benefits are a matter of "distributive justice."

. . .

"Some argue that it is unfair to offer only married couples certain socioeconomic benefits," Reilly told [a committee of Massachusetts legislators]. "That is a different question from the meaning of marriage itself. The civil union bill before this committee confuses the two issues, changing the meaning of spouse in order to give global access to all marital benefits to same-sex partners in a civil union. This alters the institution of marriage by expanding whom the law considers to be spouses. Let's not mix the two issues."

Even more recently, the papal nuncio to Spain, Archbishop Manuel Monteiro de Castro, "has surprised public opinion by defending legal same-sex unions as a 'right.'" See "Nuncio Backs 'Right' to Gay Unions," The Tablet [London], May 15, 2004, at 30: "The nuncio's words took commentators by surprise, as the Spanish bishops officially hold the view that homosexual relationships cannot receive any kind of approval. . . . 'It is right that other types of relationship are recognised,' the nuncio said. He added that those in such unions should have the same rights to social security 'as any other citizen.' But 'let's leave the term "marriage" for that to which it has always referred,' he added." See also "Sign of the Times," America, Nov. 15, 2004, at 4, 5:

Bishop George H. Niederauer of Salt Lake City did not endorse the proposed constitutional amendment in Utah, saying that he believed that state law already prohibited same-sex marriages. He said he shared concerns voiced by all three candidates for attorney general about the amendment's stipulation that "no other domestic union may be recognized as a marriage given the same or substantially equal legal effect."

Cf. Jennifer 8. Lee, "Congressman Says Bush Is Open to States' Bolstering Gay Rights," New York Times, Feb. 9, 2004 ("President Bush believes states can use contract law to ensure some of the rights that gay partners are seeking through marriage or civil union, a South Carolina congressman said Sunday."); Brian Lavery, "Ireland: Premier Backs Rights for Gay Couples," New York Times, Nov. 16, 2004 ("Prime Minister Bertie Ahern said his government might consider giving same-sex couples more rights, which would allow them to benefit from cheaper tax rates and more favorable inheritance laws.").

50. On the analogy of opposition to gay marriage to opposition to interracial marriage, see David E. Rosenbaum, "Legal License: Race, Sex, and Forbidden Unions," New York Times, Dec. 13, 2003; Nicholas D. Kristof, "Marriage: Mix and Match," March 3, 2004; Associated Press, "Blacks Split on Analogies to Gay Marriage," New York Times, Mar. 6, 2004. Cf. Josephine Ross, "The Sexualization of

Difference: A Comparison of Mixed-Race and Same-Gender Marriage," Boston College Law School, Public Law and Legal Theory Research Paper Series (2004), <http://ssrn.com/abstract=508022>.

51. Many countries already extend many or all of the benefits of marriage to same-sex unions (which are sometimes called "marriages"): Belgium (which, however, does not permit same-sex couples to adopt children), Canada, Denmark, Finland, France, Germany, Iceland, Luxembourg, the Netherlands, New Zealand, Norway, Portugal, Spain, South Africa, Sweden, Switzerland, and the United Kingdom. Moreover, the Australian states of New South Wales, Western Australia, and Tasmania and the city of Buenos Aires, Argentina, legally recognize same-sex unions. See Wikipedia: The Free Encyclopedia, <http://en.wikipedia.org/wiki.Same-sex_marriage>.

   Where do things stand in the United States? As of September 2005, while only Massachusetts recognizes same-sex "marriage," "California, Connecticut, the District of Columbia, Hawaii, Maine, New Jersey and Vermont grant persons in same-sex unions a similar legal status to those in a civil marriage by domestic partnership, civil union or reciprocal beneficiary laws." See id. Recently, the Alaska Supreme Court ruled in a unanimous decision that under the state constitution, public employers that grant spousal benefits to opposite-sex married couples must also grant spousal benefits to same-sex couples, notwithstanding that the state constitution specifically disallows same-sex marriage. Alaska Civil Liberties Union v. State of Alaska and Municipality of Anchorage, Supreme Court No. S-10459 (Oct. 28, 2005). By contrast, in the last ten years or so, the following states have amended their constitutions to forbid legal recognition of same-sex marriage: Alaska, Arkansas, Georgia, Kansas, Kentucky, Louisiana, Michigan, Mississippi, Missouri, Montana, Nebraska, Nevada, North Dakota, Ohio, Oklahoma, Oregon, Texas, and Utah. Cf. Associated Press, "Poll: Young Adults Split Over Gay Marriage," New York Times, Nov. 18, 2003:

   > Younger adults are evenly split over gay marriages, but older Americans are opposed by a 4-1 margin, according to a poll examining attitudes about homosexuality. The poll, released [today] by the Pew Research Center for the People & the Press, found that... [w]hile younger people in general were more apt to approve of gay marriage – those between ages 20 and 30 were about evenly split –... among those in their 60s and 70s, opponents outnumbered supporters by more than four to one.... The poll of 1,515 adults was taken Oct. 15–19 by the Pew Research Center on behalf of the Pew Forum on Religion and Public Life. The survey has a sampling error of plus or minus 3 percentage points.

52. See Robert N. Bellah, "Foreword" to Richard L. Smith, AIDS, Gays and the American Catholic Church xii-xiii (1994):

   > A principled rejection of gay sexuality, whether put forward by the church or any other sector of society, is morally indefensible. It has the same status today as arguments for the inferiority of women. To remain stuck in that position, as the church for the time being seems likely to do, is not only unfortunate: it makes the church collaborate in continuing forms of domination. To put it even more strongly: it makes the church collaborate in sin.

53. What about the United States? See, generally, Louis Michael Seidman, Constitutional Law: Equal Protection of the Laws (2003).

54. Cf. James P. Sterba, "Completing Thomas Sowell's Study of Affirmative Action and then Drawing Different Conclusions," 57 Stanford L. Rev. 657, 659 (2004):

   > [A]ffirmative action is a policy of favoring qualified women and minority candidates over qualified men or nonminority candidates with the immediate goals of outreach,

remedying discrimination, or achieving diversity, and the ultimate goals of attaining a color-blind (racially just) and a gender-free (sexually just) society.

55. See Beth McMurtrie, "The Quota Quandary: The United States Is Not the Only Country Struggling with Affirmative Action in University Admissions," The Chronicle of Higher Education, Feb. 13, 2004; Marion Lloyd, "In Brazil, a New Debate Over Color," The Chronicle of Higher Education, Feb. 13, 2004; Martha Ann Overland, "In India, Almost Everyone Wants to Be Special," The Chronicle of Higher Education, Feb. 13, 2004; David Cohen, "In Malaysia, the End of Quotas," The Chronicle of Higher Education, Feb. 13, 2004.

56. Jeremy Rabkin, "Private Preferences: Why Affirmative Action Won't Disappear Anytime Soon," American Spectator, November 1998, 62, 63.

57. Gratz v. Bollinger, 539 U.S. 244, 302 (2003) (Ginsburg, J., joined by Souter, J., dissenting). Cf. id. at 301: "The [U.S.] Constitution instructs all who act for the government that they may not deny to any person . . . the equal protection of the laws.' Amdt. 14, §1. In implementing this equality instruction, . . . government decisionmakers may properly distinguish between policies of exclusion and inclusion." Steven Carter has written that "whatever the source of racism, to count it the same as racialism, to say that two centuries of struggle about the most basic of civil rights has been mostly about freedom from racial categorization rather than about freedom from racial oppression, is to trivialize the lives and deaths of those who have suffered under racism." Stephen L. Carter, "When Victims Happen to Be Black," 97 Yale 420, 433–34 (1988).

58. Grutter v. Bollinger, 539 U.S. 306, 344 (2003) (Ginsburg, joined by Breyer, J., concurring) (citing Annex to G.A. Res. 2106, 20 U.N. GAOR Res. Supp. (No. 14) 47, U.N. Doc. A/6014, Art. 2(2) (1965)).

59. Fali Sam Nariman, "The Indian Constitution: An Experiment in Unity Amid Diversity," in Robert A. Goldwin et al., Forging Unity Out of Diversity: The Approaches of Eight Nations 7, 12 (1985).

60. Marc Galanter, Law and Society in Modern India 261 (1989).

61. Id. at 263.

62. Id.

63. Saras Jagwanth, "Affirmative Action in a Transformative Context: The South African Experience," 36 Connecticut L. Rev. 725, 730 (2004).

64. Nor does it mean that in the United States, there are no constitutionally sufficient reasons for the Supreme Court to do what it does: subject government's reliance on any program of race-based affirmative action to a heavy burden of justification ("strict scrutiny"). See, e.g., [Michigan cases]. Indeed, I've concluded elsewhere that there are constitutionally sufficient reasons for the Court to do so. See Michael J. Perry, We the People: The Fourteenth Amendment and the Supreme Court 97–115 (1999).

65. For the reader interested in pursuing that question, this is an excellent place to begin: James P. Sterba, "Completing Thomas Sowell's Study of Affirmative Action and then Drawing Different Conclusions," 57 Stanford L. Rev. 657 (2004). For a competing perspective, with specific reference to higher education, see Larry Alexander & Maimon Schwarzschild, "Grutter or Otherwise: Racial Preferences and Higher Education," 21 Constitutional Commentary 3 (2004).

CHAPTER 8. PROTECTING HUMAN RIGHTS IN A DEMOCRACY: WHAT ROLE
FOR THE COURTS?

1. See Introduction at x–xi.
2. State v. Makwanyane, Constitutional Court of the Republic of South Africa, 1995, Case No. CCT/3/94, [1995] 1 LRC 269.
3. See chapter 9, n. 34.
4. What about a country that is not a liberal democracy but a dictatorship – Belarus, for example: What role should the courts of such a country play in protecting human rights? The question is naive:

> [W]here governments are authoritarian and repressive, where violations are serious, systemic, and brutal, courts are least relevant. Relative to Western democracies, the judiciary's competence to review executive or legislative action may be sharply reduced or eliminated, its jurisdiction limited, its judges subjected to threat or worse, No human rights revolution was ever achieved by court decree. The struggle for human rights becomes fully political, even fully military. In many states, then, courts will be at best marginal actors on human rights issues.

Henry J. Steiner & Philip Alston, International Human Rights in Context vi–vii (2d ed. 2000).

5. This important story has been well told elsewhere. See, e.g., Douglas Greenberg et al., eds., Constitutionalism & Democracy: Transitions in the Contemporary World (1993). See also Stephen Gardbaum, "The New Commonwealth Model of Constitutionalism," 49 American J. Comparative Law 707, 711–18 (2001). Cf. John Frerejohn & Pasquale Pasquino, "Constitutional Adjudication: Lessons from Europe," 82 Texas. L. Rev. 1671 (2004); Michel Rosenfeld, "Constitutional Adjudication in Europe and the United States: Paradoxes and Contrasts," 2 I-CON 633 (2004); Mark Tushnet, "Marbury v. Madison Around the World," 71 Tennessee L. Rev. 251 92004).
6. See Constitution of the Republic of South Africa (1996), Chapter 2 ("Bill of Rights"); Chapter 8 ("Courts and Administration of Justice"). See also Christina Murray, "A Constitutional Beginning: Making South Africa's Final Constitution," 23 U. Arkansas at Little Rock L. Rev. 809 (2001); Martin Chanock, "A Post-Calvinist Catechism or a Post-Communist Manifesto? Intersecting Narratives in the South Africa Bill of Rights Debate," in Philip Alston, ed., Promoting Human Rights Through Bills of Rights: Comparative Perspectives 392 (1999). In her essay, Murray reports these interesting details:

> In March 1997, about seven million copies of the new constitution in pocket book size were distributed in South Africa. Four million went to high schools, two million were made available at post offices and another million were distributed to the police, army, prisons, and through civil organizations. These copies of the constitution were available in all eleven official languages and were accompanied by an illustrated guide, You and the Constitution, which, in thirty cheerfully illustrated pages, provided an introduction to the constitution. Murray, supra, at 837.

It is noteworthy that in the post-World War II period, the democracies of Europe have empowered the European Court of Human Rights to enforce the limitations on government power set forth in the European Convention for the Protection of Human Rights and Fundamental Freedoms. See, generally, Mark Janis, Richard Kay & Anthony Bradley, eds., European Human Rights Law: Text and Materials 64–92 (2d ed. 2000).

7. See C. Neal Tate & Torbjörn Vallinder, eds., The Global Expansion of Judicial Power (1995).

8. C. Neal Tate & Torbjörn Vallinder, "The Global Expansion of Judicial Power: The Judicialization of Politics," in Tate & Vallinder, The Global Expansion of Judicial Power, n. 7, 1, 5.

9. Id. To say that there has been a "judicialization of politics" is not to say that there has been a "judicial usurpation of politics." There has not been a usurpation, because in Canada, South Africa, the United Kingdom, and so on, it is not the courts themselves that have been the agents of judicialization but the political representatives of the people. Elsewhere, I've addressed the argument that in the modern period of American constitutional law, many important U.S. Supreme Court decisions about constitutional rights involve "the judicial usurpation of politics." See Michael J. Perry, We the People: The Fourteenth Amendment and the Supreme Court (1999).

10. Vicki C. Jackson & Mark Tushnet, Comparative Constitutional Law 414 (1999).

11. Chanock, n. 6, at 394.

12. On "welfare" rights, see the Postscript to this chapter.

13. Australia, New Zealand, and the United Kingdom are exceptions – although, now, the United Kingdom is arguably more an *apparent* exception than a *real* one, as I explain in the Appendix to this chapter. For a vigorous argument in defense of the status quo in Australia, see James Allan, "A Defense of the *Status Quo*," in Tom Campbell et al, eds., Protecting Human Rights: Instruments and Institutions (2003). See also James Allan, "Rights, Paternalism, Constitutions and Judges," in Grant Huscroft & Paul Rishworth, eds., Litigating Rights: Perspectives from Domestic and International Law 29 (2002). For an argument in opposition to the status quo in Australia, see Dianne Otto, "Addressing Homelessness: Does Australia's Indirect Implementation of Human Rights Comply with Its International Obligations," in Campbell et al., Protecting Human Rights, supra this note. For an argument that New Zealand ought to establish a system of judicial review like Canada's (I discuss Canada's system later in this chapter), see Andrew S. Butler, "Judicial Review, Human Rights and Democracy," in Huscroft & Rishworth, supra this note, at 47. See also G. W. G. Leane, "Enacting Bills of Rights: Canada and the Curious Case of New Zealand's 'Thin' Democracy," 26 Human Rights Quarterly 152 (2004). But cf. James Allan, "The Effect of a Statutory Bill of Rights where Parliament is Sovereign: The Lesson from New Zealand," in Tom Campbell at al., eds., Sceptical Essays on Human Rights, 375 (2002).

Frank Michelman has inquired in correspondence whether the regime I mean to defend in this chapter is one in which courts protect the human rights that, as a moral-realist matter, exist – or, instead, one in which courts protect the human rights (human-rights-claims) that the citizens of a liberal democracy have entrenched in their fundamental law. The latter. Indeed, although I am a moral realist, I am wary about moral-rights-talk, as distinct from legal-rights-talk. I addressed this issue in the Introduction to this book.

In any event, I doubt that there is a persuasive argument for a regime in which courts protect the human rights that, as a moral-realist matter, exist. I concur in the judgment of William J. Brennan, Jr., that if in a liberal democracy, courts are to wield the power to protect human rights, it is important that the rights be articulated in legal texts. In his H. L. A. Hart Lecture in Jurisprudence and Moral

Philosophy, delivered on May 24, 1989 at University College, Oxford, Justice Brennan
explained:

> But if America's experience demonstrates that paper protections are not a sufficient guar-
> antor of liberty, it also suggests that they are a necessary one, particularly in times of crisis.
> Without a textual anchor for their decisions, judges would have to rely on some theory of
> natural right, or some allegedly shared standard of the ends and limits of government, to
> strike down invasive legislation. But an appeal to normative ideals that lack any mooring
> in the written law . . . would in societies like ours be suspect, because it would represent so
> profound an aberration from majoritarian principles. . . . A text, moreover, is necessary
> not only to make judges' decisions efficacious: it also helps tether their discretion. I would
> be the last to cabin judges' power to keep the law vital, to ensure that it remains abreast of the
> progress in man's intellect and sensibilities. Unbounded freedom, however, is another mat-
> ter. One can imagine a system of governance that accorded judges almost unlimited discre-
> tion, but it would be one reminiscent of the rule by Platonic Guardians that Judge Learned
> Hand so feared. It is not one, I think, that would gain allegiance in either of our countries.

William J. Brennan Jr., "Why Have a Bill of Rights?," 9 Oxford J. Legal Studies 425,
432 (1989). See also Thomas B. McAffee, "The Constitution as Based on the Consent
of the Governed – Or, Should We Have an Unwritten Constitution?" 80 Oregon L.
Rev. 1245 (2001).

   Assume for the sake of discussion that there are moral (as distinct from legal)
human rights. One might be tempted to say, at this point, that if (a) the moral human
rights that the citizens of a liberal democracy – Canada, say – have concluded that
there are and have articulated in their fundamental law bear little if any relation to
(b) the moral human rights that there really are, then the courts, in protecting the
articulated, putative moral human rights, wouldn't be protecting the moral human
rights that there really are. The opposition between (a) and (b), however, is miscon-
ceived. One should say, instead, that if (a) the moral human rights that most citizens
of Canada have concluded that there are and have articulated in their fundamental
law bear little if any relation to (b) the moral human rights that other, dissenting
citizens believe that there really are, then the Canadian courts, in protecting the
articulated, putative moral human rights, wouldn't be protecting the moral human
rights that the dissenting citizens believe that there really are. True enough. But there
is little, if any reason, to doubt that most of the basic human rights articulated in
virtually every post-World War II liberal-democratic constitution as well as in the
basic international human rights documents bear not a remote but a close relationship to the moral human rights that most liberal democrats, if they believe in moral
human rights at all, believe that there really are. (Of course, this is not to say that
all the moral human rights that they believe that there are, are articulated in each
such constitution or document, or that every right articulated in each such constitution or document is one they believe to be a moral human right.) There is little
reason to doubt, too, therefore, that if courts protect the human rights articulated
in those constitutions and documents, they will be protecting many of the moral
human rights that liberal democrats, if they believe in moral human rights, believe
that there really are.
14. Larry A. Alexander, "Constitutionalism," in Martin P. Golding & William A.
    Edmundson, eds., The Blackwell Guide to the Philosophy of Law and Legal Theory
    248, 255 (2004).

15. I assume in this chapter that the judges of the courts about which we are speaking should be and are – by law, culture, or both – politically independent, in this sense: As a general matter, the judges could reasonably be expected to decide rights cases without regard to the preferences of the government, of one or another political party, or of anyone else. The Constitution of the Republic of South Africa (1996) is explicit about this. Section 165 ("Judicial Authority") provides in relevant part: "The courts are independent and subject only to the Constitution and law, which they must apply impartially and without fear, favour or prejudice. . . . No person or organ of the state may interefere with the functioning of the courts. . . . Organs of state, through legislative and other measures, must assist and protect the courts to ensure the independence, impartiality, dignity, accessibility and effectiveness of the courts." That a judge is politically independent in this sense does not mean that her decisions would not be animated in part by her political-moral values. Moreover, that we should want judges to be politically independent does not mean that we should want them, in deciding cases, to ignore their political-moral values altogether; at least, it does not mean that we believe that they will or even can ignore their values altogether.

16. One could ask the same question about entrenched legal norms that are not "human rights" norms; in the United States, for example, one could ask the same question about "separation of powers" norms, or about "federalism" norms. See, e.g., Jesse Choper, Judicial Review and the National Political Process: A Functional Reconsideration of the Supreme Court (1980). In this chapter, however, I am interested only in entrenched legal norms of a certain sort: norms that protect human beings from violations and/or unwarranted suffering.

   Notice how different the inquiry in the text accompanying this note is from the question of whether the citizens of a liberal democracy ever did give courts such a power. In the United States, it is famously controversial whether "We the People" ever did give the Supreme Court of the United States the power of judicial review, much less the power of judicial supremacy. See, e.g., Larry Kramer, The People Themselves: Popular Constitutionalism and Judicial Review (2004).

17. See Kent Greenawalt, "How Law Can be Determinate," 31 UCLA L. Rev. 1, 29 (1990): "Few, if any, writers have asserted the most extreme thesis about indeterminacy – that no legal questions have determinate answers – in clear terms, and almost no one may actually believe that thesis . . . " See also Benjamin N. Cardozo, The Nature of the Judicial Process 129 (1921): "In countless litigations, the law is so clear that judges have no discretion. They have the right to legislate within gaps, but often there are no gaps. We shall have a false view of the landscape if we look at the waste spaces only, and refuse to see the acres already sown and fruitful."

18. See Janis, Kay, & Bradley, n. 6, at 467–68 & 488–503. Even if a signatory to the European Convention has not incorporated the Convention into its domestic law, so that the Convention is not enforceable against the signatory by its own courts, the Convention is enforceable against the signatory by the European Court of Human Rights.

19. Perhaps "underdeterminate" would be the better term. See Lawrence Solum, "On the Indeterminacy Crisis: Critiquing Critical Dogma," 54 U. Chicago L. Rev. 462, 473 (1987).

20. Articulating some rights in terms that are relatively indeterminate makes good sense. See Brennan, n. 13, at 426. See also Perry, We the People, n. 9, at 29–30 (foonote material in brackets):

> The fact of legal indeterminacy – and the need, therefore, for specification – is one thing, its value another: Why might a political community, or its representatives, want to establish an indeterminate norm (a norm indeterminate in a significant number of the contexts that implicate it)? Why not issue only determinate norms? Discussing the matter of rules – in particular, legal rules – H. L. A. Hart emphasized that "a feature of the human predicament . . . that we labour under . . . whenever we seek to regulate, unambiguously and in advance, some sphere of conduct by means of general standards to be used without further official directions on particular occasions . . . is our relative ignorance of fact . . . [and] our relative indeterminacy of aim." [H. L. A. Hart, The Concept of Law 128 (2d ed. 1994).] Given that "feature of the human predicament", it makes sense that many legal (and other) norms are relatively indeterminate. "If the world in which we live were characterized only by a finite number of features, and these together with all the modes in which they could combine were known to us, then provision could be made in advance for every possibility. We could make rules, the application of which to particular cases never called for a further choice. Everything could be known, and for everything, since it could be known, something could be done and specified in advance by rule. . . . Plainly this world is not our world. . . . This inability to anticipate brings with it a relative indeterminacy of aim." [Id.] The point is not that (relatively) determinate norms cannot be achieved. [They can. One way to do so, writes Hart, "is to freeze the meaning of the rule so that its general terms must have the same meaning in every case where its application is in question. To secure this we may fasten on certain features present in the plain case and insist that these are both necessary and sufficient to bring anything which has them within the scope of the rule, whatever other features it may have or lack, and whatever may be the social consequences of applying the rule in this way." Id. at 129.] The point, rather, is that determinacy ought not always to be a goal. [This is not to say that determinacy ought never to be a goal: "To escape this oscillation between extremes we need to remind ourselves that human inability to anticipate the future, which is at the root of this indeterminacy, varies in degree in different fields of conduct . . . " Id. at 130–31. See id. at 130 et seq.] To achieve determinacy is sometimes "to secure a measure of certainty or predictability at the cost of blindly prejudging what is to be done in a range of future cases, about whose composition we are ignorant. We shall thus succeed in settling in advance, but also in the dark, issues which can only reasonably be settled when they arise and are identified." [Id. at 129–30.] We who "do ordain and establish this Constitution for the United States of America" have long understood Hart's point. Some norms comprised by the Constitution are "not rules for the passing hour," as Cardozo put it, "but principles for an expanding future. Insofar as it deviates from that standard, and descends into details and particulars, [a constitution] loses its flexibility, the scope of interpretation contracts, the meaning hardens. While it is true to its function, it maintains its power of adaptation, its suppleness, its play." [Benjamin N. Cardozo, The Nature of the Judicial Process 83–84 (1921).]

21. The Federalist Papers 229 (Clinton Rossiter ed. 1961). See Kim Lane Scheppele, Legal Secrets 94–95 (1988): "Generally in the literature on interpretation the question being posed is, What does a particular text (or social practice) *mean*? Posed this way, the interpretive question gives rise to an embarassing multitude of possible answers, a cacophony of theories of interpretation. . . . [The] question that (in practice) is the one actually asked in the course of lawyering and judging [is]: what . . . does a particular text mean *for the specific case at hand?*"

In *Truth and Method*, Hans-Georg Gadamer commented on the process of specification both in law and in theology:

> In both legal and theological hermeneutics there is the essential tension between the text set down – of the law or of the proclamation – on the one hand and, on the other, the sense arrived at by its application in the particular moment of interpretation, either in judgment or in preaching. A law is not there to be understood historically, but to be made concretely valid through being interpreted. Similarly, a religious proclamation is not there to be understood as a merely historical document, but to be taken in a way in which it exercises its saving effect. This includes the fact that the text, whether law or gospel, if it is to be understood properly, i.e., according to the claim it makes, must be understood at every moment, in every particular situation, in a new and different way. Understanding here is always application.

Hans-Georg Gadamer, Truth and Method 275 (Eng. trans. 1975).

22. "Applying," in a particular context, a norm determinate in that context should not be confused with "specifying," in a particular context, a norm indeterminate in that context. To rule that a municipal ordinance that by its terms governs "automobiles" governs "Toyota Camrys" is, as I am using the terms, to "apply" the ordinance, not to "specify" it. By contrast, to construe a constitutional provision that forbids government to prohibit any religious practice absent a compelling justification, to forbid North Carolina to prohibit the sacramental use of wine at Mass is to "specify" the (concrete, contextual meaning of the) provision. Of course, there can be cases in which it is difficult to administer the application/specification distinction.

23. Neil MacCormick, "Reconstruction after Deconstruction: A Response to CLS," 10 Oxford J. Legal Studies 539, 548 (1990). Where I've used the term "specification," MacCormick uses the Latin term "determinatio," borrowing it from John Finnis: "John Finnis has to good effect re-deployed St Thomas' concept of determinatio; Hans Kelsen's translators used the term 'concretization' to much the same effect." Id. (citing John Finnis, "On the Critical Legal Studies Movement," 30 American J. Jurisprudence 21, 23–25 (1985), and Hans Kelsen, The Pure Theory of Law 230 (Eng. trans. 1967)).

24. Put another way, it is the challenge of deciding how best to avoid the political-moral disvalue at the heart of the right.

25. Richard A. Posner, "What Am I? A Potted Plant?" New Republic, Sept. 28, 1987, at 23, 24. What Anthony Kronman has said of the process of "judgment" accurately describes the process of specifying an indeterminate legal norm. Such specification is a species of judgment.

> Good judgment, and its opposite, are in fact most clearly revealed in just those situations where the method of deduction is least applicable, where the ambiguities are greatest and the demand for proof most obviously misplaced. To show good judgment in such situations is to do something more than merely apply a general rule with special care and thoroughness, or follow out its consequences to a greater level of detail. Judgment often requires such analytic refinement but does not consist in it alone. That this is so is to be explained by the fact that we are most dependent on our judgment, most in need of good judgment, in just those situations that pose genuine dilemmas by forcing us to choose between, or otherwise accommodate, conflicting interests and obligations whose conflict is not itself amenable to resolution by the application of some higher-order rule. It is here that the quality of a person's judgment comes most clearly into view and here, too, that his or her deductive powers alone are least likely to prove adequate to the task.

Anthony Kronmann, "Living in the Law," 54 U. Chicago L. Rev. 835, 847–48 (1987).

The process of specifying a norm that is, in a particular context, indeterminate should not be confused with the different process of decoding a text that is obscure. Although both processes may be said to be processes of "interpretation", interpreting a norm, *in the sense of specifying the norm*, is not the same as interpreting a text, *in the sense of decoding the text*. Interpretation-as-specification is a different activity from interpretation-as-decoding. For a further comment on the distinction, see n. 21.

26. One kind of entrenched right against government is a right to have government do what is necessary to protect one from harm at the hands of nongovernmental ("private") actors. So to say that a right is, by its terms, a right "against government" is not to deny that protecting the right may be a way of protecting one from a nongovernmental harm.

27. For a recent example of the argument, see Erwin Chemerinsky, "In Defense of Judicial Review: A Reply to Professor Kramer," 92 California L. Rev. 1013 (2004). See also Aileen Kavanagh, "The Role of a Bill of Rights in Reconstructing Northern Ireland," 26 Human Rights Quarterly 956, 959 (1004): "[T]he advantages of [an entrenched] Bill of Rights are of special value in the context of a diverse and divided society such as Northern Ireland, in terms of empowering individuals and minorities to challenge legislation, constraining the majoritarian will, and contributing to the common good and the articulation of common, public values . . . "

28. See Mac Darrow & Philip Alston, "Bills of Rights in Comparative Perspective," in Philip Alston, n. 6, at 521–23; Saras Jagwanth, "The South African Experience of Judicial Rights Discourse: A Critical Appraisal," in Campbell, Sceptical Essays on Human Rights, n. 13, at 297 (arguing that as important as judicial review undeniably is in the new South Africa, it is not enough).

29. See, e.g., Louis Fisher, "Nonjudicial Safeguards for Religious Liberty," 70 U. Cincinnati L. Rev. 31, 92 (2001):

> The Supreme Court has competed with nonjudicial institutions for two hundred years, sometimes leading the charge for minority rights, but more often pulling up the rear. Interest groups mobilize to apply pressure to whatever branch is the most responsive to their needs. At times the courts satisfy interest group claims, and on other occasions it is the elected branches. No single branch, including the judiciary, can lay claim to having the last word, especially not in the volatile world of religious politics.

Cf. Stephen M. Griffin, "Has the Hour of Democracy Come Round at Last? The New Critique of Judicial Review," 17 Constitutional Commentary 683, 685–86 (2000): "Any fair description of the institutional environment of judicial review has to account . . . for the phenomenon of Congress on at least occasion having greater solicitide for individual rights than the supposedly rights-conscious judiciary."

30. At a conference at Harvard Law School on the occasion of the bicentennial of the birth of John Marshall, Henry Hart commented on Learned Hand's famous statement that "[a] society so riven that the spirit of moderation is gone, no court can save; . . . a society where that spirit flourishes no court need save." Quoted in Hart, Comment, in Arthur E. Sunderland, ed., Government Under Law 140 (1956). Hart said: "[T]he statement is an example – a rather clear example – of the fallacy of the undistributed middle." Id. He explained:

> What the sentence assumes is that there are two kinds of societies – one kind, over here, in which the spirit of moderation flourishes, and another kind, over here,

which is riven by dissension. Neither kind, Judge Hand says, can be helped very much by the courts. But, of course, that isn't what societies are like. In particular, it isn't what American society is like. A society is a [sic] something in process – in the process of becoming. It has always within it, as ours does, seeds of dissension. And it also has within it forces making for moderation and mutual accommodation. The question – the relevant question – is whether the courts have a significant contribution to make in pushing American society in the direction of moderation – not by themselves; of course they can't save us by themselves; but in combination with other institutions. Once the question is put that way, the answer, it seems to me, has to be yes.

Id. at 140–41. I am grateful to Ken Karst for calling this passage to my attention.

31. See Sir Gerard Brennan, "The Impact of a Bill of Rights on the Role of the Judiciary: An Australian Perspective," in Alston, n. 6, at 454, 463–64; Mac Darrow & Philip Alston, "Bills of Rights in Comparative Perspective," in id. at 465, 485; Richard A. Posner, "Review of Jeremy Waldron, Law and Disagreement," 100 Columbia L. Rev. 582, 592 (2000).

32. See Robert Dahl, Pluralist Democracy in the United States: Conflict and Consent 131 (1967) ("[C]ongressional leaders rely mainly on persuasion, party loyalty, expectations of reciprocal treatment, and, occasionally, special inducements such as patronage or public works. But none of these is likely to be adequate if a member is persuaded that a vote to support his party will cost him votes among his constituents. . . . Fortunately, for him, the mores of Congress, accepted by the leaders themselves, are perfectly clear on this point: His own election comes first."); David Mayhew, Congress: The Electoral Connection 101–02 (1974) ("[L]eaders in both houses [of the Congress] have a habit of counselling their members to 'vote their constituencies.'"); "The World of Congress," Newsweek, Apr. 24, 1989, at 28 ("Congressmen are obsessed with . . . losing an election. . . . 'Everybody here checks their spines in the cloakroom,' says Rep. Patricia Schroeder. Shorn of significant party connections, each member is his own political and policy operator. But these legislators are the world's only entrepreneurs devoted to shunning risk. Among the favorite words in everyday Capitol Hill conversation is 'cover'; it's a noun meaning a position on an issue that is structured so as to avoid any political cost."); "Congress: It Doesn't Work. Let's Fix It," Business Week, Apr. 16, 1990, at 54, 56 ("Nothing motivates members of Congress like the fear of doing something that might be criticized. So all too often they do nothing.").

33. Consider what Walter Lippman wrote a half century ago:

> With exceptions so rare that they are regarded as miracles and freaks of nature, successful democratic politicians are insecure and intimidated men. They advance politically only as they placate, appease, bribe, seduce, bamboozle, or otherwise manage to manipulate the demanding and threatening elements of their constituencies. The decisive consideration is not whether the proposition is good but whether it is popular – not whether it will work well and prove itself but whether the active talking constituents like it immediately.

Walter Lippman, The Public Philosophy 27 (1955).

34. See Keith E. Whittington, "In Defense of Legislatures," 28 Political Theory 690, 699 (2000).

35. See Darrow & Alston, n. 28, at 487 et seq. See also Whittington, n. 34, at 699.

36. Lord Scarman, "Britain and the Protection of Human Rights," New Zealand L. J. 175, 177 (1984).

37. Darrow & Alston, n. 28, at 493.
38. Quoted in Steiner & Alston, n. 4, at 48. Ken Karst has emphasized this point in his work. See Kenneth L. Karst, Belonging to America: Equal Citizenship and the Constitution 222 et seq. (1989).
39. William G. Ross, A Muted Fury: Populists, Progressives, and Labor Unions Confront the Court, 1890–1937 203 (1994) (quoting Robert A. Shortall, "The Supreme Court and Congress," America, Nov. 8, 1924, at 95). However realistic or not this view was in 1924, is the view realistic today? Or is the view too cynical about Congress and insufficiently cynical about the Supreme Court? If the view were extended to state legislatures and to courts generally – or at least to federal courts – would the view be too cynical about legislatures and insufficiently cynical about (federal) courts? Listen to Judge Posner:

> Waldron is not sufficiently realistic about the legislative process. He has too starry-eyed a view of it.... [We should recognize] that federal judges are insulated from most of the political pressures that beset elected legislatures; that these pressures sometimes reflect selfish, parochial interests, ugly emotion, ignorance, irrational fears, and prejudice; and that the judges' insulation, together with the tradition and usages of the bench and the fact that the higher federal judges are screened for competence and integrity, may confer on the judiciary a power of detached and intelligent reflection on policy issues that is a valuable complement to the consideration of these issues by ordinary lawmakers. It is even possible that an appointive judiciary such as the federal may give representation to interests that the electoral process ignores because they are not in coalition with any politically effective group.

Posner, "Review of Jeremy Waldron," n. 31, at 591. See also Alexander M. Bickel, The Least Dangerous Branch: The Supreme Court at the Bar of Politics 24–25 (1962):

> [M]any actions of government have two aspects: their immediate, necessarily intended, practical effects, and their perhaps unintended or unappreciated bearing on values we hold to have more general and permanent interest. It is a premise we deduce not merely from the fact of a written constitution but from the history of the race, and ultimately as a moral judgment of the good society, that government should serve not only what we conceive from time to time to be our immediate material needs but also certain enduring values. This in part is what is meant by government under law. But such values do not present themselves ready-made. They have a past always, to be sure, but they must be continually derived, enunciated, and seen in relevant application. And it remains to ask which institution of our government – if any single one in particular – should be the pronouncer and guardian of such values.
>
> Men in all walks of public life are able occasionally to perceive this second aspect of public questions. Sometimes they are also able to base their decisions on it; that is one of the things we like to call acting on principle. Often they do not do so, however, particularly when they sit in legislative assemblies. There, when the pressure for immediate results is strong enough and emotions ride high enough, men will ordinarily prefer to act on expediency rather than take the long view. Possibly legislators – everything else being equal – are as capable as other men of following the path of principle, where the path is clear or at any rate discernible. Our system, however, like all secular systems, calls for the evolution of principle in novel circumstances, rather than only for its mechanical application. Not merely respect for the rule of established principles but the creative establishment and renewal of a coherent body of principled rules – that is what our legislatures have proven themselves ill equipped to give us.

The question of whether to empower courts to protect rights is in part a question about comparative institutional competence. It is worth noting, therefore, that along a number of dimensions, courts in a liberal democracy may be better suited than either the legislative or executive branch of government to engage in the careful, systematic development of coherent, concrete human rights doctrines over time. With respect to the issue of coherence of doctrine over time, and in the context of the United States, Henry Hart and Herbert Wechsler observed:

> Both Congress and the President can obviously contribute to the sound interpretation of the Constitution. But are they, or can they be, so organized and manned as to be able, without aid from the courts, to build up a body of coherent and intelligible constitutional principle, and to carry public conviction that these principles are being observed? In respect of experience and temperament of personnel? Of procedure for decision? Of means of recording grounds of decision? Of opportunity for close examination of particular questions?

Paul Bator, Paul Mishkin, David Shapiro & Herbert Wechsler, Hart & Wechsler's The Federal Courts and the Federal System 82 (2d ed. 1973). With respect to the issue of concreteness of doctrine, Alexander Bickel wrote:

> [An] advantage that courts have is that questions of principle never carry the same aspect for them as they did for the legislature or the executive. Statutes, after all, deal typically with abstract or dimly foreseen problems. The courts are concerned with the flesh and blood of an actual case. This tends to modify, perhaps to lengthen, everyone's view. It also provides an extremely salutary proving ground for all abstractions; it is conducive, in a phrase of Holmes, to thinking things, not words, and thus to the evolution of principle by a process that tests as it creates.

Bickel, supra, at note 26. So, the goal of a sensible division of political labor – a division sensitive to different institutions' relative strengths and weaknesses – offers additional support for empowering courts to protect entrenched, indeterminate rights.

40. This is certainly not to say that no one is skeptical about the argument. Robert Nagel and Mark Tushnet, for example, are prominent skeptics. In commenting on a draft of this chapter, Nagel wrote that "[t]he fact that courts do not have certain deficiencies common to democratic processes does not necessarily demonstrate anything about the appropriateness of the kind of decision making that courts do engage in. . . . [S]uppose judges are not influenced by powerful electoral constituencies but instead are influenced by powerful professional reference groups whose methodologies and values also produce suboptimal results?" E-mail from Robert Nagel to Michael Perry, Apr. 9, 2002. Cf. Robert F. Nagel, Constitutional Cultures: The Mentality and Consequences of Judicial Review (1989).

In Mark Tushnet's view, the question whether judicial protection of rights is, on balance, a good idea or a bad one "is ultimately empirical. . . . [Y]ou have to compare the number and importance of the occasions on which legislatures get the right and wrong answers to the number and importance of the occasions on which courts get the right and wrong answers." E-mail from Mark Tushnet to Michael Perry, Apr. 5, 2002. (In support and elaboration of this point, Tushnet called my attention to this essay: Wojciech Sadurski, "Judicial Review and the Protection of Constitutional Rights," 22 Oxford J. Legal Studies 275 (2002).) According to Tushnet, the argument for empowering courts to protect rights does not pay sufficient heed to the number and importance of occasions on which legislatures get the right answers and the number and importance of occasions on which courts get the wrong answers.

In addressing Tushnet's "ultimately empirical" question, however, we must be wary about generalizing across different countries. The United States is not Canada is not the United Kingdom is not South Africa is not India – and so on. Similarly, we must be wary about generalizing across different historical periods. Notice, moreover, that the question is at least partly counterfactual: "What would the legislature have done, in [specify country], during [specify historical period], if there had been no judicial review?" Or: "What would the courts have done... if there had been judicial review?" I don't know how one can hope to answer such questions with anything approaching confidence. And if one can't, then one must decide – that is, a liberal democracy must decide – how to resolve the doubt: in favor of judicial protection of rights, or against it.

41. Richard H. Pildes, "Forms of Formalism," 66 U. Chicago L. Rev. 607, 613 (1999).

42. See Constitution of the Republic of South Africa, Chapter 2 ("Bill of Rights"); Chapter 8 ("Courts and Administration of Justice").

43. Mark Tushnet, "Judicial Activism or Restraint in a Section 33 World," 52 U. Toronto L. J. 65 (2003) (review of Kent Roach, The Supreme Court on Trial: Judicial Activism or Democratic Dialogue? (2001)).

44. Darrow and Alston Mule, and respond to, several arguments about why empowering courts to protect rights is problematic: it leads to the judicialization of politics; it also leads – indeed, it *therefore* leads – to the politicization of the judiciary; it contributes to an exaggerated "rights-consciousness," which is a bad thing; judges are, in general, too conservative to protect rights; litigation is too costly a vehicle for protecting rights. See Darrow & Alston, n. 28, at 511 et seq.

45. The idea of democracy at work in this claim is Shumpeterian:

> [Joseph] Shumpeter... proposes the following, more modest definition of democracy: "the democratic method is that institutional arrangement for arriving at political decisions in which individuals acquire the power to decide by means of a competitive struggle for the people's vote." The people influence political decisions by voting in elections and "do not control their political leaders in any way except by refusing to reelect them or the parliamentary majorities that support them."...
>
> The politician is vulnerable to losing his office unless he continuously manages to attract votes. This creates an incentive for him to pay attention to what voters want. And this incentive guarantees that, in a democracy, the government will not act in a way that attracts the wrath of an electoral majority – or, if it does, that it won't keep it up for long.

Andrew Koppelman, "Talking to the Boss: On Robert Bennett and the Counter-Majoritarian Difficulty," 95 Northwestern U.L. Rev. 955, 956–57 (2001) (quoting Joseph A. Shumpeter, Capitalism, Socialism, and Democracy (3d ed. 1950)). According to Koppelman, "[Joseph] Shumpeter is entirely free of... mushy sentimentalism about majoritarianism..." Id. at 956.

46. Jeremy Waldron, "A Right-Based Critique of Constitutional Right," 13 Oxford J. Legal Studies 18, 50–51 (1993). For Waldron's more recent, extended discussion of the issues, see Jeremy Waldron, Law and Disagreement, chs. 10–13 (1999).

47. For a discussion of such an argument, see Darrow & Alston, n. 28, at 498 et seq.

48. Cf. Waldron, n. 46, at 28 (criticizing the "disabling of representative institutions"). Waldron has argued that "once it becomes unclear or controversial what the people have committed themselves to, there is no longer any basis in the idea of precommitment for defending a particular interpretation against democratic objections."

Waldron, Law and Disagreement, n. 46, at 266; see id. at 255–81. Waldron's argument seems to me irrefutable.

49. James Bradley Thayer, John Marshall 106–07 (1901).

50. Bickel, n. 29, at 24.

51. For an argument that the Australian experience belies the generalization that rights are not likely to be optimally protected in a democracy unless politically independent courts are empowered to protect them, see Allan, "A Defense of the *Status Quo*," n. 13. Dianne Otto disagrees. See Otto, n. 13.

52. Again, Australia, New Zealand, and the United Kingdom are exceptions.

53. See, e.g., Cooper v. Aaron, 358 U.S. 1 (1958).

54. By contrast, a decision by the Supreme Court that a law (policy, act) is constitutional is subject to a different rule: If legislators believe that a law would be unconstitutional, they may decline to enact the law on that basis even if in the judgment of the Supreme Court the law would not be unconstitutional. Similarly, if the President of the United States or a governor of a state believes that a law is unconstitutional, he may decline to enforce the law on that basis even if in the Court's judgment the law is not unconstitutional. Or am I reading the doctrine of judicial supremacy too narrowly? For a broader reading, see Mark Tushnet, "*Marbury v. Madison* and the Theory of Judicial Supremacy," in Robert P. George, ed., Great Cases in Constitutional Law 17 (2000).

> An official who refuses to act on constitutional grounds – who vetoes a bill rather than signs it, who refuses to prosecute for violating the antisediton act – is defying the courts just as much as a person who acts pursuant to a statute the courts have held unconstitutional.
>
> In short, the fact that our constitutional system does not have a way to get the courts to review some official decisions that conflict with the courts' constitutional interpretations does not really counter the theory of judicial supremacy. It identified an awkward procedural "defect" in our constitutional system without rejecting the theory directly.

Id. at 28. In any event, the doctrine of judicial supremacy, however broad or narrow it may be, should not be confused with the different and extremely problematic doctrine of judicial *exclusivity* that the present Supreme Court seems, implicitly, to have embraced. The Court has been acting as if it is not only the supreme, but also the exclusive, expositor of constitutional meanings. See generally Larry D. Kramer, "Foreword: We the Court," 115 Harvard L. Rev. 4 (2001). See also Robert C. Post & Reva B. Siegel, "Protecting the Constitution from the People: Juricentric Restrictions on Section Five Power" 78 Indiana L. J. 1 (2003).

55. But what if the Canadian Supreme Court ruled against, not a law, but, say, some practice engaged in by Royal Mounted Police? Even then the Court does not have the last word: If the Parliament disagrees with the Court's opinion that the practice is unconstitutional, the Parliament can enact a law authorizing, or even requiring, the practice, and expressly declaring that the law shall operate notwithstanding the Charter provision on which the Court relied. In that indirect sense, section 33 covers not only laws enacted by the Parliament or provincial legislatures, but all governmental acts.

56. Walter F. Murphy, "Constitutions, Constitutionalism, and Democracy," in Greenberg et al., Constitutionalism & Democracy, n. 5, at 3, 17.

57. See Paul C. Weiler, "Rights and Judges in a Democracy: A New Canadian Version," 18 J. L. Reform 51, 79–80 (1984).

58. Id. at 83–84.
59. For discussion of yet another option, see Gardbaum, n. 5, at 727–32 (discussing New Zealand). Speaking of Canada, the United Kingdom, and New Zealand, Gardbaum writes:

> Rather than a mutually exclusive choice between two incompatible poles, the Commonwealth model suggests the novel possibility of a continuum stretching from absolute legislative supremacy to the American model of a fully constitutionalized bill of rights with various intermediate positions in between that achieve something of both. Moreover, although all three of the Commonwealth bills of rights reject the American model in that they seek to render the protection of a bill of rights consistent with their traditional conceptions of democracy and parliamentary supremacy, each does so in a different way and thus occupies a different position on the continuum between the two poles. . . .
> . . .
> Analytically and institutionally, the major impact and contribution of the new model is to open up a range of intermediate possibilities where none were previously thought to exist. The new question might become, not which of the two polar positions shall we occupy, but where on the spectrum should we be.

Id. at 710, 744–45. Gardbaum adds: "Almost certainly, there can be no global answer to this question, for ultimately the choice will likely depend, at least in part, on normative preferences among the values that are likely to be culturally and historically specific." Id. at 745.
60. My question here is about the *domestic* legal system of a liberal democracy. A liberal democracy's participation, by treaty, in a transnational legal system for the protection of rights – for example, the United Kingdom's participation in the European Human Rights System – poses different issues, issues beyond the scope of this chapter.
61. Gardbaum, n. 5, at 741.
62. The ideal, we might say, of parliamentary or legislative ultimacy. It is not surprising, as a historical matter, that Canada and the United Kingdom take the argument from democracy – which is, in effect, an argument for parliamentary sovereignty and against judicial supremacy/ultimacy – more seriously than does the United States. As Gardbaum explains:

> [T]here is . . . an important aspect of the real tension between [American-style] judicial review and popular sovereignty that – for historical reasons – is not fully appreciated in the United States and has resulted in a failure to comprehend fully why the claims of legislative supremacy were, and continue to be, so powerful and compelling to so many other countries. In Europe and elsewhere, legislative supremacy is often understood as the institutional manifestation of popular sovereignty, the notion that all political power derives from and remains with the people. Moreover, popular sovereignty is not generally viewed as an empty political truism for it was typically the concrete and hard-fought result of centuries of struggle between the people on the one hand, and the monarch (usually supported by church and aristocracy) over where ultimate power lay. During the course of this struggle, popular sovereignty was generally institutionalized in the legislature and monarchical power in the executive and judiciary. Legislative supremacy thus reflected the historical triumph of the people against rival claims to supremacy of the Crown and a narrow political elite.
> By contrast, in the United States (the product of a colonial revolution rather than a people's one in this sense), popular sovereignty has been a given from its founding and as a result tends to seem like a truism for it is hard to contemplate the alternatives,

even though, of course, the revolution was fought and the Constitution framed in the immediate context of one of them. Accordingly, the institutions of government do not have the same histories or sets of social meanings. And in particular, legislatures are not conceived of in the same way as the *distinctive* collective organ of the people. Rather, they are one among several organs of the government set up as necessary evils, and in principle no less alien or "of us" – and probably more dangerous – than the executive branch, both of which are to be viewed with pragmatic suspicion and played off against each other. In this context, placing legal limits on the legislature does not seem like placing limits on "ourselves" or transferring power from the people; rather it seems no different than placing legal limits on the executive – both are limits that the people impose upon their elected leaders.

Id. at 740–41.

63. Michael J. Perry, The Constitution, the Courts, and Human Rights 113 (1982). See also Gardbaum, n. 5, at 710: "By attempting to create joint responsibility and genuine dialogue between courts and legislatures with respect to fundamental rights, the new [Commonwealth] model [of constitutionalism] promises both to reinject important matters of principle back into legislative and popular debate and to provide a radically direct resolution of the countermajoritarian difficulty associated with judicial review." Cf. Kent Roach, "Constitutional. Remedial and International Dialogues About Rights: The Canadian Experience," <http://ssrn.com/abstract=621245> (2004).

Let me be clear: I am not making the obviously silly suggestion that such interinstitutional dialogue is the only path to a more self-critical and mature political morality. It can be, however, one important path. Cf. Tsvi Kahana, "The Notwithstanding Mechanism and Public Discussion: Lessons from the Ignored Practice of Section 33 of the Charter," 44 Canadian Public Administration 255, 281 (2001): "Nothing prevents the public from engaging in rigorous public debate, even in areas where the court has said nothing; nothing guarantees that the public will engage in such deliberation even if the court does rule on an issue. The argument that I am making is that while not absolutely necesssary and sufficient on its own, a Supreme Court decision prior to the [legislature's invocation of section 33] increases the chances of an informed public discussion."

The Canadian Charter of Rights and Freedoms has been in force since 1982. How well, or how poorly, has the system of judicial penultimacy – that is, section 33 – been functioning in Canadian politics? Has the ideal articulated in the text accompanying this note been realized, to some extent at least, in Canada? There is no consensus. Stephen Gardbaum has argued that section 33 has done little to create a genuine dialogue between the Canadian judiciary on the one hand, in particular the Supreme Court of Canada, and Parliament and provincial legislatures on the other. In Gardbaum's view, the Canadian Supreme Court's voice and will are virtually as dominant in Canada as the United States Supreme Court's voice and will are in the United States. See Gardbaum, n. 5, at 719–27. Mark Tushnet seems to concur: "To an outsider, effective legislative responses to the Canadian Supreme Court's most controversial decisions seem as rare as effective responses to equally controversial decisions by the U.S. Supreme Court." Tushnet, "Judicial Activism or Restraint in a Section 33 World," n. 43; see also Mark Tushnet, "Policy Distortion and Democratic Debilitation: Comparative Illustration of the Contermajoritarian Difficulty," 94 Michigan L. Rev. 245, 275–301 (1995).

By contrast, Peter Hogg, Dean of the Osgoode Hall Law School, York University, Toronto, has argued that section 33 is functioning very well indeed. Hogg refers to "a study published in 1997 [that] found 65 cases in which the courts had struck down or directly amended a federal or provincial law under the *Charter of Rights* since its adoption in 1982 . . . " Peter W. Hogg, "*The Charter* Revolution: Is It Undemocratic?" 12 Forum Constitutionnel 1, 2 (2001/2002) (referring to Peter W. Hogg and Allison A. Bushel (now Thornton), "The Charter Dialogue Between Courts and Legislatures," 35 Osgoode Hall L. J. 75, 81 (1997)). Based on this study, and on judicial events after 1997, Dean Hogg concludes:

> [T]he intervention of courts does not close down the marketplace of ideas, and a public debate usually follows any important *Charter* decision. That debate often increases public awareness of minority perspectives (consider for example the strong support that now exists for same-sex rights), which in turn influences the form that any legislative response takes. [Under the *Charter*,] the legislature usually has a good deal of discretion as to the appropriate response to a Charter decision, and, bearing in mind public opinion, will normally want to replace a law that has been struck down with one that accomplishes the policy objective but is more inclusive of minorities and less intrusive of guaranteed rights. . . . In those rare cases where government simply cannot abide the Court's interpretation of the *Charter*, reversal is usually legally possible, and can be accomplished politically where public opinion is particularly strong . . . Where public opinion is less strong or is divided, government may choose to leave the decision in place . . . This kind of interaction between . . . the decisions of the Court, the debate in the public media and the ultimate response by the legislature is by no means undemocratic. The claim that judicial review under the *Charter of Rights and Freedoms* is "undemocratic" cannot be sustained.

Hogg, "The *Charter* Revolution," supra this note, at 7–8 (passages rearranged). In a recent book, Kent Roach, Professor of Law at the University of Toronto, joins Dean Hogg and others who conclude that section 33 is functioning well. See Kent Roach, The Supreme Court on Trial: Judicial Activism or Democratic Dialogue (2001).

We need not resolve this disagreement between Professors Gardbaum et al. and Dean Hogg et al. As Jeffrey Goldsworthy has argued, even if section 33 has not functioned well in Canadian politics – even if it has not operated in a dialogue-enhancing, democratizing way – the principal reasons for this are not inherent; rather, they are peculiar to Canadian politics and do not indicate that a similar provision could not or would not operate in a dialogue-enhancing, democratizing way elsewhere. See Jeffrey Goldsworthy, "Judicial Review, Legislative Override, and Democracy," 38 Wake Forest L. Rev. 451, 470 (2003).

Gardbaum predicts that judicial penultimacy will function better in the United Kingdom under the HRA than (in his judgment) it has in Canada under the Charter. See Gardbaum, n. 5, at 732–39. Gardbaum's prediction is puzzling, given his report that Prime Minister Blair's Labor Government

> has repeatedly stated its belief that the normal course of action would be that [a declaration of incompatibility] "will almost certainly prompt Government [whichever party is in power] and Parliament to change the law." . . . In parliamentary debate, government ministers acknowledged that only with respect to highly controversial matters of principle, such as abortion, could it foresee not amending or repealing legislation in response to a court declaration of incompatibility. See Hansard for October 21, 1998, debate involving Jack Straw, the Home Secretary: "In the overwhelming majority of cases, regardless of which party was in government, I think that Ministers would examine the matter and say, 'a

declaration of incompatibility has been made, and we shall have to accept it. We shall have to remedy the defect in the law spotted by the Judicial Committee of the House of Lords.'"

Id. at 733–34 & n. 105.

64. Cf. Tushnet, "Judicial Activism or Restraint in a Section 33 World," n. 43: "The concerns articulated by proponents of parliamentary sovereignty can be rearticulated as grounds for urging constitutional courts in strong-form systems [of judicial review] to be restrained rather than activist."

65. James Bradley Thayer, "The Origin and Scope of the American Doctrine of Constitutional Law," 7 Harvard L. Rev. 129 (1893). See generally "One Hundred Years of Judicial Review: The Thayer Centennial Symposium," 88 Northwestern U. L. Rev. 1–468 (1993). (Thayer's essay is reprinted in Leonard W. Levy, ed., Judicial Review and the Supreme Court: Selected Essays 43–63 (1967). My citations to Thayer's essay are to the essay as reprinted by Levy.)

> Felix Frankfurter described [Thayer], his teacher, as "our great master of constitutional law." Thayer, said Frankfurter, "influenced Holmes, Brandeis, the Hands (Learned and Augustus) . . . and so forth. I am of the view that if I were to name one piece of writing on American Constitutional Law – a silly test maybe – I would pick an essay by James Bradley Thayer in the *Harvard Law Review*, consisting of 26 pages, published in October, 1893, called 'The Origin and Scope of the American Doctrine of Constitutional Law'. . . . Why would I do that? Because from my point of view it's a great guide for judges and therefore, the great guide for understanding by non-judges of what the place of the judiciary is in relation to constitutional questions."

Leonard W. Levy, "Editorial Note," in Levy, supra this note. See also Paul Kahn, Legitimacy and History: Self-Government in American Constitutional Theory 84 (1992):

> Thayer was a friend and professional colleague of Oliver Wendell Holmes, first in law practice and then at Harvard, where Thayer taught for thirty years. Louis Brandeis was a student of Thayer's, and Felix Frankfurter, who just missed Thayer at Harvard, acknowledged Thayer's substantial influence. Of Thayer's most famous essay in constitutional law, "The Origin and Scope of the American Doctrine of Constitutional Law," Holmes wrote, "I agree with it heartily and it makes explicit the point of view from which implicitly I have approached the constitutional questions upon which I have differed from some other judges."

66. Thayer, "The Origin and Scope of the American Doctrine of Constitutional Law," n. 65, at 54, 59. Thayer's most prominent judicial disciple was Felix Frankfurter, who wrote in his dissenting opinion in *West Virginia State Board of Education v. Barnette* (in which the Court struck down a public school regulation, challenged by a Jehovah's Witness, that compelled students to salute the flag and recite the Pledge of Allegiance): "Only if there be no doubt that any reasonable mind could entertain can we deny to the states the right to resolve doubts their way and not ours. . . . I think I appreciate fully the objections to the law before us. But to deny that it presents a question upon which men might reasonably differ appears to me to be intolerance. And since men may so reasonably differ, I deem it beyond my constitutional power to assert my view of the wisdom of this law against the view of the State of West Virginia." West Virginia State Board of Education v. Barnette, 319 U.S. 624, 661–62, 666–67 (1943). As Justice Frankfurter understood, a Thayerian approach to the specification of indeterminate constitutional norms affords relatively little opportunity for a judge's own values to influence her resolution of the conflict at hand.

To afford relatively little opportunity is not to afford no opportunity.

> ...Thayer's rule, like all guideposts, is not self-applying. Even limited by the rule of administration, judges, like criminal juries, might differ over what constitutes a reasonable doubt; the possibilities, the stuff of which reasonable doubts are made, do not always strike all men, however reasonable, alike. Even under Thayer's rule of administration, then, the freedom and the burden of decisionmaking remain. But that freedom is narrowed, and that was Thayer's aim. He sought to reduce the scope of judicial freedom without diminishing the judicial duty and burden of judging.

Sanford Gabin, Judicial Review and the Reasonable Doubt Test 45–46 (1980).

According to Thayer, the deferential approach is fitting when a federal court reviews, for federal constitutionality, federal action, or when a state court reviews, either for federal constitutionality or for state constitutionality, state action, but not when a federal court reviews, for federal constitutionality, state action, in which case (according to Thayer) a non-deferential approach is fitting. See Thayer, "The Origin and Scope of the American Doctrine of Constitutional Law," n. 65, at 62–63. Limiting the deferential approach in the way Thayer did makes little sense, however, and most commentators who discuss Thayer's conception of proper judicial role fail even to note the limitation. See, e.g., Bickel, n. 39, at 35–46; Wallace Mendelson, "The Influence of James B. Thayer upon the Work of Holmes, Brandeis, and Frankfurter," 31 Vanderbilt L. Rev. 71 (1978); but see Charles Black, Decision According to Law 34–35 (1981). (Even Felix Frankfurter failed to note, much less to heed, the limitation – as his dissent in *Barnette* makes clear.) Sanford Gabin has explicitly argued that "the reasonable doubt test should be applied not just to all national legislation but, contrary to Thayer's prescription, to all state legislation as well." Gabin, supra this n., at 5.

67. See Bickel, n. 39, at 34–46.
68. See Kahn, n. 65, at 85–87.
69. Paul Kahn has encapsulated Thayer's point: "[T]he more the Court tries to represent the people, the more the people cease to function as the popular sovereign." Id. 87. For Kahn's commentary on Thayer's argument, see id. at 85–89. Moreover, according to Thayer, a non-deferential – aggressive – judicial approach to enforcing constitutional norms would weaken the capacity of the people and their representatives to deliberate about contested constitutional questions as responsibly as they should. Thayer elaborated the point in a book on John Marshall:

> [T]he exercise of judicial review, even when unavoidable, is always attended with a serious evil, namely, that the correction of legislative mistakes comes from the outside, and the people thus lose the political experience, and the moral education and stimulus that comes from fighting the question out in the ordinary way, and correcting their own errors. The tendency of a common and easy resort to this great function, now lamentably too common, is to dwarf the political capacity of the people, and to deaden its sense of moral responsibility.
>
> ...
>
> And if it be true that the holders of legislative power are careless or evil, yet the constitutional duty of the court remains untouched; it cannot rightly attempt to protect the people by undertaking a function not its own. On the other hand, by adhering rigidly to its own duty, the court will help, as nothing else can, to fix the spot where responsibility lies, and to bring down on that precise locality the thunderbolt of popular condemnation. ... For that course – the true course of judicial duty always – will powerfully help to bring the people and their representatives to a sense of their own responsibility.

Thayer, John Marshall, n. 49, at 106–07, 109–10. Many modern students of American judicial review have shared Thayer's concern. For example, Alexander Bickel wrote that "[t]he search must be for a [judicial] function . . . whose discharge by the courts will not lower the quality of the other departments' performance *by denuding them of the dignity and burden of their own responsibility.*" Bickel, n. 39, at 24 (emphasis added). Cf. Allan C. Hutchinson, "Waiting for Coraf (or the Beatification of the Charter)," 41 U. Toronto L. J. 332, 358 (1991): "By endlessly waiting for CORAF, we place ourselves *in waiting;* it inculcates a servile and sycophantic attitude in people. Such a practised posture of dependence is anathema to the democratic spirit. It is infinitely better to run the unfamiliar risks of genuinely popular rule than to succumb to the commonplace security of distant authority." For a more recent, but none the less critical, statement by Hutchinson, see Allan C. Hutchinson, "Supreme Court Inc: The Business of Democracy and Rights," in Gavin W. Anderson, ed., Rights & Democracy: Essays in UK-Canadian Constitutionalism 29 (1999).

70. Mark Tushnet's and Jeremy Waldron's respective arguments against American-style judicial review are each at least partly Thayerian in character. See Mark Tushnet, Taking the Constitution Away from the Courts, chs. 6–7 (1999); Waldron, Law and Disagreement, n. 46, chs. 10–13.

71. See n. 10.

72. Tushnet, "Judicial Activism or Restraint in a Section 33 World," n. 43.

73. Id.

74. Goldsworthy, n. 63, at 456.

75. Id.

76. See Ariel L. Bendor & Zeev Segal, "Constitutionalism and Trust in Britain: An Ancient Constitutional Culture, A New Judicial review Model," 17 American U. Int'l L. Rev. 683, 721 (2002):

> The fact that the British courts are not empowered to strike down primary legislation might actually encourage them to issue declarations of incompatibility. The non-pure judicial review power might make the British courts more robust in exercising their powers than their counterparts in pure judicial review systems. In doing so, the courts might contribute to a stronger protection of civil liberties.

77. See n. 63 and accompanying text.

78. Weiler, n. 57, at 80.

79. Id. at 84–85. For Weiler's argument, see id. at 79–86. Senator Robert M. La Follette presumably would have been sympathetic to Professor Weiler's suggestion. Speaking to a convention of the American Federation of Labor in 1922, Senator La Follette proposed "a constitutional amendment to permit Congress to reenact any federal statute that the Court had declared unconstitutional . . . " Ross, n. 39, at 194. "Although La Follette's proposal presumably would have permitted Congress to reenact the law by a majority vote, La Follette eventually came to advocate the [American Federation of Labor's] proposal to permit reenactment only by a two-thirds vote of both houses." Id. at 194 n. 3.

> Even though La Follette never introduced a measure to permit Congress to override judicial nullification of legislation, a measure that embodied part of the plan advocated by La Follette and the AFL was introduced in the House by Republican James A. Frear of Wisconsin in February 1923. Frear proposed [a constitutional] amendment that would

have permitted Congress to enact a law to set aside by a two-thirds vote any Supreme Court decision that invalidated a federal statute.

Id. at 199–200.

80. Bickel, n. 39, at 25–26.

81. Section 33 of the Canadian Charter represents such an effort on the assumption that Canada's "notwithstanding clause should only be employed in a remedial way, *after* legislation has already been considered by the courts and struck down; it should not be used preemptively, to block anticipated judicial review altogether. . . . [S]ection 33 is intended to allow a further stage in the dialogue between courts and legislatures as to the meaning of *Charter* rights, not to prevent such dialogue altogether." Brian Slattery, "A Theory of the Charter," 25 Osgoode Hall L. J. 701, 742 (1987). (The quoted language is Slattery's characterization of the position argued by Donna Greschner and Ken Norman in their article: "The Courts and Section 33," 12 Queen's L. J. 155, 190 et seq. (1987).) For another argument that section 33 should be invoked only reactively, not preemptively, see Kahana, n. 63. Guido Calabresi has called the Canadian Constitution, in consequence of section 33 of the Charter, "a wonderful example of an essentially Bickellian constitution. Guido Calabresi, "Foreword: Antidiscrimination and Constitutional Accountability (What the Bork-Brennan Debate Ignores)," 105 Harvard L. Rev. 80, 124 (1991).

82. Thayer, John Marshall, n. 49, at 106–07.

83. See n. 84.

84. See Sanford Levinson, "The Audience for Constitutional Meta-Theory (or, Why, and to Whom, Do I Write the Things I Do?)," 63 U. Colorado L. Rev. 389, 406–07 (1992): "[T]he United States Constitution can meaningfully structure our polity if and only if *every* public official – and ultimately every citizen – becomes a participant in the conversation about constitutional meaning, as opposed to the pernicious practice of identifying the Constitution with the decisions of the United States Supreme Court or even of courts and judges more generally." See also Mark Tushnet, Taking the Constitution Away from the Courts, chs. 6–7 (1999); Mark Tushnet, "Scepticism about Judicial Review: A Perspective from the United States," in Campbell, Sceptical Essays on Human Rights, n. 13, at 359; Waldron, Law and Disagreement, n. 46, chs. 10–13. Cf. Cass Sunstein, The Partial Constitution 354 (1993) (expressing "hope for newly reinvigorated deliberation about constitutional commitments – deliberation that will occasionally take place in the courtroom, but more often, and far more fundamentally, through democratic channels").

85. In the United States, during the period from the 1890s to the 1930s, there were many proposals to curb judicial power to strike down legislation as unconstitutional, including proposals of regimes in which unpopular judicial decisions could be overridden. None of the proposals, however, was adopted. For the definitive discussion of the various proposals, see Ross, n. 39. See also Gerald Gunther, Learned Hand: The Man and the Judge 213 et seq. (1994) (discussing Theodore Roosevelt's proposal for popular control of judicial power and Learned Hand's response). Cf. William G. Ross, "The Resilience of *Marbury v. Madison*: Why Judicial Review Has Survived So Many Attacks," 38 Wake Forest L. Rev. 733 (2003).

86. See Tushnet, Taking the Constitution Away from the Courts, n. 70, chs. 6–7; Waldron, Law and Disagreement, n. 46, chs. 10–13. Waldron attributes this claim to Mark

Tushnet and then seems himself to affirm it: "[P]opulist constitutional politics, freed from court-centered legalism, tends to project a progressive and liberating vision (rather than a tight-fisted libertarian one) on to the founding commitments of the American republic." Jeremy Waldron, "A Question of Judgment," Times Lit. Supp., Sept. 28, 2001, 7 (reviewing Mark Tushnet, Taking the Constitution Away from the Courts (1999)). According to Tushnet, "progressives and liberals are losing more from judicial review than they are getting." Tushnet, Taking the Constitution Away from the Courts, n. 70, at 172.

87. Cf. Douglas Laycock, "The Benefits of the Establishment Clause," 42 DePaul L. Rev. 373, 376 (1992): "Some of the time, judicial review will do some good. Judges did nothing for the Mormons, but they may have saved the Jehovah's Witnesses and the Amish. If judges can save one religious minority a century, I consider that ample justification for judicial review in religious liberty cases."

88. Posner, "Review of Jeremy Waldron," n. 31, at 592.

89. The qualifier "for the United States" is important:

> There is no reason to suppose that the issue [whether American-style judicial review is a good idea] should be resolved the same way in two different countries, even countries that share the same language and the same basic legal and political heritage. That depends on all sorts of emprical questions and judgmental imponderables involving the political and legal cultures of the two countries and the career path of judges and legislators in them.

Id.

90. Something Alexander Bickel said about judicial review itself is tangentially relevant here: "It will not be possible fully to meet all that is said against judicial review. Such is not the way with questions of government. We can only fill the other side of the scales with countervailing judgments on the real needs and the actual workings of our society and, of course, with our own portions of faith and hope. Then we may estimate how far the needle has moved." Bickel, n. 39, at 24.

91. Cécile Fabre, Social Rights under The Constitution: Government and the Decent Life 3 (2000). For a fuller articulation of these rights, see id. at 107–08. See also Isfahan Merali & Valerie Oosterveld, eds., Giving Meaning to Economic, Social, and Cultural Rights (2001).

92. See Matthew 25:40. Cécile Fabre has sketched an additional reason why the citizens of a liberal democracy should entrench (some) welfare rights: Fabre takes note of the argument that because welfare rights "to adequate minimum income, housing, and health care are not part of the *concept* of democracy, . . . constitutionalizing them amounts to upholding rights at the expense of democracy". She then notes, however, that such rights "are, in a limited number of cases, necessary conditions for a democracy's functioning and survival, and [therefore] in those cases constitutionalizing them is true to the value of democracy even though it constrains the democratic majority;" moreover, "the right to adequate education is a defining feature of the concept of democracy and a necessary condition for its functioning and survival, and . . . constitutionalizing it therefore does not conflict with democracy." Fabre, n. 91, at 4–5. See id. at 110–51.

93. See n. 14 and accompanying text.

94. Irish Constitution, Article 45 (1).

95. Indian Constitution, Article 37.

96. See Constitution of the Republic of South Africa (1996), Chapter 2 ("Bill of Rights"); Chapter 8 ("Courts and Administration of Justice").

97. For an interesting discussion of the question, see Mark Tushnet, "Social Welfare Rights and the Forms of Judicial Review," 82 Texas L. Rev. 1895 (2004).

98. Michael Walzer, "Philosophy and Democracy," 9 Political Theory 379, 391–92 (1981). See id. at 392–93. But cf. Jeremy Waldron, Law and Disagreement 234 (1999): "It is wrong . . . to contrast the kinds of demands made in the name of political rights and the kinds of demands made in the name of economic and social rights. . . . [R]ights of both sorts require the institution and operation of administrative systems; both involve manpower and resources; both presuppose a relatively stable and well-organized society; and both require governments and government officials to do certain things under certain conditions, not merely to refrain from doing certain things."

99. Mark Tushnet, Taking the Constitution Away from the Courts 169 (1999). For examples, see Cass R. Sunstein, "Against Positive Rights," 2/1 East European Constitutional Rev. 35 (1993); Lawrence Sager, "The Domain of Constitutional Justice," in Larry Alexander, ed., Constitutionalism: Philosophical Foundations 235 (1998); Frank B. Cross, "The Error of Positive Rights," 48 UCLA L. Rev. 857 (2001). (Cass Sunstein subsequently recanted – or certainly seemed to. See Cass R. Sunstein, "Social and Economic Rights? Lessons from South Africa," 11 Constitutional Forum 123 (2001).)

100. See Fabre, n. 91, ch. 5. See also Kim Lane Scheppele, "A Realpolitik Defense of Social Rights," 82 Texas L. Rev. 1921 (2004); Marius Pieterse, "Possibilities and Pitfalls in the Domestic Enforcement of Social Rights: Contemplating the South African Experience," 26 Human Rights Quarterly 882 (2004). But cf. Michael J. Dennis & David P. Stewart, "Justiciability of Economic, Social, and Cultural Rights: Should There Be an International Complaints Mechanism to Adjudicate the Rights to Food, Water, Housing, and Health?" 98 American J. Int'l L. 462 (2004) (answering in the negative).

101. In South Africa, however, a system of judicial ultimacy is already in place with respect to the protection of *all* constitutionally entrenched rights, even welfare rights. If a court's power to protect constitutionally entrenched welfare rights is the power of judicial ultimacy, the case for its exercising that power in a deferential (Thayerian) fashion is, in my judgment, overwhelming. But, of course, not everyone agrees. Cf. Mark S. Kende, "The South African Constitutional Court's Construction of Socio-Economic Rights: A Response to Critics," 19 Connecticut J. Int'l L. 617 (2004) (responding to those who argue that the South Africa's Constitutional Court hasn't been sufficiently "activist" in enforcing welfare rights).

102. See Luke Clements & Philip A. Thomas, eds., "Special Issue: The Human Rights Act: A Success Story?" 32 Journal of Law & Society 1–201 (2005).

103. "In this Act 'the Convention rights' means the rights and fundamental freedoms set out in (a) Articles 2 to 12 and 14 of the Convention, (b) Articles 1 to 3 of the First Protocol, and (c) Articles 1 and 2 of the Sixth Protocol, as read with Articles 16 to 18 of the Convention." HRA, Article 1 (1). "Those Articles are to have effect for the purposes of this Act subject to any derogation or reservation . . . " HRA, Article 1 (2).

104. It has been argued that the judiciary's power under section 3(1) is so large that in effect "[p]arliamentary sovereignty has given way to judicial sovereignty." Alison L.

Young, "Judicial Sovereignty and the Human Rights Act 1998," 61 Cambridge L. J. 53, 65 (2002).

> [W]hen is it impossible to interpret statutes in a manner compatible with Convention rights? . . . Section 3 (1) reaches a limit when protecting Convention rights requires implied repeal [of a challenged statute]. Yet, when we invesitigate this boundary more thoroughly, we discover that it is so malleable as to amount to no limit at all. Control over the extent to which Convention rights are protected through statutory interpretation rests firmly in the hands of the judiciary.

Id. at 53. This conclusion, if correct, reinforces my conclusion later that judicial power to protect rights is much stronger in the United Kingdom, under the Human Rights Act, than first appearances might have led one to believe. I am grateful to Jeff Goldsworthy for pointing this out to me.

105. This statement oversimplifies a complex procedural scheme. See HRA, Article 10 & Schedule 2 ("Remedial Orders"). See also Gardbaum, n. 5, at 733–34:

> Once a declaration [of incompatibility] has been made, HRA creates no legal duty on either Parliament or the government to respond in any way, but it does empower the relevant minister to make a "remedial order" under section 10 and Schedule 2. This "fast track" procedure permits a minister to amend incompatible legislation by order laid before and approved by both Houses of Parliament. [Gardbaum adds, in a footnote at this point, that "[t]he detailed procedures for a remedial order are extremely complex. See Section 10 and Schedule 2. They were also among the most controversial aspects of the bill and the Government was forced to amend its original scheme, which permitted less parliamentary supervision of remedial orders."] HRA obviously did not need to empower Parliament to amend or repeal such legislation since the power clearly already exists. . . . Under Section 19, whenever a new piece of legislation is being considered in Parliament, the relevant Minister must make a statement in writing before its Second Reading either that in his or her view the Bill is compatible with the Convention rights or that although he or she is unable to make such a statement, the government nevertheless wishes to proceed with the Bill.

106. Several such cases (and many others that are less high profile) are included in the materials compiled by Janis, Kay, & Bradley, n. 6.

107. Gardbaum, n. 5, at 733–34. Gardbaum reports that the quoted "language is taken from the Government's White Paper of October 24, 1997. Section 2.10." Id. at n. 105.

> In parliamentary debate, government ministers acknowledged that only with respect to highly controversial matters of principle, such as abortion, could it foresee not amending or repealing legislation in response to a court declaration of incompatibility. See Hansard for October 21, 1998, debate involving Jack Straw, the Home Secretary: "In the overwhelming majority of cases, regardless of which party was in government, I think that Ministers would examine the matter and say, 'a declaration of incompatibility has been made, and we shall have to accept it. We shall have to remedy the defect in the law spotted by the Judicial Committee of the House of Lords.' . . . Although I hope that it does not happen, it is possible to conceive that some time in the future, a particularly composed Judicial Committee of the House of Lords reaches the view that provision for abortion in . . . the United Kingdom . . . is incompatible with one or another article of the convention. . . . My guess – it can be no more than that – is that whichever party was in power would have to say that it was sorry, that it did not and would not accept that, and that is was going to continue with the existing abortion legislation."

Id.

108. In an earlier draft, I said not "might be otherwise" but "would likely be otherwise". In correspondence, Richard Kay has suggested to me that "internal political factors will be just as important [as the prospect of an adverse decision by the European Court of Human Rights]. The UK lacks a constitutional protection of rights but nonetheless still has a strong 'rights culture.' I suspect that alone would put strong pressure on the government to respond. This is especially true when the declaration comes from domestic judgments and not from a bench of 'foreigners.' Consequently I disagree with your statement that the situation 'would likely be otherwise' if the UK were not bound by treaty to the ECHR." Letter from Richard Kay to Michael Perry, Feb. 26, 2002.

109. On the European Human Rights System, see Janis, Kay, & Bradley, n. 6.

110. On the right of individual petition, see Article 34 of the Convention.

CHAPTER 9. HOW SHOULD THE SUPREME COURT RULE?

1. See Furman v. Georgia, 408 U.S. 238, 239 (1972). The first ten amendments to the Constitution, known as the Bill of Rights, were drafted in 1789 and took effect in 1791. Although the various provisions of the Bill of Rights were directed only to the federal government, not to the governments of the states, it is now constitutional bedrock that the Fourteenth Amendment makes the most important provisions of the Bill of Rights applicable to the states. So it is not just the federal government but state government too that may not, inter alia, prohibit the free exercise of religion (First Amendment), abridge the freedom of speech (First Amendment), or inflict cruel and unusual punishments (Eighth Amendment). On the idea of constitutional bedrock, see Michael J. Perry, We the People: The Fourteenth Amendment and the Supreme Court 19–23 (1999). For the most impressive argument in support of the still-controversial historical claim that the Fourteenth Amendment was meant to make the most important provisions of the Bill of Rights applicable to the states, see Michael Kent Curtis, No State Shall Abridge: The Fourteenth Amendment and the Bill of Rights (1986). Cf. Perry, We the People, supra this note, at 77–80.

2. See Vasan Kesavan & Michael Stokes Paulsen, "The Interpretive Force of the Constitution's Secret Drafting History," 91 Georgetown L. J. 1113, 1144–45 (2003): "[The original meaning/understanding approach] asks not what the Framers or Ratifiers meant or understood subjectively, but what their words would have meant objectively – how they would have been understood by an ordinary, reasonably well-informed user of the language, in context, at the time, within the relevant political community that adopted them." See also Keith E. Whittington, "The New Originalism," 2 Georgetown J. L. & Public Policy 599 (2004).

> [T]he new originalism is focused less on the concrete intentions of individual drafters of constitutional text than on the public meaning of the text that was adopted. . . . It is the adoption of the text by the public that renders the text authoritative, not its drafting by particular individuals. This is not to say that the history of the drafting process is irrelevant – it may provide important clues as to how the text was understood at the time and the meaningful choices that particular textual language embodied – but it is not uniquely important to the recovery of the original meaning of the Constitution. Similarly, the discovery of a hidden letter by James Madison revealing the "secret, true meaning of a constitutional clause would hardly be dispositive to an originalism primarily concerned

with what the text meant to those who adopted it. The Constitution is not a private conspiracy.

Id. at 610–11. Cf. Stanley Fish, "There is No Textualist Position," 42 San Diego L. Rev. 629, 649–50 (2005):

- A text means what its author intends.
- There is no meaning apart from intention.
- There is no textualist position because intention is prior to text; no intention, no text.
- There is no choice between intentional meaning, conventional meaning, dictionary meaning, and the meaning imputed to the ordinary, or exceptional, or reasonable man, only choices between alternatively posited intentions. Dictionaries and conventions do not have intentions; the ordinary or exceptional or reasonable man did not author the text you are interpreting.
- If you are not trying to determine intention, you're not interpreting; but sometimes interpreting is not what you want to be doing (although before you do something else, you should be sure you have good reasons).
- The intentions of readers, except for the intention to determine intention, do not count as interpretations, but as rewritings.
- None of the above amounts to a method. Knowing you are after intention does not help you find it; you still have to look for evidence and make arguments. And thinking that it is something else you are after will not disable you if you are really interpreting; for then you would be seeking intention even if you said you were not.
- Interpretation is not a theoretical issue, but an empirical one, and, therefore, all the debates about interpretation should stop. (Fat chance!)

See also Steven Knapp & Walter Benn Michaels, "Not a Matter of Interpretation," 42 San Diego L. Rev. 651 (2005).

3. See 5 The Founders Constitution 377 (1987) (House of Representatives, Amendments to the Constitution, 17 Aug. 1789):

Mr. SMITH, of South Carolina, objected to the words "nor cruel and unusual punishments;" the import of them being too indefinite.

Mr. LIVERMORE. – The clause seems to express a great deal of humanity, on which account I have no objection to it; but as it seems to have no meaning in it, I do not think it necessary. . . .

The question was put on the clause, and it was agreed to by a considerable majority.

See also William J. Brennan, Jr., "Constitutional Adjudication and the Death Penalty: A View from the Court," 100 Harvard L. Rev. 313, 323 (1986): "[T]he language of the eighth amendment was taken from the English Bill of Rights of 1689, but we do not know why the framers were particularly attracted to that language or, for that matter, exactly what the language signified to the English."

4. That is, torture *as punishment* as distinct from torture as a means of getting information.

5. See Atkins v. Virginia, 536 U.S. 304, 311 (2002): "The Eighth Amendment succinctly prohibits '[e]xcessive' sanctions." Three years later, the Court wrote that "the Eighth Amendment guarantees individuals the right not to be subjected to excessive sanctions. The right flows from the basic 'precept of justice that punishment for crime

should be graduated and proportioned to [the] offense.'" Roper v. Simmons, 543 U.S. 551, 560 (2005) (quoting Weems v. United States, 217 U.S. 349, 367 (1910)).

6. See Benjamin Wittes, "What Is 'Cruel and Unusual'?" Policy Review, December 2005 & January 2006:

> The hallmark of cruelty . . . is the needless infliction of pain and suffering. Judging whether a punishment is cruel, therefore, requires an assessment of whether the suffering it entails is necessary for some legitimate government purpose or whether it is senseless. On its face, this inquiry is not a complicated one: A punishment reasonably tied to the goal of deterrence or disabling a criminal from further harm to society is not cruel, however unpleasant it may be. A punishment that goes beyond these goals to wanton violence, irrational harshness, gross disproportionality, or needlessly degrading humiliation can reasonably be described as cruel for constitutional purposes. The essential quality of the cruelty, in other words, is that the punishment in question goes somehow beyond any reasonable punitive purpose.

7. See Trop v. Dulles, 356 U.S. 86, 100–01 n. 32 (1958): "If the word 'unusual' is to have any meaning apart from the word 'cruel' . . . the meaning should be the ordinary one, signifying something different than which is generally done."

8. Furman v. Georgia, 408 U.S. 238, 279 (1972) (Brennan, J., concurring) (internal citation omitted).

9. See Marc L. Miller & Ronald F. Wright, Criminal Procedures: Cases, Statutes, and Executive Materials 190–91 (2003): "In Coker v. Georgia, 433 U.S. 584 (1977), the Supreme Court struck down the death penalty as a sentencing option in the rape of an adult woman; . . . the constitutional basis for the decision was the Eighth Amendment's prohibition of cruel and unusual punishments. Since then only murder convictions have led to death sentences."

10. See Atkins v. Virginia, 536 U.S. 304 (2002).

11. See Roper v. Simmons, 543 U.S. 551 (2005).

12. See Michael J. Perry, The Constitution in the Courts: Law or Politics? 45–46 (1994).

13. See Antonin Scalia, A Matter of Interpretation: Federal Courts and the Law 46, 132, 145–47 (1997).

14. Nor does it mean that the power to impose capital punishment is constitutionally enshrined. See Perry, The Constitution in the Courts, n. 12, at 46 (1994):

> The [People's] expectation that reliance on the death penalty would persist into the future and their decision, given that expectation, to regulate imposition of the death penalty do not constitute a decision to authorize reliance on the death penalty, to *constitutionalize* the death penalty – in that sense, they do not constitute a decision to exempt the death penalty from possible prohibition by the Eighth Amendment.

See also Brennan, n. 3, at 324:

> [The Fifth Amendment] does not, after all, declare that the right of Congress to punish capitally shall be inviolable; it merely requires that when and if death is a possible punishment, the defendant shall enjoy certain procedural safeguards. . . . [W]hat one can fairly say is that they sought to ensure that *if* there was capital punishment, the process by which the accused was to be convicted would be especially reliable.

See, generally, Shannon D. Gilreath, "Cruel and Unusual Punishment and the Eighth Amendment as a Mandate for Human Dignity: Another Look at Original Intent," 25 Thomas Jefferson L. Rev. 559, 571–84 (2003).

15. Whittington, n. 2, at 610. See also Andrew Oldenquist, "Retribution and the Death Penalty," 20 U. Dayton L. Rev. 335, 340–43 (2004) (criticizing Scalia's interpretive approach to the Eighth Amendment).

> Scalia points out that the Framers didn't think that capital punishment was cruel because they allude to it as an option in the same document in which they prohibit cruel and unusual punishments. But why does it matter whether they thought capital punishment was cruel? What should guide us is what they explicitly prohibit or mandate in the Constitution. And if the Framers' opinions about capital punishment do not count, surely neither do the opinions of late eighteenth century reasonable bystanders. Where is the evidence that the Framers intended that their own acceptance of capital punishment should determine our interpretation of the Eighth Amendment? And even if they, or the reasonable bystanders of the time, considered burying alive but not hanging to be cruel, it doesn't follow that this is what the Eighth Amendment means or implies. It certainly isn't what it *says*. . . . Awe at writing a document to guide a new nation through future generations, together with respect for the judgment of future generations, may well have moved them not to want to restrict us by their personal opinions about what is cruel or what is an unreasonable search, and this awe and respect may account for the abtractness of much of the Bill of Rights.

Id. at 341.

16. See Perry, The Constitution in the Courts, n. 12, at 79–81.

17. Whittington, n. 2, at 610–11.

18. I would not want to be charged with defending the proposition that capital punishment is intrinsically barbaric; in particular, I would not want to be charged with defending the proposition that no matter what the deterrent effect, capital punishment is barbaric.

19. See Chapter 4 at 46–47.

20. Trop v. Dulles, 356 U. S . 86, 100–01 (1958). In 1995, in a case in which the Constitutional Court of the Republic of South Africa declared capital punishment unconstitutional, the president of the court wrote: "Although the United States Constitution does not contain a specific guarantee of human dignity, it has been accepted by the United States Supreme Court that the concept of human dignity is at the core of the prohibition of 'cruel and unusual punishment' by the Eighth and Fourteenth Amendments." State v. Makwanyane and Another, 1995 (6) BCLR 665, 695 (Constitutional Court).

21. Roper v. Simmons, 543 U.S. 551, 560 (2005).

22. Furman v. Georgia, 408 U.S. 238, 273 (1972) (concurring op'n).

23. See Chapter 4 at 47–48, 50.

24. Cf. Franklin E. Zimring, "The Unexamined Death Penalty: Capital Punishment and Reform of the Model Penal Code," 105 Columbia L. Rev. 1396, 1409 (2005): "In some Southern states, inadequate defense and appellate lawyers and judges willing to use procedural defaults to nullify substantive legal claims have created much higher rates. For example, Virginia's, Texas's, and Missouri's rates of execution are more than thirty times those of Ohio, Pennsylvania, and California."

25. The Supreme Court began a four-year moratorium on capital punishment in 1972 (see Furman v. Georgia, 408 U. S . 238 (1972)) and ended it four years (see Gregg v. Georgia, 428 U. S. 153 (1976)). ("The Supreme Court's decision in *Furman* effectively declared unconstitutional the death penalty statutes then in place in 40 states and commuted the sentences of 629 death row inmates around the country. Because only Justices Brennan and Marshall asserted that the death penalty was per se

unconstitutional, the opinions of Justices Stewart, White, and Douglas suggested that states could rewrite their death penalty statutes to remedy the constitutional problems." Miller & Wright, n. 9, at at 184–85.) In the more than thirty years since the moratorium ended, the following states have executed fewer than five persons (the number executed is in parentheses): Colorado (1), Connecticut (1), Idaho (1), Kansas (0), Kentucky (2), Maryland (4), Montana (2), Nebraska (3), New Hampshire (0), New Jersey (0), New Mexico (1), New York (0), Oregon (2), Pennsylvania (3), South Dakota (0), Tennessee (1), Washington (4), Wyoming (1). In the same period, the U.S. government has executed 3 persons and the U.S. military, none.

26. Benjamin Wittes has suggested determining the "unusualness" of a punishment by "set[ting] the number of states at three-quarters of the number of states in the Union, currently 38. This corresponds to the number of states required to amend the Constitution." Wittes, "What Is 'Cruel and Unusual'?" n. 6.

27. Cf. Joan F. Hartman, "'Unusual' Punishment: The Domestic Effects of International Norms Restricting the Application of the Death Penalty," 52 U. Cincinnati L. Rev. 655 (1983).

28. Cf. Roper v. Simmons, 543 U.S. 551, 575 (2005): "Our determination that the death penalty is disproportionate punishment for offenders under 18 finds confirmation in the stark reality that the United States is the only country in the world that continues to give official sanction to the juvenile death penalty."

29. The list of retentionist countries excludes twenty-four countries that Amnesty International categorizes as "abolitionist in practice": "countries which retain the death penalty for ordinary crimes such as murder but can be considered abolitionist in practice because they have not executed anyone during the last 10 years and are believed to have a policy or established practice of not carrying out executions. The list also excludes countries that have made an international commitment not to use the death penalty."

30. In 2004, there were at least 3,797 executions in twenty-five countries around the world. China, Iran, the United States, and Vietnam were responsible for 94 percent of these known executions: China (at least 3,400 executions), Iran (approximately 159), Vietnam (approximately 64), and the United States (59). The next four were Saudi Arabia (33), Pakistan (15), Kuwait (9), and Bangladesh (7). Id.

31. The name "Texas" seems apt: "Texas . . . accounts for more than a third of all executions in the United States. Last year [2004], it carried out 23 of the 59 executions in the country; no other state approached double figures." Editorial, "No Airtight Case for Death," The Birmingham News, Nov. 10, 2005, at 8A.

32. The Supreme Court has addressed this issue. See Atkins v. Virginia, 536 U.S. 304, 319 (2002):

> With respect to retribution – the interest in seeing that the defender gets his just deserts – the severity of the appropriate punishment necessarily depends on the culpability of the offender. . . . If the culpability of the average murderer is insufficient to justify the most extreme sanction available to the State, the lesser culpability of the mentally retarded offender sure does not merit that form of retribution.

See also Roper v. Simmons, 543 U.S. 551, 571 (2005):

> Whether viewed as an attempt to express the community's moral outrage or as an attempt to right the balance for the wrong of the victim, the case for retribution is not as strong with a minor as with an adult. Retribution is not proportional if the law's most severe

penalty is imposed on one whose [moral] culpability or blameworthiness is diminished, to a substantial degree, by reason of youth and immaturity.

33. The Supreme Court has addressed this issue, too. See Atkins v. Virginia, 536 U.S. 304, 319–20:

> With respect to deterrence – the interest in preventing capital crimes by prospective offenders – it seems likely that capital punishment can serve as a deterrent only when murder is the result of premeditation and deliberation. [The] same cognitive and behavioral impairments that make [the mentally retarded] morally less culpable – for example, the diminished ability to understand and process information, to learn from experience, to engage in logical reasoning, to control impulses – . . . also make it less likely that they can process the information of the possibility of execution as a penalty and, as a result, control their conduct based upon that information. Nor will exempting the mentally retarded from execution lessen the deterrent effect of the death penalty with respect to offenders who are not mentally retarded. Such individuals are unprotected by the exemption and will continue to face the threat of execution.

See also Roper v. Simmons, 543 U.S. 551, 571–72 (2005) (making similar point with respect to minors).

34. Moreover, both executions of the mentally retarded and executions of minors were rare in the United States before the Supreme Court ruled that such executions violate the Eighth Amendment. See Atkins v. Virginia, 536 U.S. 304, 313–16 (2002) (the mentally retarded); Roper v. Simmons, 543 U.S. 551, 564–67 (minors).

35. 536 U.S. 304.

36. 543 U.S. 551.

37. Sanford Gabin, Judicial Review and the Reasonable Doubt Test 45–46 (1980).

38. There are two sentences in Section 1 of the Fourteenth Amendment. The first sentence provides: "All persons born or naturalized in the United States, and subject to the jurisdiction thereof, are citizens of the United States and of the State wherein they reside." There is no disagreement about what this sentence was meant to accomplish: to "overturn[] the Dred Scott decision by making *all persons* born within the United States and subject to its jurisdiction citizens of the United States" (and of the state wherein they reside). Slaughter-House Cases, 83 U.S. (16 Wall.) 36, 73 (1872). In *Dred Scott v. Sandford*, 60 U.S. (19 How.) 393 (1857) – surely the single most infamous case in American constitutional law – the Supreme Court ruled, inter alia, that "a man of African descent, whether a slave or not, was not and could not be a citizen of a State or of the United States. . . . That [the] main purpose [of the first sentence of Section 1 of the Fourteenth Amendment] was to establish the citizenship of the negro can admit of no doubt. The phrase, 'subject to its jurisdiction' was intended to exclude from its operation children of ministers, consuls, and citizens or subjects of foreign States born within the United States." 83 U.S. (16 Wall.) at 73. On *Dred Scott*, see Don E. Fehrenbacher, The Dred Scott Case: Its Significance in American Law and Politics (1978). For a shorter commentary, see Don E. Fehrenbacher, "Dred Scott v. Sandford, 19 Howard 393 (1857)," 2 Encyclopedia of the American Constitution 584 (Leonard W. Levy, Kenneth L. Karst, & Dennis J. Mahoney, eds., 1986).

39. See Perry, We the People, n. 1, ch. 3.

40. 14 Statutes 27 (1866).

41. See Perry, We the People, n. 1, at 52–53.

42. See id. at 54–57.

43. Slaughter-House Cases, 83 U.S. (16 Wall.) 36, 73 (1872).

44. Id. On *Dred Scott*, see Don E. Fehrenbacher, The Dred Scott Case: Its Significance in American Law and Politics (1978). For a shorter commentary, see Don E. Fehrenbacher, "Dred Scott v. Sandford, 19 Howard 393 (1857)," 2 Encyclopedia of the American Constitution 584 (Leonard W. Levy, Kenneth L. Karst & Dennis J. Mahoney, eds., 1986).

45. That treats them less well, that is, with respect to *non-political* privileges and immunities. The principal political privilege is the right to vote. See Perry, We The People, n. 1, at 67–69.

46. See id. at 57–80.

47. Or if the differential treatment is based on a negative but accurate generalization about those the law treats less well, if government can, without serious cost, avoid reliance on the generalization. See, e.g., United States v. Virginia, 518 U.S. 515 (1996).

48. The reader familiar with the Supreme Court's equal protection and substantive due process cases will notice that:

   • The Court's equal protection doctrine is grounded substantially in the requirement that differential treatment not be based on a demeaning view about those the law treats less well or on a negative but accurate generalization about those the law treats less well, if government can avoid reliance on the generalization without serious cost.
   • The Court's substantive due process doctrine is grounded substantially in the requirement that the costs the law visits on those who are treated less well not be disproportionate to the benefits the law achieves.

49. In *Lochner v. New* York, 198 U.S. 45 (1905), the Supreme Court famously applied the "regulation for the public good in a reasonable fashion" requirement (though the Court pegged the requirement to the due process clause rather than to the privileges or immunities clause). However, the Court failed to apply the requirement in a deferential (Thayerian) way and thereby usurped the legislative function. See id. at 65 (Harlan, J., joined by White & Day, JJ., dissenting); id. at 74 (Holmes, J., dissenting).

50. See n. 63 and accompanying text.

51. See Perry, We the People, n. 1, at 152–53.

52. See Griswold v. Connecticut, 381 U.S. 479 (1965).

53. H. Tristram Engelhardt, Jr., "Moral Knowledge: Some Reflections on Moral Controversies, Incompatible Moral Epistemologies, and the Culture Wars," 10 Christian Bioethics 79, 84 (2004).)

54. Peter Singer, The President of Good and Evil: The Ethics of George W. Bush 37 (2004).

55. Laurence H. Tribe, "Will the Abortion Fight Ever End: A Nation Held Hostage," New York Times, July 2, 1990, at A13.

56. Richard A. Posner, Sex and Reason 337 (1992).

57. John Hart Ely, "The Wages of Crying Wolf: A Comment on *Roe* v. *Wade*," 82 Yale L. J. 920, 923 (1973).

58. 410 U.S. at 155.

59. See, e.g., Michael Gazzaniga, "Op-Ed: All Clones Are Not the Same," New York Times, Feb. 17, 2006.

60. Garry Wills, "The Bishops vs. the Bible," New York Times, June 27, 2004. On the the enduring absence of a consensus to which Will refers, compare Robert P. George & Patrick Lee, "Acorns and Embryos," The New Atlantis, Fall 2004/Winter 2004, <http://www,thenewatlantis.com/archive/7/georgeleeprint.htm>, with Michael S. Gazzaniga, "The Thoughtful Distinction Between Embryo and Human," The Chronicle Review, Apr. 8, 2005. See also Anthony Kenny, "Life Stories: When an Individual Life Begins – and the Ethics of Ending It," Times Lit. Supp., Mar. 25, 2005, at 3. Jesuit moral theologian Richard McCormick foresaw that because of this dissensus about the moral status of the fetus – in particular, about the fetus' s moral status during early pregnancy – "public policy [would] remain sharply contentious and the task of legislators correspondingly complex." Richard A, McCormick, SJ, "The Gospel of Life," America, Apr. 29, 1995, at 12, 13. See also John Langan, SJ, "Observations on Abortion and Politics," America, Oct. 25, 2004: "[T]he fact of continuing and intense public disagreement [underlines] how far we are from having a broad public consensus against the practice [of abortion] and of how difficult it would be to . . . enact a legal prohibition against it." Cf. Clifford Longley, "'The Church Hasn't Yet Made a Mature Appraisal of What Democracy Demands,'" The Tablet [London], May 7, 2005, at 11: "The criminal justice system . . . only works when there is at least a minimal degree of assent by the public to the moral framework in which it operates. . . . [W]hat you have to persuade the majority of is not just that your moral principle is correct but that it is right to insist that the minority which does not agree with it must nevertheless comply with it too."

61. Cf. Jon Stewart, America (the Book): A Guide to Democracy Inaction 90 (2004) (describing *Roe v. Wade*, 410 U.S. 113 (1973): "The Court rules that the right to privacy protects a women's decision to have an abortion and the fetus is not a person with constitutional rights, thus ending all debate on this once-controversial issue."

62. See n. 48.

63. Washington v. Glucksberg, 521 U.S. 702, 765–65, 768 (1997) (Souter, J., concurring in the judgment). Compare this statement by the Canadian Supreme Court:

> Parliament has enacted this legislation after a long consultation process that included a consideration of the constitutional standards outlined by this Court . . . While it is the role of the Court to specify such standards, there may be a range of permissible regimes that can meet these standards. It goes without saying that this range is not confined to the specific rule adopted by the Court pursuant to its competence in the common law.

Regina v. Mills, 3 S.C.R. 668 at para. 59 (1999).

64. In *Roe,* the Court rejected Texas's contention that "life begins at conception and is present throughout pregnancy, and that, therefore, the State has a compelling interest in protecting that life from and after conception." The Court said that "[w]e need not resolve the difficult question of when life begins. . . . [T]he judiciary, at this point in the development of man's knowledge, is not in a position to speculate as to the answer." 410 U.S. at 159. The right question, however, was not what answer the judiciary, or anyone else, should give, but only whether Texas wasn't constitutionally free to give the answer it did. That others would give a different answer – or no answer – is beside the point. As John Ely wrote, "[t]he problem with *Roe* is not so much that [the Court] bungles the question it sets itself, but rather that it sets itself a question the Constitution has not made the Court's business." Ely, n. 57, at 943. The Court went on to say that "we do not agree that, by adopting one theory of life,

Texas may override the rights of the pregnant woman that are at stake." 410 U.S. at 162. But as Richard Epstein appropriately responded: "It makes no sense to hold in conclusionary terms that 'by adopting one theory of life, Texas may [not] override the rights of the pregnant woman that are at stake.' That formulation of the issue begs the important question because it assumes that we know that the women's rights must prevail even before the required balance takes place. We could as well claim that the Court, by adopting another theory of life, has decided to override the rights of the unborn child." Richard Epstein, "Substantive Due Process by Any Other Name: The Abortion Cases," 1973 Supreme Court Rev. 159, 182.

The crucial question was this: *Why* wasn't Texas free – free as a *constitutional* matter, free *under the Fourteenth Amendment* – to proceed on the basis of the assumption that a pre-viable unborn child has the same moral status as a post-viable unborn child or a born child? The Court did not address that question – or, if it matters, addressed it only in the most conclusory terms. Again, Ely: "The Court grants that protecting the fetus is an 'important and legitimate' governmental goal, and of course it does not deny that restricting abortion promotes it. What it does, instead, is simply announce that that goal is not important enough to sustain the restriction." Ely, supra this note, at 942. See id. at 924–25 (explaining why, if the Court wanted to "second-guess legislative balances . . . when the Constitution has designated neither of the values in conflict as entitled to special protection[,] . . . *Roe* seems a curious place to have begun"). If the correct answer is that Texas and other states *are* constitutionally free to proceed on the basis of the assumption that a pre-viable unborn child has the same moral status as a post-viable unborn child or a born child, then the pregnant woman does not have "at stake" the right against a state that the Court had in mind, because there is no such right: a constitutional right to non-interference by the state with her decision to have an abortion.

65. It's no secret that the principal critics of the Court's decision in *Roe* have been "pro-life" on the question of whether pre-viability abortions should be a crime. The most powerful critique of the decision, however, was written by someone who did not fit that profile, someone who announced, in his critique, that "as a legislator" he would "vote for a statute very much like the one the Court ends up drafting." See Ely, n. 57. (The quoted language is at p. 926.) Ely's unequivocal judgment – delivered in April 1973, just three months after the Court decided *Roe* – was that the Court's ruling in *Roe* is "a very bad decision[,] . . . because it is bad constitutional law, or rather because it is *not* constitutional law and gives almost no sense of an obligation to try to be." Id. at 947.

Ely is not the only politically liberal constitutional scholar who charged that the Court's decision in *Roe* was illegitimate. In 1976, Archibald Cox, who served as Solicitor General of the United States under Presidents Kennedy and Johnson, complained that in *Roe*

> the Court failed to establish the legitimacy of the decision by articulating a precept of suffi-
> cient abstractness to lift the ruling above the level of a political judgment . . . Nor can I artic-
> ulate such a principle – unless it be that a State cannot interfere with individual decisions
> relating to sex, procreation, and family with only a moral or philosophical State justifica-
> tion: a principle which I cannot accept or believe will be accepted by the American people.

Archibald Cox, The Role of the Supreme Court in American Government 113 (1976). In 1979, another liberal constitutional scholar, Gerald Gunther, wrote that although

"*Brown v. Board of Education* was an entirely legitimate decision[,] . . . I have not yet found a satisfying rationale to justify *Roe v. Wade* . . . on the basis of modes of constitutional interpretation I consider legitimate." Gerald Gunther, "Some Reflections on the Judicial Role: Distinctions, Roots, and Prospects," 1979 Washington U. L. Q. 817, 819.

So, one need be neither "pro-life" nor a politically conservative constitutional scholar to conclude that *Roe v. Wade* constitutes one of the greatest – and, therefore, one of the worst – judicial usurpations of American politics in the period since World War II.

66. A demeaning claim – a claim that falsely attributes a deficit of some kind to a person in virtue of, say, her being a women – should not be confused with a negative but accurate generalization about the members of a group. An example of the former: Women are, as such, not fit for the practice of law. An example of the latter: Women are, in general, less strong than men. A law or policy based on a demeaning claim about those the law/policy treats less well is not the only sort of law/policy that fails to serve the public good *in a reasonable fashion*. So too does a law/policy based on a negative but accurate generalization about the members of a group *if government can, without serious cost, avoid reliance on the generalization*. See, e.g., United States v. Virginia, 518 U.S. 515 (1996).

67. Baker v. State [of Vermont], 744 A.2d 864, 870 (Vt. 1999). For a fuller specification of the benefits in question, see id. at 883–84. See also Goodridge v. [Massachusetts] Department of Public Health, 798 N.E.2d 941, 955–57 (Mass. 2003).

68. See Michael J. Perry, Under God? Religious Faith and Liberal Democracy 20–52 (2003).

69. See id. at 55–80. Cf. Nicholas D. Kristof, "Lovers Under the Skin," New York Times, Dec. 3, 2003: "A 1958 poll found that 96 percent of whites disapproved of marriages between blacks and whites. . . . In 1959 a judge justified Virginia's ban on interracial marriage by declaring that 'Almighty God . . . did not intend for the races to mix.' "

70. 388 U.S. 1 (1967).

71. See Christopher Wolfe, "Why the Federal Marriage Amendment Is Necessary," 42 San Diego L. Rev. 895 (2005). Compare Michael J. Perry, "Why the Federal Marriage Amendment Is Not Only Not Necessary, But a Bad Idea: A Response to Christopher Wolfe," 42 San Diego L. Rev. 925 (2005). Cf. Adam Liptak, "Caution in Court for Gay Rights Groups," New York Times, Nov. 12, 2004; John M. Broder, "Groups Debate Slower Strategy on Gay Rights," Dec. 9, 2004.

72. Consider Richard Posner's position that

> [it is not] the business of the courts to buck public opinion that is as strong as the current tide of public opinion against gay marriage. . . . Because the basis in conventional legal materials for creating a constitutional right . . . to gay marriage is extremely thin, opponents cannot be persuaded that the creation of [this right] by courts is anything other than a political act by a tiny, unelected, unrepresentative, elite committee of lawyers.

Richard Posner, "Gay Marriage – Posner's Response to Comments," The Becker-Posner Blog, July 24, 2005, <http://becker-posner-blog.com/>.

To avoid misunderstanding, it bears emphasis that nothing I have said here means that a *state* supreme court should not interpret the antidiscrimination provision of the state constitution to require the state to recognize same-sex unions. Posner finds the "argument for recognizing homosexual marriage quite persuasive," but he nonetheless thinks that the Supreme Court should not require states to extend the benefit of law to same-sex unions: Such "a radical social policy . . . is deeply offensive to the vast majority of its citizens. . . . [For the Court to do so] would be an unprecedented example of judicial immodesty." Richard A. Posner, "Should There Be Homosexual Marriage, And If So, Who Should Decide?" 95 Michigan L. Rev. 1578, 1584–85 (1997). Posner's preference is for "[letting] a state legislature or an activist (but elected, and hence democratically responsive) state court adopt homosexual marriage as a policy in one state, and let the rest of the country learn from the results of its experiment. That is the democratic way . . . " Id. at 1585–86.

Because of two state court rulings – one by the Vermont Supreme Court in 1999 and the other by the Supreme Judicial Court of Massachusetts in 2003 – Vermont and Massachusetts now both recognize same-sex unions. In Vermont, the recognized unions are called "civil unions"; in Massachusetts, "marriages." The Vermont Supreme Court ruled that the right "to the common benefit and protection of the law guaranteed by . . . the Vermont Constitution" requires the state legislature to extend the benefit of law to same-sex unions. Baker v. State [of Vermont], 744 A.2d 864, 869–70 (Vt. 1999). The court concluded its ruling with these words: "The extension of the Common Benefits Clause to acknowledge plaintiffs as Vermonters who seek nothing more, nor less, than legal protection and security for their avowed commitment to an intimate and lasting human relationship is simply, when all is said and done, a recognition of our common humanity." Id. at 889. The Massachusetts court introduced its ruling with these words:

> Marriage is a vital social institution. The exclusive commitment of two individuals to each other nurtures love and mutual support; it brings stability to our society. For those who choose to marry, and for their children, marriage provides an abundance of legal, financial, and social benefits. In return it imposes weighty legal, financial, and social obligations. The question before us is whether, consistent with the Massachusetts Constitution, the Commonwealth may deny the protections, benefits, and obligations conferred by civil marriage to two individuals of the same sex who wish to marry. We conclude that it may not. The Massachusetts Constitution affirms the dignity and equality of all individuals. It forbids the creation of second-class citizens. . . . [The Commonwealth] has failed to identify any constitutionally adequate reason for denying civil marriage to same-sex couples.

Goodridge v. [Massachusetts] Department of Public Health, 798 N.E.2d 941, 948 (Mass. 2003).

In 2005, the legislature of another New England state – Connecticut – became the first to extend the benefit of law to same-sex unions without being told by its state judiciary to do so. See Associated Press, "Civil Union Law Takes Effect in Connecticut," New York Times, Oct. 1, 2005. Moreover, California, the District of Columbia, Hawaii, Maine, and New Jersey "grant persons in same-sex unions a similar legal status to those in a civil marriage by domestic partnership, civil union or reciprocal beneficiary laws. See Wikipedia: The Free Encyclopedia, <http://en.wikipedia.org/wiki.Same-sex_marriage>. Recently, the Alaska Supreme Court ruled, in a unanimous decision, that under the state constitution public employers that grant spousal benefits to opposite-sex married couples must also grant spousal benefits to same-sex couples, even though the state constitution specifically disallows same-sex marriage. Alaska Civil Liberties Union v. State of Alaska and Municipality of Anchorage, Supreme Court No. S-10459 (Oct. 28, 2005).

73. Posner, "Gay Marriage – Posner's Response to Comments, n. 72.
74. Cf. Posner, "Should There Be Homosexual Marriage," n. 72, at 1586: "When the Supreme Court moved against public school segregation, it was bucking a regional majority but a national minority (white southerners). When it outlawed the laws forbidding racially mixed marriages, only a minority of states had such laws on their books." More recently, Posner wrote that "*Brown [v. Board of Education,* 347 U.S. 483 (1954)] would have been unthinkable – and in my pragmatic view unsound – had the case arisen in 1900 rather than the 1950s, because in 1900 the vast majority of the American population would have considered compelled racial integration of public schools improper." Posner, "Gay Marriage – Posner's Response to Comments," n. 72.

75. Alexander M. Bickel, The Least Dangerous Branch: The Supreme Court at the Bar of Politics 24 (1962).
76. 347 U.S. 483 (1954). Cf. Charles L. Black, Jr., Decision According to Law 33 (1981) (describing *Brown* as "the decision that opened our era of judicial activity").
77. Cf. John Hart Ely, Democracy and Distrust: A Theory of Judicial Review (1980).
78. As Gerard Lynch has written, "to most lawyers of my generation, *Brown* is a touchstone for constitutional theory fully as powerful as *Lochner* was for a previous generation." Gerard Lynch, Book Review, 63 Cornell L. Rev. 1091, 1099 n. 32 (1983). Mark Tushnet has said much the same thing: "For a generation, one criterion for an acceptable constitutional theory has been whether that theory explains why *[Brown]* ... was correct." Mark V. Tushnet, "Reflections on the Role of Purpose in the Jurisprudence of the Religion Clauses," 27 William & Mary L. Rev. 997, 999 n. 4 (1986). See also Gregory Bassham, Original Intent and the Constitution: A Philosophical Study 105 (1992): "The acid test of originalism, as indeed of any theory of constitutional adjudication, is its capacity to justify what is now almost universally regarded as the Supreme Court's finest hour: its decision in *Brown v. Board of Education.*" But see John Harrison, "Reconstructing the Privileges or Immunities Clause," 101 Yale L. J. 1385, 1463 n. 295 (1992): "I do not think that my theory of the 14th Amendment stands or falls with [its ability to accommodate the Court's decision in *Brown*]. Man is not the measure of all things, as Socrates replied to the Sophists, and neither is Brown v. Board of Educ.... An interpretation of the Constitution is not wrong because it would produce a different result in *Brown.*"

SUMMATION

1. John R. Searle, "Social Ontology and Free Speech," The Hedgehog Review, Fall 2004, 55, 66.
2. Bernard Williams, "Republican and Galilean," New York Rev., Nov. 8, 1990, at 45, 48 (reviewing Charles Taylor, Sources of the Self: The Making of Modern Identity (1989)).

Index